A Few Reasonable Words

A Few Reasonable Words

Selected Writings

Henry Regnery

with an introduction by
George A. Panichas

Intercollegiate Studies Institute
Wilmington, Delaware
1996

Copyright ©1996 by the Intercollegiate Studies Institute

Library of Congress Catalog Card Number
96–75871

ISBN 1-882926-13-7

Published in the United States by:

Intercollegiate Studies Institute
3901 Centerville Road
P.O. Box 4431
Wilmington, DE 19807-0431

Manufactured in the United States of America

One ought, every day at least, to hear
a little song, read a good poem, see
a fine picture, and, if it were possible,
to speak a few reasonable words.

—Goethe

Contents

Introduction

George A. Panichas .... *XI*

I

This Liberal Age: A Critical Appraisal *3*
Albert J. Nock: An Appreciation *32*
Richard M. Weaver: Advocating Right Reason *52*

II

Russell Kirk: Making of the Conservative Mind *83*
Emerging Conservatism:
    Kilpatrick, Morley, and Burnham *121*
The Responsibility of the Educated:
    A Graduation Address *142*

III

Historical Revisionism and World War II:
    Part I *157*

Historical Revisionism and World War II:
  Part II 186
Winston Churchill: A Question of Leadership 210

IV

Hermann Schnitzler: Remembering a Great Teacher 235
Max Picard: A Tribute 253
Richard Strauss: A Classic of Our Time 262

V

T.S. Eliot, Ezra Pound, and Wyndham Lewis:
  A Creative Friendship 287
George F. Kennan: A Gift to America 321
Alexander Solzhenitsyn: The Man and the Problem 339

Notes 359

Acknowledgements

The author and the publisher gratefully acknowledge the publications in which the essays in this volume first appeared.

"This Liberal Age: A Critical Appraisal" first appeared as "The Age of Liberalism" in *Modern Age,* Spring 1975.

"Albert J. Nock: An Appreciation" was first published in *Modern Age,* Winter 1971.

"Richard M. Weaver: Advocating Right Reason" was originally published as "Richard Weaver: A Southern Agrarian at the University of Chicago" in *Modern Age,* Spring 1988.

"Russell Kirk: Making of the Conservative Mind" first appeared as "Russell Kirk and the Making of the Conservative Mind" in *Modern Age,* Fall 1977.

"Emerging Conservatism: Kilpatrick, Morley, and Burnham" first appeared in *Modern Age*, Summer 1978.

"The Responsibility of the Educated" was a graduation address given at Rockford College in 1960.

"Historical Revisionism and World War II: Parts I & II" were published in *Modern Age,* Summer and Fall 1976.

"Winston Churchill: A Question of Leadership" originally appeared as "War and Leadership" in *Modern Age,* Summer 1989.

"Hermann Schnitzler: Remembering a Great Teacher" was originally published as "Remembering a Great Teacher" in *Modern Age*, Summer 1995.

"Max Picard: A Tribute," in its present form, appears here for the first time.

"Richard Strauss: A Classic of Our Time" was first read as a lecture in 1976.

"T.S. Eliot, Ezra Pound, and Wyndham Lewis: A Creative Friendship" was first published as "Eliot, Pound, and Lewis: A Creative Friendship" in *Modern Age*, Spring 1972.

"George F. Kennan: A Gift to America" was first published as "A Gift to America" in *Modern Age*, Summer 1994.

"Alexander Solzhenitsyn: The Man and the Problem" was originally published as "The Problem of Alexander Solzhenitsyn" in *Modern Age*, Spring 1981.

Introduction

Henry Regnery has earned a distinguished and lasting place in the annals of American publishing. As a longtime independent publisher—he founded the Henry Regnery Company in 1947—he sought to make available to the reading public the works of great writers that might otherwise not have appeared in print. For him the power of words and the responsibility of writers were absolutely interdependent, and the books that appeared under his imprint amply illustrated the truth of this criterion. The books he published were essentially, though not exclusively, conservative in orientation, and focused largely on acute philosophical, educational, literary, religious, socio-political, economic, and cultural issues, especially as these related to the modern era in the years directly following World War II. Some of the European and American authors whose writings he published were those of religious thinkers like Max Picard, Romano Guardini, and Gabriel Marcel; of educational commentators like Robert M. Hutchins and

Mortimer Smith; of literary artists like Ezra Pound, Wyndham Lewis, and Roy Campbell; of socio-political critics like Montgomery Belgion, Raymond Aron, and Ernst Jünger; and of literary and cultural critics like Eliseo Vivas and Richard M. Weaver. It is worth adding here that Henry Regnery's *Memoirs of a Dissident Publisher* (1978) endures as a valuable autobiographical document in the history of publishing and also of conservative thought.

It was the publication, in 1953, of Russell Kirk's *The Conservative Mind* that perhaps marked the highest degree of vision on the part of the Henry Regnery Company. No other book in modern intellectual and political history has had more impact on the destiny of the conservative movement in the United States or more affected the direction of the conservative political imagination. "Kirk not only offered convincing evidence that conservatism was an honorable and intellectually respectable position, but that it was an integral part of the American tradition." Thus writes Henry Regnery in a long essay on Russell Kirk's achievement and significance included in this volume of selected essays composed and published during the past three decades. This essay includes a detailed and often fascinating narration of the publishing history of *The Conservative Mind*, as recited by the publisher himself. The essay, which contains incisive commentary on other books subsequently written by Kirk and published by the Henry Regnery Company, concludes with these words:

> In a disorderly age he has tirelessly and elo-
> quently made clear the necessity and sources of
> order; against the false prophets who proclaim
> that all values are relative and derive from will and
> desire, he shows their immutability; and to those
> who believe that man is capable of all things, he
> teaches humility and that the beginning of wis-
> dom is respect for creation and the order of being.

These preceding words give to us the measure of the major and intrinsic concerns of the essays that Henry Regnery devotes to other American conservative figures found in the first two sections of this book and whose works he also published. As in the Kirk essay, the separate essays on Albert J. Nock and on Richard M. Weaver, as well as a joint essay examining particular books by James Jackson Kilpatrick, Felix Morley, and James Burnham, seen in the special context of an "emerging conservatism" in the 1950s, exhibit the kind of critical seriousness and percipience exemplifying the other essays in this book. In the essays that immediately follow, he gives witness not only as a publisher of books of high civilizational value, and which testify incontestably to his standards of discrimination, but also as a writer who possesses literary talent and critical axioms, and who addresses himself to the same urgent problems of the modern world that the books he published also ad-dressed. Indeed, what makes this book especially stimulat-ing is to have on view here the lucid, fertile ways and workings of a mind concerned, critically and judgmentally, with the world of books and ideas, with the men who create books and shape ideas, and with epochal events in modern history which impinge on our common humanity and which, in the end, incite the books and the ideas that speak of the modern human condition. It is this fundamental, overarching concern which gives this book its unity of outlook and helps define its aims and values.

The essays in this book, it can be said, chart an intellectual journey in the modern world, and invite the reader to take part in the journey. A reader who accepts this invitation will be the richer for it; indeed, a younger generation of readers will find in these essays, individually and collectively, a trustworthy guide who, above all, ably describes the temper of the period following World War II and of events during and after the war that "represented the final triumph of liberalism." The lead essay in this book, "This Liberal Age," should be required reading for younger readers shaped and conditioned by the sham promises of new and fair deals, let alone the new morality, and the new age that "terrible simplifiers" have long been laboring to establish in place of first causes and first principles. Henry Regnery's keen historical sense, no less than his moral sense, cannot but have a restorative effect on readers endlessly exposed to the liberal tales of a terrestrial paradise. In an age in which specious ideologies thrive, such an encounter is bound to give needed shock to the mind.

For an author the search for historical truth must be a disinterested endeavor, even when, as he admits, this search becomes yet another lost cause. "Whether writing and publishing the historical truth brings any immediate practical results or not," he writes, "if we believe in anything, we must believe that the truth is worthwhile for its own sake. If a free society is to survive, is to have any meaning, men must be made accountable for their activity, we must know what our leaders did, said, and agreed to do in our name." These words, in fact, faithfully express his aims as a publisher of books, as well as a writer himself of essays, questioning decisions made by political leaders, like Franklin D. Roosevelt and Winston Churchill, that helped shape the peace after 1945. And both as the publisher of books like Charles C. Tansill's *Back Door to War* (1952) and George N. Crocker's *Roosevelt's Road to Russia* (1959), and as the writer of a two-part essay, the longest in this book, "Historical Revisionism and World War II," he presents the case for historical revisionism with conviction. In an era when ideology and political correctitude control and manipulate the academy, the world of newspapers, publishers, and reviewing practices, and increasingly the electronic media, Henry Regnery's example of dissent has much corrective value.

A Few Reasonable Words, the title given to this book, catches the spirit of the author's preoccupations, and of the subject and themes the essays as a whole center on throughout. It is a title entirely appropriate for a writer who deliberately avoids ideological extremes, who counsels clear and disciplined thought, who speaks in sensible terms and tones, always forcefully but also always restrainedly. The title also crystallizes the moral measure of an author who presents to his reader a selection from the various essays he has written over the years, possessing as he does both a keen historical sense and an active moral sense. In this respect, a reader would do well to ponder especially the short essay, originally given as a commencement address in 1960, "The Responsibility of the Educated." In title and content, this essay augments and sharpens the main title and direction of the book, and ultimately points to the author as a man of prudence and of probity, those quiet virtues underpinning the entire book itself.

Reasonable words and responsible acts are mutually necessary: are, in fact, what a world in disarray desperately requires if a humane civilization in a modern setting is not to dissolve altogether. "The Responsibility of the Educated" is an essay that provides a reader with a cogent purview of the author's basic position, of the values and principles that he affirms and that he counsels as an antidote to our present troubles. Here he speaks out with much feeling and candor, in the vital context of "What I Believe." It is an essay that essentializes Henry Regnery's position and beliefs. In it we hear the conjoining voice of a determined publisher, committed writer, and concerned American citizen alerting his listeners to instances of poor leadership and, in turn, poor decisions that have incalculable consequences in the life of a nation and also the course of history. Citing the dismal story and aftermath of the Yalta, Teheran, and Potsdam conferences (and of the great personages taking part in them), he goes on to lament the fact that the educated, then and now, have not fulfilled their responsibility in speaking out against vacillating governmental policies and political programs and agendas that lack moral roots and convictions. Above all, he stresses that our national leaders have not lived up to the standards of the

Founding Fathers who knew that

> ...history was a struggle for power, for existence, for advantage, that life itself is struggle, and that to see it otherwise is rank self-deception. But they also knew that the task of civilization is to bring, in so far as it is possible, order and justice out of the chaos of the struggle for existence. They knew that man is imperfect, that human institutions are equally imperfect, and that to expect perfection from the one was as futile and deceptive as to demand perfection from the other.

The last two sections of the book reveal a distinct literary dimension, as the author concentrates on gifted individuals who comprise his representative men, so to speak: in short, men whose ideas, values, and standards he esteems and recommends to readers. The essays in these sections give an added dimension to those that precede in the form of reminiscences, tributes, and critical appraisals. He thus adds to the socio-political and historical aspects of the earlier essays a more evocative tone and a more sapiential thrust. Through his representative men he seeks primarily to convey paradigms of character, of thought, of attitude that reinforce and refine his inclusive emphasis on the intellectual and moral uses of responsibility. A spirit of affirmation prevails here, and the men whose lives and attainments he respects and salutes often serve as a counter-poise to some of the conditions and circumstances he has delineated in the earlier essays and sections. One will readily discern, too, how these men act as inspiring guides and good influencers in Henry Regnery's own life and work, helping him to appreciate more fully and deeply higher concepts of character and culture, of culture and society, and of art and thought. These representative men, it can be said, instill loyalty to first principles, now often dislodged or abandoned by our intellectual and political leaders.

That the author is a man of measure—of restraint, reserve, reticence—is clearly observed in the essays as a whole, both in style and in content. Romantic excesses and indulgences, which he doubtlessly connects with a vulgar liberalism, repel him. For Henry Regnery, Goethe's belief that in limitations one first shows himself the master is a central and impelling belief. Indeed, the crisis of modernity, as his essays demonstrate, often stems from a rejection of the law of limitations—a rejection fanned in turn by the insistence that everything is possible. The dispassionate note that one encounters in his writings must not, however, be seen as overruling any expression of emotion or strong sympathy. Two essays, in particular, the autobiographical essay on "Hermann Schnitzler," originally written as a testimony of gratitude, and an appreciation of "Richard Strauss," which views the German composer as a classic of our time, illustrate, respectively, his capacity for human affection and intense aesthetic rapport. The first of these essays confirms the undying truth of an ancient Greek poet's declaration that a man counts it a great joy if he but have the shadow of a friend. The second salutes an outstanding modern composer of symphonic poems and operas, and celebrates a life that "came about as close to complete success and fulfillment as is permitted to man, flawed and imperfect creature that he is." The essay on Schnitzler, it should be noted, shows the author's literary sensitivity at its best; and that on Strauss, his lifelong musical interests. Clearly, he wrote these essays with considerable personal joy, which is certain to touch and transform a reader.

The men whose lives Henry Regnery honors in memory are, as he makes plain, also men of our time who were able to resist, in civilized and creative ways, the modern spirit of doubt, change, disillusionment, destruction, decadence. In their examples he asks us to find the strength and the courage we need to contend with the sickness of the modern world. No less compelling, in this respect, is his short but trenchant tribute to the Swiss-German philosopher and metaphysician, Max Picard. It was Hermann Schnitzler who first introduced him to Picard's writings, of which the Regnery Company eventually published, in English translation, *Hitler in Our Selves* (1948), *The Flight from God* (1952), and *The World of Silence* (1953). The beautiful and wise soul which he recognized in Picard (whom he visited on several occasions, which he vividly re-creates in his tribute) conflates with Picard's writings and ideas.

Henry Regnery's own decision to become a full-time publisher owed much to his wish to publish Picard's *Hitler in Our Selves*, a book which helps explain the catastrophe that overtook European civilization, and which diagnoses its breakdown. Though essentially concerned with Nazism as a German phenomenon, this remarkable, prophetic book sees Hitlerism as a terrifying portent and symptom of the general crisis of modern man, especially the spiritual chaos into which modern civilization has fallen, with its attendant discontinuity, fragmentation, destructiveness, apostasy, and the despotism of worldliness. Henry Regnery writes that, by publishing Picard's books, he was giving Americans "the opportunity to come under the influence of an extraordinary man who has something to offer we very much need." Clearly, Picard's books have considerable relevance in the present time, when there is no longer any point of orientation and when the Hitler in our selves now transmutes into the nihilism in our selves. If his circumspect comments do nothing more than alert a reader to even one of Max Picard's books, they will have done a good deed.

The men, both Americans and Europeans, whom he admires and celebrates, are men who had a common calling, a common vocation: to tell us truths about our modern world, about ourselves, and about our origins. Henry Regnery sees their writings and thought not only as gifts to a modern world in dire need of moral direction and renewal, but also as a fervent defense of civilized values. In a long and percipient essay on the results of their "creative friendship," for example, he elucidates in detail how T. S. Eliot, Ezra Pound, and Wyndham Lewis in the first half of the twentieth century responded to what the latter spoke of as "the threat of extinction to the cultural tradition of the West." It is exactly this threat at an ever-increasing scale which concerns Henry Regnery and shapes the thrust of his essays in their parts and in their whole, in general and in particular. That this threat has also become even more pronounced and pervasive in the years since the end of World War II is, in fact, what especially troubles and preoccupies him in this book and what gives to it a far greater sense of urgency and timeliness. In no way, how-ever, does the possibility of the total annihilation of our sacred patrimony, and thus the final victory of those whom Russell Kirk aptly identifies as "enemies of the permanent things," daunt him. Despite the debasement and deteriora-tion that he sees in our midst, he does not succumb to despair, he refuses to surrender to the kingdom of enmity. His faith in the principles of order and the dignity and value of human life, and his affirmation of the higher meaning of existence, do not desert him, whatever the threats of the "antagonist world," to recall Edmund Burke's phrase.

For Henry Regnery the union of what can best be termed the critical spirit and the creative spirit is essential to a civilized society, and to the idea of order. Such a union deters sloppiness, chaos, excess, debasement. It is the luminous presence of this union, however transient it was, that he observed in his book *Creative Chicago* (1993), particularly as found in the achievement of Louis Henri Sullivan, one of America's greatest architectural geniuses. When this union thrives, vision finds its fulfillment in what Sullivan calls "the beneficence of power"—of power and responsibility, one could add. But when such a union falters, the losses to civilization can be disastrous, even fatal. In *A Few Reasonable Words* the author particularly exam-ines figures of achievement and significance in the light of how each assumes the responsibility of vision and choice. Yet he is profoundly and invariably aware of the hard, tensive realities that grip life, and does not fail to warn of what takes place when the critical and the creative spirit is sundered, and how the rhythm of disintegration, in one's self and in the world, besets the human situation. Still, it is characteristic of his attitude and outlook that the negative is subordinated to his emphasis on human effort, on aspiration, on ascent. In this connection, Simone Weil, whose celebrated essay on "*The Iliad*, or The Poem of Force," he read with deep admiration when it was first translated into English by Mary McCarthy and published in Dwight Macdonald's magazine *Politics* in November 1945, provides the appropriate note here: "The world is a closed door. It is a barrier. And at the same time it is the way through."

The essays in this book bear witness to the author's constancy of faith and purpose. And those whose writings and ideas he illuminates in his essays exemplify the dynamics of this constancy. Thus, with George F. Kennan, American statesman and sage, and the subject of the penultimate essay in this book, Henry Regnery, quoting from Kennan's *Around the Cragged Hill: A Personal and Political Philosophy* (1993), registers his own "basic preferences...for the small over the great, for the qualitative over the quantitative,...for the discriminate over the indiscriminate, and for the varied over the uniform, in most major aspects of social life.'" And with Kennan he also agrees that, "'if we are to have hope of emerging successfully from the great social bewilderment of this age, weight must be laid predominantly upon the spiritual, moral, and intellectual shaping of the individual.'" That which elicits his greatest attention and respect, as *A Few Reasonable Words* reveals again and again, is the example of a writer and his work patiently striving, often in the face of powerful ideological opposition, to achieve the fulfillment of vision and thus to portray the human spirit at its highest point of excellence. Particularly alarming to him is the suppression of life-values in the interest of ideology, in short, of corrupt politics and morality emerging in the garb of the "New Order" and the "New Man."

Appropriately, *A Few Reasonable Words* concludes with an essay on Alexander Solzhenitsyn, who possesses the inner courage and creative faith that Henry Regnery admires in a dissident writer who, refusing to capitulate to totalitarian rule, insists that we need "to subordinate our interests to moral criteria." Indeed, the essay on Solzhenitsyn returns us to the first essay in the book, "This Liberal Age," by reminding us of the power of the liberal left and of its disdain for a writer like Solzhenitsyn who has a prophetic calling to which he remains absolutely loyal as he shatters the illusions of the apologists for a bankrupt Marxism-Leninism, as well as of the social engineers and utopists who endlessly strive to create a new heaven and a new earth. Solzhenitsyn, he contends, has always presented a "problem" to the liberal mind, desperate in its effort to replace man's vision of God with the vision of man without God. In Solzhenitsyn, he sees the might of the word in the struggle between good and evil. In him, too, he sees the example of a writer who accepts not only the moral responsibility of his calling, but also the full consequences of that acceptance.

Of the fourteen essays included in *A Few Reasonable Words* eleven of them were originally commissioned for publication in *Modern Age: A Quarterly Review*, between the years 1971 and 1995. With Russell Kirk, it will be remembered, Henry Regnery was instrumental in the founding of *Modern Age* in 1957, and he has steadfastly maintained interest in its purposes and direction. In his recently published *The Sword of Imagination: Memoirs of a Half-Century of Literary Conflict* (1995), Kirk memorably recalls the challenges and the difficulties of an undertaking aspiring to inform and persuade. "Certain Modernist excesses incited...[us]," he recalls, "to found a periodical comparable to the vanished *Bookman* and the *American Review* that might publish reflections on the permanent things and offer some intellectual resistance to a reckless neoterism.... *Modern Age* was intended to become, in considerable part, an American protest against the illusions of Modernity; and so it has remained." Henry Regnery's book must be read, then, in light of what Kirk has to say about the mission and ethos of *Modern Age*. His essays, in the form of both articles and reviews, validate the importance of a quarterly review in the intellectual community, and particularly at a time when *les clercs* have disowned their charge. In their content, above all, the essays further illustrate, by enlarging and enriching, the worth of a journal of opinion, of dissent to be more exact, in providing a focus of ideas and a center of resistance for those disturbed by the drift of modern civilization in the last half of the twentieth century.

We live in a time of history when morality of mind, let alone moral virtues, is not held in high regard; and when the trivial and the tawdry are predominant tendencies in the social and cultural life of a nation and its people. To our peril, we stubbornly refuse to recognize the transcendent power of morality which José Ortega y Gasset invokes in words that have increasingly fallen into silence: "For morality is always and essentially a feeling of subordination and submission to something, a consciousness of obligation and service." Henry Regnery has steadfastly refused to be a part of this silence. *A Few Reasonable Words* depicts the resoluteness and integrity of this brave man of thought. In the essays here, written in a crisp, direct, unadorned style, without any affectation or pretension, an appreciative reader will discover those exceptional qualities, or endowments, that are intimately associated with morality of mind: in short, the insight and the sapience, the critical intelligence and the courage of judgment that characterize the keen-sighted few who labor for the survival of humane values of civilization.

—George A. Panichas

I

This Liberal Age: A Critical Appraisal

Albert J. Nock: An Appreciation

Richard M. Weaver: Advocating Right Reason

Albert J. Nock

Richard M. Weaver

1

This Liberal Age:
A Critical Appraisal

We live in a time dominated by words: the printed word in the form of books, magazines, and newspapers; the spoken word brought to us by radio and television. From the morning newspaper to the commentator on evening TV, from the first-grade primer (or basal reader, to use the ugly contemporary description) to the latest work of Arthur Schlesinger, Jr., or John Kenneth Galbraith, we are subjected to a constant flood of words, not of the *word*, which, as the embodiment of truth and the primal order of being was *In the beginning*, but of words; words intended to implant opinions, to make us do or believe something we would not have done or believed otherwise. It is this fact of words which characterizes our time, which differentiates it from all others, and which has made those who, in one way or another, control the dissemination of words the real rulers of our society.

The lords of the media, as was demonstrated as long ago as the Spanish-American War, can start wars, or, with the black art of public relations, can turn an unknown utility lawyer who makes a superficial impression into a great statesman, as was done with Wendell Willkie, or make an amiable Illinois lawyer, who had been a mediocre governor but was a polished speaker with a great facility for phrase making, and, as John Dos Passos put it, "held all the fashionable views,"[1] into a world figure, as was done with Adlai Stevenson. We are told that the president of the United States is the most powerful man in the world, but as the fate of Richard Nixon demonstrated, the media are more powerful still. Nixon was the first man for generations to become president in defiance of the media, but they were able—admittedly with his help—to destroy him. Without the enormous barrage of publicity the combined forces of press, TV, and radio were able to concentrate on Watergate, it would have made no greater impact on public opinion than, say, the Bobby Baker case during the administration of Lyndon Johnson. Those who control press, TV, and radio have become the fourth branch of government, and in many ways have the greater influence and power.

There is, then, the fact of this great instrument which modern technology and business organization have created, and the further fact that the viewpoint and general position of those who have controlled it since the 1930s have been predominantly liberal, a combination of circumstances, we must face it, which is the most striking feature of the landscape of our time. During the fight over intervention in the war that had broken out in Europe in 1939, the America First Committee and those of similar persuasion without doubt had the bulk of the American people behind them, but the press that counted—the *New York Times*, the *New York Herald-Tribune*, the *Washington Post*, *Harper's*, the *Atlantic*, the *Nation*, the *New Republic*, *Time*—were on the other side, and, needless to say, carried the day. It was possible to win the Republican nomination in 1940 for Wendell Willkie, who three months before was virtually unknown, in preference to Robert Taft, who was a national figure, because that is what those who controlled the press wanted. It was not because Willkie was a stronger candidate or a better man than Taft. Rather, it was because his views were more acceptable to the small but powerful group that was in a position to pull the strings of public opinion, which is not, of course, the opinion of the public, but of those able to make themselves heard.

Writing of American participation in World War I, Albert J. Nock remarked, "We cannot help remembering that this was a liberal's war and a liberal's peace." World War II and the peace that followed it represented the final triumph of modern liberalism. With a four-term president in the White House, almost complete control of the means of communication, and the colleges and universities largely under their influence, the liberals had the world at their feet. But, one may well ask, Who are the liberals? What do they want? What do they stand for? As for who they are, Mrs. Roosevelt and Justice Warren were liberals, as were Adlai Stevenson and President Kennedy; Arthur Schlesinger, Jr., is a liberal, so are John Kenneth Galbraith and Clark Kerr.

Justice William O. Douglas and Hugh Hefner are liberals (and it is only in a time dominated by the values of liberalism that such a man as Hefner could have made his way, with his "Playboy philosophy," to fame and fortune). The Civil Liberties Union is a liberal organization, the Ford Foundation shows a strong preference for liberal causes, the *New York Times* and the *Washington Post* are liberal newspapers, the *Nation* is a liberal magazine, and Americans for Democratic Action a liberal political pressure group. What the liberals want, what they stand for, is more difficult to describe precisely, all the more so because their position often changes, is not consistent within itself, and not every liberal spokesman agrees with every other, but certain basic ideas and principles can be discerned.

The liberal, to begin with an important aspect of his position, takes a benign view of man, at least in the abstract; the idea of original sin he regards as medieval and with abhorrence. Man, he believes, whatever the theologians may say, is basically good; what tendency toward evil he may show is a result of social influences, not of any innate human flaw. Where the evil influences in society came from if man is basically good he does not explain. The liberal believes that all human and social problems are capable of solution, and in spite of his tendency to blame society for criminal or malicious behavior instead of the perpetrator, he has an almost mystical faith in the power of government and an equally strong distrust of private power. "The diversity of private power, its independence, its actual popularity in the culture at large seems to the left to be subversive of true order. Public power is endowed by the liberal-rationalist with natural superiority and with a kind of immaculateness that has theistic reverberations,"[2] as Ronald Berman points out in his *America in the Sixties*. With public power, the liberal believes, anything is possible: the age-old problem of race relations can be solved by forcibly integrating schools and neighborhoods, the problem of poverty by a government program, of ignorance by requiring everyone to go to school, of health by socialized medicine. Even the secondary differences between the sexes can seemingly be abolished by government action.

In his Message to Congress on January 24, 1944, President Roosevelt announced a "Second Bill of Rights" which would guarantee the "right" of everyone not only to a useful and remunerative job, a decent home, a good education, protection from fear of old age and unemployment, but also to good health. Such promises, ridiculous as they may sound—to whom does one go to claim one's "right" to good health?—are not at all inconsistent with the liberal position as it has been represented over the years. It is no more absurd to guarantee everyone the "right" to good health than to guarantee the freedom from fear, which was one of the "Four Freedoms" we were assured we fought World War II to attain, and which the liberal intelligentsia accepted without a qualm or murmur of protest.

Roy Campbell, with the poet's facility for getting at the substance of things, once remarked that if a dog bites a man, the liberal automatically takes the side of the dog; likewise automatically, Campbell went on to say, he takes the side of the criminal against the policeman, of the striker against the employer, of the black man against the white. Mrs. Roosevelt, by way of example, said that she would never cross a picket line; when Caesar Chavez announces a boycott of table grapes, the liberal intelligentsia, whether they know anything or not of the facts of the case, dutifully stop eating grapes. If a boycott of lettuce is demanded, as one man they stop eating lettuce. Any revolutionary adventurer, whether Castro, Lumumba, Nkrumah, Sukarno, Allende, is greeted with uncritical acclaim as the saviour of his people so long as he invokes the proper anti-imperialist, democratic, class-struggle incantations; when one after another turns out to be the usual self-serving, power-seeking opportunist, it makes no difference, the next to appear evokes the same uncritical enthusiasm.

His political heroes—Adlai Stevenson, John F. Kennedy, Eugene McCarthy, George McGovern—appear to the liberal not as ordinary men seeking votes, but trailing clouds of glory, endowed with the gift of prophecy, and especially with that gift the liberal seems to regard with special favor, charisma. The liberal's capacity for self-delusion is almost unlimited, and experience seems to have little or no effect on him. He came back from Russia in the twenties and thirties with tales of having "seen the future and it works"; now he comes back from Communist China with the same breathless enthusiasm.[3]

The Nuremberg Trials, we were assured, were going to introduce the reign of law among the nations, in spite of the rather obvious fact that at least one of the judges came into court with unclean hands and that one of the basic principles of Western justice, the prohibition of *ex post facto* law, had been ignored. The United Nations charter was greeted as the herald of a new era of peace and freedom, although one of the chartering nations at the time was in the process of depriving its smaller Western neighbors, with the usual methods of military occupation, mass arrests, and deportations, of their freedom and national existence. The causes are endless—industrial democracy, progressive education, school rooms without walls, civil rights demonstrations, freedom marches, open housing, one man-one vote, integration—and each promises the millennium, and the failure of one cause merely whets the liberal's appetite for the next.

But why should otherwise intelligent, normal people who are probably endowed with more than the usual share of good will and the spirit of generosity be so singularly lacking in the ability to see things as they are, to accept the human condition for what it is? It is an old and well established principle of logic that a false premise leads to a false conclusion—admit that the moon is made of green cheese, Norbert Wiener used to say, and it is possible to prove that Murphy is the pope. The liberal begins with the premise of the innate goodness of man and his ultimate perfectibility, all human experience notwithstanding, and finds himself, unwittingly, defending a system of government which engages in mass terror and slave labor camps, and depends for its very existence on a vast system of secret police.

There is more, however, than his inadequate conception of the nature of man that limits the liberal's grasp of reality: the basis of his system of values is faulty. The dominant philosophical position in this country for the past two generations at least has been the naturalism of, among others, John Dewey. Not all naturalists are liberals, although Dewey himself was, and not all liberals are naturalists, but there is certainly justification for the assertion that modern American liberalism has been strongly influenced by the philosophy of naturalism, that naturalism is, in fact, the philosophy of liberalism. Values, according to naturalistic philosophy, are determined by desires; there is no such thing as good or evil in itself, since values have no reality outside experience. As Eliseo Vivas has written, "There was much argument among naturalistic moralists about which desires could be satisfied and how they could be satisfied to produce value. But they agreed on the basic notion that it was desires that constituted value and therefore no desire in and by itself was either good or bad."[4] Margaret Mead's *Coming of Age in Samoa*, for example, described the habits of a primitive people. What right do we have, the author implied, to say that the traditional attitudes of Western civilization toward sexual relations and morality are better? It is all a matter of custom, of what people actually do, not of what they ought to do, which was also the underlying assumption of the Kinsey Report. Values, therefore, are not normative, but merely reflect a given state of affairs. The ultimate consequence of all this is the "Pleasure Principle" of the student revolutionaries, from which emanated such pearls as the following: "In SDS, f.....g is a statement of community, and there's a lot of inter-f.....g, but it's not casual. Sex comes out of a relationship, and is used to build a relationship stronger."[5] From John Dewey to Margaret Mead to the student revolutionaries and the SDS was a perfectly logical development, although not one that Dewey himself would in any way have wanted or welcomed.

From all this derives the liberal attitude toward evil: for the liberal, evil is not an existential fact, but a social problem, which is doubtless one of the reasons liberals found it so difficult, if not impossible, to recognize Stalin and Soviet Russia for what they were. So long as the Communists arrayed themselves in the garments the liberals approved of—anti-colonialism, equality, a democratic constitution, the abolition of exploitation—the liberals were quite willing to overlook, or forgive, what they actually did, if they were able to perceive it at all. One of the most flagrant examples of such myopia and self-delusion, but one that is by no means unique, is Joseph E. Davies's *Mission to Moscow*, and particularly the acclaim it received from the liberal press. George F. Kennan has described the indignation of the professional staff of the U.S. Embassy in Moscow when Davies arrived in 1936 as ambassador—they all seriously considered resigning in protest.[6] The quality of the book itself, and of Davies's competence as an observer, may be judged by his comments concerning the great purge trials of the old Bolsheviks, which he witnessed:

> On the face of the record in this case it would be difficult for me to conceive of any court, in any jurisdiction, doing other than adjudging the defendants guilty of violation of the law as set forth in the indictments and as defined by the statutes.[7]

As if that was not enough: "The prosecutor [Vyshinsky] conducted the case calmly and generally with admirable moderation."[8] Kennan, on the other hand, who attended the trials as Ambassador Davies's interpreter, speaks of "Vyshinsky's thundering brutalities."[9] Davies saw him differently: "The Attorney General is a man of about 60 and is much like Homer Cummings; calm, dispassionate, intellectual, and able and wise. He conducted the treason trial in a manner that won my respect and admiration as a lawyer."[10] One more quotation should be sufficient to put *Mission to Moscow* and its author in proper perspective:

> Stalin is a simple man, everyone says, but a man of tremendous singleness of purpose and capacity for work. He holds the situation in hand. He is decent and clean-living and is apparently devoted to the purpose of the projection of the socialist state and ultimate communism, with sufficient resiliency in his make-up to stamp him as a politician as well as a great leader.[11]

The book was bad enough, but Davies, let us not forget, was an ambitious, superficial man whose single claim to distinction was a very rich wife. In his reports to Washington, as well as those in his book, he was only serving the purpose for which President Roosevelt had sent him to Moscow. However, much worse than the book was its utterly irresponsible reception by the liberal claque. *Foreign Affairs* commended it as "...one of the best informed books to appear in recent years on Soviet Russia";[12] *Pacific Affairs* described it as "...a book of exceptional importance";[13] the *Saturday Review of Literature* as "...one of the most significant books of our time";[14] and Walter Duranty, who had for many years been the Moscow correspondent of the *New York Times,* proclaimed: "To me the charm of this book is first of all its acuteness. How well Davies understood, and how accurately he judged!"[15] (How accurately Duranty was in the habit of judging may be surmised from the following, quoted in *Time,* February 15, 1943: "I see Mr. Stalin as the clear-minded statesman who looks at East and West— both ways at once.") Perhaps the most significant and revealing comment about the book is the following, which appeared on the jacket: "The most important contribution to the literature on the Soviet Union"; this blurb came from no less an objective authority than Maxim Litvinov, Commissar for Foreign Affairs. Finally, to make the story more or less complete, it should be mentioned that *Mission to Moscow* was a selection of the Book-of-the-Month Club and was made into a much publicized movie.

It would be no problem to give many examples of such self-delusion, but one more may be sufficient to illustrate the point I am trying to make and to show one aspect of the general temper of the time. In its account of the Yalta Conference *Time* found itself able to say (February 19, 1945): "By any standards, the Crimean Conference was a great achievement." Now this was the conference, it seems scarcely necessary to mention, where the basic decisions, which were later ratified at Potsdam, were made which resulted in all of Eastern Europe coming under the domination of Communist Russia—the three Baltic countries, Poland, Eastern Germany, Czechoslovakia, Hungary, Romania, and Bulgaria—and by that time there could not, or need not, have been any doubt about what this meant. In addition, it was agreed that Eastern Poland would be ceded to Russia, with the Polish population of the area to be moved westward, and that all German territory east of the Oder-Neisse would go to Poland with the exception of the northern half of East Prussia, which went to Russia—this included such historically German cities as Konigsberg, Breslau, Stettin and Danzig—and that the German population of over seven million would be driven out. The Yalta Conference, without doubt, resulted in one of the most monstrous international agreements in history.[16] How, then, could *Time* describe it as "a great achievement?" Because, to quote *Time* again, "there was a special recognition of certain precepts which Americans have always held dear, and which would reassure many a citizen that World War II was not being fought in vain," namely, "free and unfettered elections by universal suffrage and secret ballot," and "the principle of collective security." So long as the verbal garment was beyond reproach—free and unfettered elections, collective security—the substance could be ignored.

By the end of World War II, liberalism had become an orthodoxy, an orthodoxy "so profoundly self-righteous," as John Dos Passos, speaking from direct experience, described it, "that any critic became an untouchable."[17] While the liberals constantly affirmed their devotion to tolerance and to the idea of what they called "the open society," their tolerance did not, as a rule, include criticism of the truth, and liberalism was the embodiment of truth. The response to two books that appeared during this period and which questioned the very basis of the liberal position will give an impression of some of the obstacles ideas that did not fit the prevailing and accepted thought patterns had to overcome to gain attention.

In 1944 the University of Chicago Press published an unassuming looking, scholarly book without fanfare of any kind and in a very small first printing, which soon became the center of discussion and shook the liberal position to its foundations. This was F. A. Hayek's *Road to Serfdom*. It had first been published in England—Hayek at the time was professor of economics at the University of London—and had been rejected by several American publishers, in one case on the basis of the report of a reader who stated that, although he thought the book would enjoy a good sale, it was "unfit for publication by a reputable house."[18] The thesis of the book, simply stated, was that centralized economic planing—socialism, in other words—must inevitably lead to complete collectivism and the loss of personal freedom. The book was quite obviously the work of a serious scholar whose interest was not indulgence of ideological polemics but the preservation of the free society. The *New York Times*, to its everlasting credit and the astonishment of many, gave the book an excellent and favorable review in a prominent place by Henry Hazlitt, and the *Reader's Digest* made its ideas widely available by means of a skillful condensation. Such attention quickly mobilized a counterattack. Alvin H. Hansen, then much quoted as a "leading authority" on economic questions, pronounced categorically in the pages of the *New Republic*: "Hayek's book will not be long lived. There is no substance in it to make it long lived."[19] The *Library Journal* spoke of its "abstract presentation and poor organization,"[20] but the major attack came from Professor Herman Finer of the University of Chicago in a polemical, abusive book called *The Road to Reaction*, which is of much less interest now, except as a period piece, than the acclaim it inspired. The Kirkus Book Review Service, which was then, and still is, widely used by libraries in the selection of books, described the Finer book as "An exciting book—and a much needed one—the atomic bomb to explode the reactionaries' *Mein Kampf*, Hayek's *Road to Serfdom*."[21] In the *New York Times*, S. E. Harris of the Harvard faculty of economics welcomed Finer's polemic with the words, "This brilliant, persuasive volume...exposes his [Hayek's] fallacies and errors of fact." Finer, of course, was "a world authority," and his book one "no reader can afford to disregard."[22]

The American success of *Road to Serfdom* surprised no one more than its author, who had written it with the English situation in mind; publication by a university press in a very small first printing would in any case almost have guaranteed a limited sale ordinarily. The force of its argument and the coherence of its presentation, plus the fortunate circumstance of the Hazlitt review in the *New York Times* and the condensation in the *Reader's Digest* made it an enormously influential book—and one which, in spite of Alvin Hansen's confident prediction, has become a classic in the literature of economic and political theory.

My second example was also published by the University of Chicago Press, Richard Weaver's *Ideas Have Consequences*. Weaver was a rather obscure professor of English in the college of the University of Chicago when the book was published in 1948; the fact that the Director of the Press, W. T. Couch, chose to publish the book and to put all the resources of the press behind it was not, in my opinion, unrelated to his rude dismissal several years later. It was Weaver's purpose to try to discover why it was, as he put it, that

> ...in the first half of the twentieth century, we look about us to see hecatombs of slaughter; we behold entire nations desolated by war and turned into penal camps by their conquerors; we find half of mankind looking upon the other half as criminal. Everywhere occur symptoms of mass psychosis. Most portentous of all, there appear diverging bases of value, so that our single planetary globe is mocked by worlds of different understanding.[23]

The thesis of the book was that Western civilization had taken a wrong turn in the fourteenth century with William of Occam's questioning of universals; from this beginning came the gradual erosion of belief in objective truth and in the reality of transcendental values which brought us to our present predicament. This argument the author developed with great skill and care and in a style appropriate to his subject.

Ideas Have Consequences was a book, therefore, concerned with an enormously significant problem, and offered a serious, well-grounded analysis of its nature. How, then, did the liberal reviewers respond? Exactly as one might have expected. Howard Mumford Jones, for example, reviewing the book in the *New York Times*[24] accused Weaver of "irresponsibility," to which Weaver replied:

> The way for a writer to show responsibility is to make perfectly clear the premises from which he starts. His statements can then be judged with reference to those principles. I proceeded at some length to make explicit the grounds of my argument, and I have no reason to feel that they are left unclear. I maintain, as Jones correctly infers, that form is prior to substance, and that ideas are determinants.[25]

Charles Frankel, in a review as condescending as it was superficial, found Weaver's thesis "trivial, if not self-contradictory,"[26] and the reviewer for the *Annals of the American Academy*, J. D. Hertzler, while conceding that there were a "number of things one definitely applauds," concluded with the remark, "the nostalgia for and flight to the ideas and 'conditions' of the Middle Ages leaves one cold."[27]

The book is not without faults—there are exaggerations, for example, which Howard Mumford Jones took great delight in pointing out—but it was written under the cloud of Auschwitz, Yalta, Hiroshima, the mass air raids, unconditional surrender, and at a time when civilization seemed bent on destroying itself, a situation that would incline a man as sensitive to the world around him as Weaver was to take an rather apocalyptic view. Anyone, however, who uses such words as "irresponsible" or "trivial" to describe this book says more about himself than the book, and whatever the liberal reviewers may have said, *Ideas Have Conse-*

quences, years after its publication, is still being read, and still has much to say to us, as the following sentence from the last chapter will indicate:

> And, before we can bring harmony back into a world where everything seems to meet "in mere oppugnancy," we shall have to regard with the spirit of piety three things: nature, our neighbors—by which I mean all other people—and the past.[28]

While my primary purpose here is to describe the temper of the period immediately following World War II, one cannot help but pose the question, How did it happen? Why was it that a substantial part of those who dominated the communication of ideas should have been, in their basic attitudes and values, in opposition to the attitudes and values which had been regarded and accepted as a traditional and basic element of American society? Jefferson had taught, and Americans believed, that "the government is best which governs least"; now the group that set the patterns of thought were telling us that social justice required more and more government supervision of every aspect of life; what came to be called, derisively, the "Puritan ethic"—faith, prudence, temperance, self-reliance, the drive to "get ahead," to improve one's self—was represented as anti-social and detrimental to the public good. How could it have happened that in a matter of only a few years such an attitude toward morality, taste, and behavior as represented by Hugh Hefner's "Playboy philosophy" and by the "pleasure principle" of the revolutionary students could not only have won general acceptance, but become almost an integral part of American life? Pornography, once "the last resort of those disqualified from social life," as Ronald Berman put it, had won the sanction of some of the leading people of society—can one imagine Justice Hughes or Justice Taft writing for a pornographic magazine, as Justice Douglas has seen fit to do?

Joseph Schumpeter and F. A. Hayek agree on the term "intellectuals" to describe people who presume to speak for us, who mold opinion and tell us what to think and believe, and this, no doubt, is as good a description as any. Hayek defines intellectuals as "secondhand dealers in ideas,"[29] and Schumpeter as "people who wield the power of the spoken and written word, and one of the touches that distinguishes them from other people who do the same is the absence of direct responsibility for practical affairs."[30] Schumpeter gives a witty, interesting, and convincing explanation of why so many intellectuals have become socialist (he uses socialist and liberal interchangeably), which includes the following two observations:

> ...the intellectual group cannot help nibbling, because it lives on criticism and its whole position depends on criticism that stings; and criticism of persons and current events will, in a situation in which nothing is sacrosanct, fatally issue in criticism of classes and institutions...;[31]

and the fact that mass education has made a large number of people psychologically incapable of working on the level of their talents, but has trained them for nothing else, thus creating a large group of dissatisfied people who feel themselves outside normal society.

Having described the intellectual as a "secondhand dealer in ideas," Hayek makes the important point that intellectuals are inclined "to judge all particular issues in the light of certain general ideas,"[32] and that such general ideas usually consist of a rather confused, ill-digested conglomerate of concepts which have been current and fashionable and which, though they may derive from new truths, are often incorrectly applied and only partially understood. As examples of such intellectual fashions he mentions the theory of evolution, the idea of the predominant influence of environment over heredity, the theory of relativity, the power of the unconscious, equality, the superiority of planning over the results of spontaneous development. And since the intellectual is the means by which ideas and opinions reach the public, "the 'climate of opinion' of any period," Hayek goes on to say, "is thus essentially a set of very general preconceptions by which the intellectual judges the importance of new facts and opinions."[33]

Hayek further points out that the intellectual's preference for generalizations also contributes to his preference for socialism, for public power as opposed to private power. He prefers "broad visions, the specious comprehension of the social order as a whole which a planned system promises"[34] to the tiresome comprehension of technical details and practical problems which the proper understanding of the workings of a free society requires.

Granting that the intellectuals are as they have been described, how was it possible for them to attain the dominant role in our society that has been ascribed to them? Why is it, for example, that the propertied class, which supports the universities, has not only permitted them to be largely taken over by a group that teaches an orthodoxy completely antithetical to its own, but goes right on supporting the universities after this has been pointed out? Why is it, as Schumpeter put it, that "the bourgeoisie," as he calls the propertied class, "besides educating its own enemies, allows itself in turn to be educated by them?" Schumpeter's explanation is that "the bourgeois order no longer makes any sense to the bourgeoisie itself and that, when all is said and nothing is done, it does not really care."[35] This may be true, but it is only a part of the explanation, and perhaps a small part.

The infection started and was propagated in the colleges and universities. Eliseo Vivas was the assistant during the thirties, when the process was just getting underway, of a very well known and influential professor at one of the great Midwestern universities. This man was head of the department of philosophy, a friend of a powerful political family of the state, who had played an influential part in the ousting of a president of the university and in the selection of his successor. He was a man of no scholarly distinction, but a superb speaker who, as Vivas describes it,

> ...employed his superior rhetorical powers in dishing out the thin gruel that he took to be philosophic wisdom—relativism and atheism. He was at his best before large audiences, especially when the audience was not altogether with

him: the voice became softer and deeper, the attitude more gentle, the manner more appealing, expressing a generous desire to lead his students to a better life than their conservative parents had led, if they accepted his reasonable views. His appeal was to the unconventional and critical resentment of the students to the status quo. He addressed the students in a humor they could not miss and in a quasi-poetical language that was as corny as it was middle-to-low brow. He suggested to them, clearly but never explicitly, that he and they were victims of an irrational system, hedging them around with absolutes and false theology. The students loved him and his message.[36]

Vivas was then a teaching assistant and like many other young academics of that time deeply involved in a flirtation with Marxism, which in his case, however, did not lead to a commitment. In speaking of his own teaching in those far-off days of the early thirties, he remarks: "Viewed from the outside, his teaching was quite successful. Students crowded his courses and their reactions to his teaching were always strong.... But was he really a teacher at all? He was not teaching philosophy; he was carrying on a relentless job of propaganda for his own views."[37] Because he and many of his colleagues at the time, he goes on to say, "...put more effort into getting their own ideas accepted than they did in training students to judge for themselves, they could not be called teachers. They were indoctrinators."[38]

The great question, of course, is how all this affected the students. Many of them, as Vivas said, came to the university, especially in those days, filled with political, religious, moral, and social views which, as he put it, "were not merely naive but absurd." It was the teacher's duty to "lead them to think, since all they did was to parrot the nonsense they had learned at home.... But how far to crack their ignorance? Above all, how to crack it? It was all too easy for a teacher with his dialectical hammer to split open the student's mind and spill his beliefs on the ground, leaving him feeling total devastation, emptiness, acute and angry pain. Furthermore, neither he nor his friends," Vivas goes on to say, speaking of his own teaching, "distinguished between the millennial, fragrant, respectable orthodoxies that had sustained the civilization they claimed to champion, and the smelly little ones. For him and his friends all orthodoxies except their own were little and smelly. Their own views, they complacently believed, were not an orthodoxy, they were the truth.... Stripped roughly of the coverage of his beliefs, the student's personality underwent a shock from which sometimes he never successfully recovered. The upshot was that the 'smelly little orthodoxies' that were discarded from students were displaced by devastating cynicism, and since the need to believe was not eradicated when his beliefs were shown up, the student was often ready to fall for the strong dogmatism that was at hand, Marxism."[39] The process Vivas describes was going on, to a greater or less degree, in every college and university in the country, and grew in intensity as time went on, with the SDS and the student revolutionaries of the 1960s one of its more spectacular, but by no means most significant results. It was through this process that liberalism in its modern form became the reigning orthodoxy of the country.

But I have still not answered the question, Why did the propertied classes, who supply the money, permit it to happen? If Schumpeter's explanation, that they do not care, is not sufficient, what is the reason? On the face of it, it would seem that the non-university community should have no difficulty eliminating what Schumpeter calls its "enemies" from the educational institutions—it supplies the money, and the trustees, who are largely from outside the university, in theory, at least, control the institution itself. But how are such people to know what really goes on, and even if they know, what can they do about it? Such a professor of philosophy as Vivas described without doubt had a thoroughly corrupting influence. But how could a member of the legislature, let us say, or a trustee, prove it? And even if he could, what could he do? We live, we are told, in an "open society," where nothing is sacred, in which all questions are "open questions." If nothing is sacred, if all questions are open questions, what is subversive? The universities have made themselves, to a large degree, autonomous by their insistence on tenure, on academic freedom—which is interpreted as academic license—and on the principle that faculty are to be appointed on the basis of scholarly competence alone, without regard to background, point of view, or moral values, all of which has made the professor impregnable and disarmed the university itself. Much the same thing has happened, on a modified scale, in the public high schools.

One of the principal reasons for the development of this situation, which Schumpeter describes as "the bourgeoisie permitting itself to be educated by its enemies," is that "the bourgeoisie" has little or no understanding of the influence or importance of ideas. There are many reasons for this, one of which is doubtless inadequate education. As Eric Voegelin put it:

> It will be sufficient to state that the students have good reason to revolt; and if the reasons they actually advance are bad, one should remember that the educational institutions have cut them off from the life of reason so effectively that they cannot even articulate the causes of their legitimate unrest.[40]

Furthermore, a man who has spent his life in practical pursuits, as most of us do, whose judgements are necessarily made on the basis of everyday considerations, finds it difficult not only to think in terms of abstractions, but to attach much importance to them. Then there is the attitude of the successful businessman toward the intellectual: for rather obvious reasons, and unfortunately for the businessman, he is inclined not to take the intellectual seriously, and considering the general impression made by intellectuals as a group, this is not difficult to understand. Why should a man who has successfully run a substantial business, which means dealing with numerous and constantly changing situations and confronting antagonists of every kind, from labor union officials to government bureaucrats, take a man seriously who chases after one half-understood idea after another and probably cannot even balance his own checkbook, to say nothing of giving another man a job or showing a profit at the end of the year and keeping the ship afloat in every kind of weather? The businessman may be justified in considering himself a better man than the intellectual, but it is the intellectual who has the last word. The intellectual is in a position to undermine the basis of order in society without the businessman, or society as a whole, for that matter, even being aware of what is going on. It is the man of business and affairs who has given the intellectual the source of his power and influence—the vast, elaborate communications network and the enormous system of mass education—but because he has little or no understanding of the role of ideas in the life of society, he has lost all control and influence over what he has created.

There is a further consideration in all this which should also not be forgotten: in any encounter between a professor or academic administrator and the ordinary citizen, the latter is almost invariably at a hopeless disadvantage. The professor enters the fray with the great prestige, whether deserved or not, associated with learning and a life devoted to the higher things, while the ordinary citizen, who pays for it all, appears as the man who has spent his life grubbing for money. In addition, the professor, by the nature of his training and the practice of his profession, is far more skillful in expressing himself verbally than the average citizen. Some years ago, to give an example, a member of the state legislature of Illinois became concerned about what was going on in the universities, and, as we should know by now, with good reason. He made some speeches about

Communism, which were probably wide of the mark, and instituted an investigation. One of the first witnesses to be called was the president of the University of Chicago who, needless to say, was far better equipped for such an encounter than any member of the legislature. When the question of Communist influence in the universities came up, which was probably a rather insignificant factor in the problem, the university president innocently remarked that he didn't know much about Communism, would the chairman of the committee kindly explain it to him, give him a precise definition? None of the committee were able to make a satisfactory answer, even if they knew. The president of the university quickly made fools of the committee, the press was amused, and the world of intellectuals congratulated itself on having won another battle against the common man; but had it? The president of a university occupies a position of great honor and prestige, also of responsibility. Would it not have been better, and more in keeping with his position as the head of an educational institution the rest of the community supports, to have tried to help the members of the committee instead of making them appear foolish? There was something wrong with the universities, which the state legislator instinctively realized, even if he put his finger on the wrong place. Our whole situation, and that of the universities also, would be far better off now if the universities, instead of contemptuously rejecting any form of criticism or questioning, had taken an honest look at themselves from the standpoint of their true purpose and responsibility to society as a whole. But members of the academy are not, as a rule, characterized by the virtue of humility.

Perhaps the two words that best characterize the climate of opinion in our country in the period immediately following World War II are arrogance and its concomitant, self-delusion. We had played the decisive part in a great victory; our economic and military power were without equal. Hitler had ignominiously taken his own life; his Thousand-Year Reich was in ruins and had surrendered unconditionally. What was left of Germany was completely at our mercy. The situation of Japan was similar, but not quite so drastic. Rather than ascribing victory to our vastly greater industrial and human resources, it was easy to believe (and we succumbed to the temptation) that it had come about because we were morally better.

In the war crimes trials following the war we set out not only to demonstrate the crimes of our enemies, but to establish a new concept of international law which would institute the reign of order among nations, an order based on law which would be maintained by the United Nations under the benign influence and care of the two remaining great powers, the United States and Soviet Russia. To make it all seem plausible, certain facts had to be overlooked— war crimes, for example, and crimes against humanity were tacitly assumed to have been committed by the Axis powers alone; the Hitler-Stalin Pact of 1939, which had paved the way for the outbreak of war, and the support of the Axis powers by World Communism until Hitler's attack on Russia in 1941, were conveniently forgotten. Since the only morally admissible form of government was democracy, it was necessary to picture Soviet Russia as at least an incipient democracy—there was much talk of its "democratic" constitution, and of Stalin as a kindly father-figure: "Good old Uncle Joe."

We provided Japan with a new, democratic constitution, and set out to "reeducate" the Germans; we were going to convert them from autocratic, goose-stepping Prussians into peace-loving democrats, in our image. Our democratic institutions, our free press, our system of education, had proven their superiority by our victory, and, hence, should be the model for the whole world, and certainly for the countries we had defeated in the war which were now, it seemed, as putty in our hands.

Stability of international monetary relations was assured by the Bretton Woods Agreement. We would henceforth be masters of our own fate in monetary matters also; no longer would we be slaves to the vagaries of the gold standard. Gold, we were told on the highest authority, was a "barbarous relic," and would henceforth be used only for filling teeth, wedding rings, and other forms of jewelry.

In domestic matters it was assumed that we were equally successful in having found answers to the problems that had beset mankind for generations. A "full-employment" act was passed by the federal government which would banish the specter of unemployment. Since a college education had demonstrably helped some to obtain a better position in life, it would be made available to all—as a somewhat sceptical editorial writer put it at the time, the government was not only going to guarantee a college education for everyone, but that everyone would graduate at the head of his class. There were still a few problems, of course—"pockets of poverty" here and there, segregation in the South, inadequate education and medical care for some, but it was confidently believed that all these things could be taken care of by passing laws, by supreme court decisions, and new, imaginative government programs.

When all these things are taken into account, the reader will perhaps agree that I was not greatly overstating the case when I said: "World War II and the peace that followed it represented the final triumph of liberalism."

2

Albert J. Nock:
An Appreciation

Albert J. Nock is something of an acquired taste, but for those who do not mind his strongly held opinions, his prejudices, and his numerous dislikes, he can be refreshing and stimulating. Most of his books are now out of print, and the journal he edited in the early twenties, the *Freeman*—considered by some to have been the best magazine ever published in this country—is a collector's item. However, a small group of believers keeps his memory alive, and the fortunate person who for the first time happens to come upon his *Memoirs* has the exhilarating feeling of having made an important literary discovery.

Although rather surprised to find himself in his later years classified as a conservative, Nock without doubt contributed substantially to the development of modern conservatism, and the spectacle of the generation in revolt which was raised on the baby books of Dr. Spock, taught in progressive schools on Dick and Jane, and educated in colleges and universities almost completely dominated by liberalism, makes a reconsideration of Nock's views on such subjects as education, the state, and the place of the individual in society particularly timely.

Nock was born in Brooklyn in 1870, the only child of an Episcopal minister. He came from a large family, and grew up in a secure, established environment. The family later moved to a lumber town in Michigan on the shores of Lake Huron, where Nock spent the rest of his boyhood. From the time the ice froze in the fall until the spring thaw, the town was completely isolated. He describes it affectionately as a self-reliant, independent place, full of characters; indeed, it seems to have been an ideal community to grow up in for a person of Nock's temperament. During his youth he was sent to a boarding school in Illinois where he received good training, and then to a small college in New York State, St. Stephen's, which, from his account, must have been a no-nonsense sort of place. Students were expected to have a fluent reading knowledge of Greek and Latin on arrival; the course of study consisted, in Nock's words, of "Readings and expositions of Greek and Roman literature; mathematics up to the differential calculus; logic; metaphysics; a little work on the sources and history of the English language." That was all; there were no courses in English, for instance—English was one's mother tongue and a student was expected to use it properly; as for English literature, that was in the library. After college, Nock seems to have played professional baseball for several years while doing graduate work, and at the insistence of his mother, who is reputed to have been a rather purposeful woman, became, as his father had been, an Episcopal minister. He served in several parishes, but never seems to have been entirely satisfied with the calling of pastor, and in 1909 left the ministry to join the staff of the *American* magazine.

The *American* magazine had grown out of the reform movement of the early 1900s, and included on its staff Ida Tarbell, Lincoln Steffens, Ray Stannard Baker, Finley Peter Dunne, William Allen White, and John Reed. Nock wrote frequently for the *American* and had a hand in the planning of many articles. He was by then a follower of Henry George, was active in some of the groups that promoted George's ideas, and by this means extended his circle of friends and acquaintances beyond that of the *American*. For example, he met Brand Whitlock, the reform mayor of Cleveland, and became a close, life-long friend. Another acquaintance of this period was William Jennings Bryan who, while Secretary of State in the first Wilson administration, asked Nock to make several trips to Europe on his behalf. The first months of World War I he spent in Brussels with his friend Brand Whitlock, who had become the American ambassador to Belgium.

Many of Nock's associations during those years must have been with liberals and reformers, but any inclination he may have had in those directions was soon dispelled. Mr. Wilson's eagerness to get into the European war, the peace that followed it—an "orgy of looting," Nock later described it—the enthusiasm of liberals for such "reforms" as the income tax and the direct election of senators, and finally the penchant of liberals to solve all social problems by legislation soon cured him of any temptation he may have harbored to embrace liberalism. He was later to write in the *Freeman*:

> We can not help remembering that this was a liberal's war, a liberal's peace, and that the present state of things is the consummation of a fairly long, fairly extensive, and extremely costly experiment with liberalism in political power.

During the war he served on the editorial staff of the *Nation*, then edited by Oswald Garrison Villard, and enjoyed the distinction of having caused a whole issue to be suppressed by Mr. Wilson's post office department because of an article critical of Samuel Gompers. In 1920 he became the founding editor of the *Freeman*, a weekly journal of comment and criticism, which was supported financially by Francis Neilson, a former member of Parliament who had opposed the war, resigned his seat, emigrated to America, and married a Chicago Swift. According to Nock's account, when a young writer asked him about the magazine's editorial policy, and particularly whether there were any "sacred cows," he replied that there were three, "as untouchable and sacred as the Ark of the Covenant." These, he went on to say, were as follows: "You must have a point. You must make it out," and finally, "you must make it out in eighteen carat, impeccable, idiomatic English."

When the *Freeman* was discontinued in 1924 Nock enjoyed a considerable reputation in literary circles—there was still in those days something which could be called a republic of letters. He had no difficulty finding publishers for his books, although none of them made any concession to popularity or current intellectual fashions and all, he said, lost money. He had, however, a ready outlet for his witty, pungent essays in such magazines as *Harper's*, the *Atlantic*, the *American Mercury*, the *Century*, until World War II made Nock's kind of realism unwelcome. He wrote biographies of three of the men he greatly admired—Rabelais, Jefferson, and Henry George—and edited an edition of the selected writings of another, Artemas Ward. Nock also edited a complete edition of Rabelais, for which the biography, later published as a separate book, was written as the Introduction. The book on Jefferson is still a useful, interesting, and penetrating study. The *Rabelais* is said to be somewhat dated by recent scholarship, but it is well worth reading, if for no other reason than Nock's love of the subject and its fine writing. There are several collections of essays, and near the end of his life, in 1943, he published his last, and perhaps best book, *The Memoirs of a Superfluous Man*.

From all accounts, Nock was a man of considerable charm—distinguished looking, a brilliant conversationalist, proud of his skill as a billiard player, but intensely jealous of his privacy, and rather inaccessible except to those few favored by his friendship. According to one apocryphal story, the best way to get a message to him during the *Freeman* days was to leave it under a certain stone in Central Park, but it does seem to be true that he would go to a different town to mail letters to make it difficult for his correspondents to disturb his privacy. His oldest and most intimate friend had no idea that Nock had been married and had two sons until he happened, by chance, to meet them on a ship. Nock spent much of his time between the two wars in Europe, chiefly in Belgium and France; but for all his dislike of the self-confident, rich, rather arrogant America of the time, he was, with his scepticism, his realism tempered by idealism, his independence, a true Jeffersonian American.

With the wreckage of the liberal theory of education all about us, it is refreshing and instructive to go back to Nock's rather heretical views on the subject. Much of his *Memoirs* is devoted to education, and he wrote a beautifully worked-out book on the topic, based on a series of lectures he gave at the University of Virginia in 1931, *The Theory of Education in the United States*. Nock's views on education begin with a sharp distinction between intelligence and what he called "sagacity." It was the gift of sagacity and cleverness, he said, which made it possible for frail, weak *Homo sapiens* to survive in a hostile environment; it was sagacity which "enabled man to build up the prodigious apparatus of civilization." He seemed rather doubtful that intelligence or wisdom had much to do with this process. Intelligence, on the other hand, is required if man is "to civilize himself, or even to understand what civilization means." Unfortunately, Nock thought, having been given the sagacity and cleverness to build the elaborate mechanism of civilization, man has never had at his disposal the intelligence to give civilization sufficient direction and purpose; it is the lack of balance between these two gifts which makes human societies so unstable. Corresponding to his distinction between sagacity and intelligence, Nock distinguishes two kinds of training—that which is functional and that which is formative. It is formative training which can, in his opinion, truly be called education, but only the intelligent are capable of being educated. Functional training, he said, can produce an Edison, while education may produce an Emerson. These two pairs of distinctions, between intelligence and sagacity on the one hand and education and training on the other, are central to Nock's critique of contemporary education in America.

The title Nock chose for his autobiography, rather characteristically, was *The Memoirs of a Superfluous Man*. He was superfluous, he went to some length to explain, because, having belonged to the last American generation that offered what he considered to be a proper education, he was an educated man, and America had no place for such a man—he was an anachronism. A society devoted to what he called "economism"—the social philosophy "which interprets the whole sum of human life in terms of the production, acquisition, and distribution of wealth"—needed Edisons, Henry Fords, Andrew Carnegies, all clever, sagacious men, but none of them educated, nor in his opinion intelligent. But what was such a society to do with an educated man? In a society essentially neolithic, as Nock thought ours to be, there is no place for an educated or educable person which a trainable person could not fill. In making such observations Nock, of course, was indulging in a considerable amount of conscious overstatement, but when one compares the curriculum, say, of Michigan State

University with its courses in beginning and advanced fly casting, with that offered to Nock at St. Stephen's College, the exaggeration does not appear so great.

But what for Nock were the marks of intelligence? "The person of intelligence," Nock wrote in his *Theory of Education in the United States*, "is the one who always tends to 'see things as they are,' the one who never permits his view of them to be directed by convention, by the hope of advantage, or by an irrational and arbitrary authoritarianism." To this he added, "...and thus we may say that there are certain integrities at the root of intelligence which give it somewhat the aspect of a moral as well as an intellectual attribute." Wyndham Lewis came close to saying the same thing in his observation that "...the ability to *perceive* the true—which is under everybody's nose but not seen by everybody—is confined to people of considerable intelligence."

If it is only those of intelligence, those who "always tend to see things as they are" who are capable of being educated, what did Nock understand education to be? For him, the purpose of education is to produce a disciplined and experienced mind, and the means to do this is the study of the literatures of Greece and Rome, which "comprise," he said, "the longest and fullest continuous record available to us of what the human mind has been busy about in practically every department of spiritual and social activity." It was "these studies," he went on to say,

> which were regarded as formative because they are maturing, because they powerfully inculcate the views of life and the demands on life that are

appropriate to maturity and that are indeed the specific marks, the outward and visible signs, of the inward and spiritual grace of maturity. And now we are in a position to observe that the establishment of these views, and the direction of these demands is what is traditionally meant, and what we citizens of the republic of letters mean, by the word education; and the constant aim at inculcation of these views and demands is what we know under the name of the great tradition in education.

Nock was of the opinion that education in the spirit of the great tradition had virtually disappeared in the United States; it had become a victim of Gresham's law which, he thought, applied not only to money, but to everything else. When the idea became generally accepted that because higher education was of benefit to some, it should be made available to all, then training had to be substituted for education, because it is only the few who are capable of being educated. "When we consider what the average is, we are quite free to say that the vast majority of mankind cannot possibly be educated." Perhaps Nock's greatest heresy was to question the usefulness of trying to teach everyone to read. It was a noble intention, he admitted, and his much admired Jefferson was in favor of it, but considering the results—the sort of things most people read, and the effect of popular literacy on the general level of writing and publishing, Nock was not at all sure that it had been worth the effort. "Henry Adams," to quote Nock again, said that the succession of Presidents from Washington to Grant was almost enough in itself to upset the whole Darwinian theory.... So one may say that the course of the *North American Review* from its illustrious editorship under Sparks, Everett, Dana, Lowell, Adams, down to the present time, is quite enough to upset the notion that universal literacy is an absolute good. The *North American Review* stands today as intellectual America's monument to the genius of Sir Thomas Gresham.

Nock's advice, needless to say, was not sought by any presidential commissions on higher education, nor did another university follow the example of the University of Virginia by inviting him to expound his views on the subject. With such disasters as that of Cornell before us, however, his firmly held opinion that everyone is not capable of being educated does not seem so preposterous as it may have in the 1900s. Nock would not be at all surprised at the turmoil and dissension now prevalent in colleges and universities; he would no doubt say that these are the necessary and inevitable consequences of the misguided attempt to educate people completely incapable of meeting the demands of higher education—they quite naturally feel threatened and out of place, and those capable of doing university work feel cheated by the watered-down curriculum mass education has made necessary.

Nock had no objection to what he called "functional" training, nor did he deny it its proper place in society; what he did object to was confusing training with education, which he thought was detrimental to both and in fact placed real education in danger of extinction—Gresham's law again. Nock's two pairs of distinctions—intelligence as opposed to sagacity, and training as opposed to education—are no doubt too finely drawn, but they are useful nevertheless and could certainly be helpful in resolving the major crisis in which our educational establishment now finds itself. Do the people who glibly assert that higher education should be available to everyone really know what they are talking about, and are we really doing all those people who are sent in masses to gigantic universities at public expense a kindness, when what most of them need is a chance to learn to make a living to enable them to earn an honorable place for themselves in society? Nock's distinctions may be drastic, and are certainly unwelcome to many, but they are honest, and were made by a man who tried to "see things as they are."

It should not be assumed that because of his use of the word "economism" to characterize the dominant attitude in the United States that Nock would have had anything in common with such ADA types as, for example, John Kenneth Galbraith. While it is true that he did not have a high opinion of men typified by Henry Ford, Andrew Carnegie, or Jay Gould, at the sight of a liberal he "sweat with agony." It was the liberals who were loading up the statute books, as he said, with social legislation, thereby increasing the power of the state at the expense of society, reducing the individual to a "condition of complete state servitude," and "bringing forth the monster of collectivism,

ravenous and rampant." He had no illusions about either
liberals or liberalism, and his objection to the Henry Fords
and Andrew Carnegies of the world was not that they had
been spectacularly successful in producing goods and making money, but that for them these were the principle aims
of life. Nock was a classicist; he believed that man should
strive to create a society that would bring the various aspects
of life into a harmonious whole. In one of his *Freeman*
essays, which is included in a small collection of essays
called *The Book of Journeyman,* he states this idea beautifully:

> The Great Tradition contemplates a harmonious
> and balanced development in human society of
> the instinct of workmanship (the instinct for
> progressive material well-being, with which in-
> dustry and trade are concerned); the instinct of
> intellect and knowledge; the instinct of religion
> and morals; the instinct of beauty and poetry; the
> instinct of social life and manners.

Nock, as mentioned before, was a Jeffersonian American:
he admired the self-reliance, the independence, the strong
sense of individual worth which, in his mind, the Jeffersonian
American represented, and which he remembered from the
Lake Huron lumber town of his boyhood, which did not
even have a police force, and did not need one. But the
America dominated by "economism" was something else
again—"It [economism] can build a society which is rich,
prosperous, powerful, even one which has a reasonably
wide diffusion of material well-being. It cannot build one

which has savour and depth, and which exercises the irresistible power of attraction that loveliness wields."

Nock's attitude toward the state was solidly Jeffersonian, and is succinctly expressed in the title of a collection of his essays on the subject, *Our Enemy, the State*. Nock believed that there were three inexorable laws in all realms of human affairs, in politics, culture, social organization or whatever: Gresham's law; the law of diminishing returns; and the law of exploitation (to which he gave the name, after the friend who formulated it for him, Epstean's law). Epstean's law, he thought, operates with the same immutability as the other two in human behavior, or as the law of gravitation in physics—"Man tends always to satisfy his needs and desires with the least possible exertion." The trouble with all political theory, in Nock's opinion, was that none took these three laws of human behavior into account: the theory of republicanism, for example, is based on a conception of man not as he is, but as he ought to be, and is therefore doomed to failure.

> Republican society must follow the historic pattern of gradual rise to a fairly high level of power and prestige, and then a rather sudden lapse into dissolution and displacement in favour of some other society which in turn would follow the same pattern.

Because of Epstean's law, Nock argued, the state always tends to become a well-organized system of exploitation; for the same reason all schemes to improve the lot of man by state action are doomed to failure—those in control will always distort such schemes for the purpose of satisfying their own needs and desires with the least possible exertion. How amused Nock would have been by the "War on Poverty." When a representative of a Chicago newspaper some months after this program had gotten under way was investigating the spending of "poverty" money in a county in Southern Illinois, he reported that when he remarked to the man in charge that most of the money was apparently being used to give jobs to deserving Democrats, the latter with remarkable candor replied, "But isn't that what it's for?"

Nock thought that to understand the workings of the state it was necessary to understand the difference between state power and what he called "social power." The more or less spontaneous mobilization of the resources of individuals to meet an immediate need is social power; Nock gave as an example the voluntary help extended at the time of the Johnstown flood. Our private schools, colleges, and universities, hospitals, art galleries, symphony orchestras are all expressions of social power. The state, Nock thought, uses every contingency as an excuse to assume such powers to itself, but every increase in state power, which involves coercion, is at the expense of social power. How far we have gone in this direction, as Nock predicted we would, is illustrated by the plight of most private institutions—schools, colleges, universities, hospitals, art galleries, symphony orchestras. The state, by its power of unlimited taxation, takes such a large share of the national product that all such institutions now face a choice between extinction or state support on terms set by the state. But, as Nock said,

It is unfortunately none too well understood that, just as the state has no money of its own, so it has no power of its own. All the power it has is what society gives it, plus what it confiscates from time to time on one pretext or another; there is no other source from which state power can be drawn.

The growth of state power, he went on to say, is always at the expense of social power—as the state waxes, society wanes, and since the state derives its power from coercion, while social power is voluntary, the whole process comes down to the substitution of force for freedom.

Nock believed that there are no accidents in history; events move with the iron law of necessity from cause to effect.

Because the nineteenth century was what it was the twentieth century must be what it is...there is no way of cutting in between cause and effect to make it something different from what it must be.

Because of the enormous growth of state power he saw under the New Deal, he did not hold out much hope for American society. He thought that the process of collectivism would continue, was irreversible, in fact, and would probably end in military despotism.

Closer centralization; a steadily growing bureaucracy; state power and faith in state power steadily increasing, social power and faith diminishing;

the State absorbing a continually larger proportion of the national income; production lan-
guishing, the State in consequence taking over
one 'essential industry' after another, managing
them with ever-increasing corruption, ineffi-
ciency and prodigality, and finally resorting to a
system of forced labor.

So Nock, writing in 1935, saw the future. It has not yet gone
that far, but who is to say that the chain of events is not
developing as he saw it?

Nock called himself an individualist. Where, in his
inexorable chain of cause and effect, does the individual
find himself, what is he to do about it all? Nock came to the
conclusion, after a fairly long and active life, that something
he had learned from a misplaced German aristocrat who
was working as a church janitor in the Michigan lumber
town of his boyhood, and who, in turn, had it from
Montaigne, summed it all up very well:

Human beings are very much what they are, and
their collective society is very much what it is, and
nothing of any conceivable consequence can be
done about either.

We are left, therefore, with ourselves. "In a word," he wrote,

ages of experience testify that the only way society can be improved is by the individualist method
which Jesus apparently regarded as the only one
whereby the Kingdom of Heaven can be established as a going concern; that is, the method of

each one doing his very best to improve one.

In another place, he expressed the same idea by saying that the only way to improve society is to try to present it with one improved unit.

Along the same lines as his view of the individual in society is his theory of the Remnant, which he developed in an essay called "Isaiah's Job," which has often been reprinted and is included in William F. Buckley's anthology of conservative writing, *Keeping the Tablets*. In the essay on the Remnant, it seems quite clear that Nock, consciously or unconsciously, was explaining his own position as a writer. God's instructions to Isaiah, as paraphrased by Nock, were to take care of the Remnant, the

> ...obscure, unorganized, inarticulate, each one rubbing along as best he can. They need to be encouraged and braced up, because when everything has gone completely to the dogs, they are the ones who will come back and build up a new society, and meanwhile your preaching will reassure them and keep them hanging on.

It is not the mass man, Nock thought, to whom anyone having something to say should direct his attention, but the Remnant, a word, he said, Plato had used in exactly the same way it was used by Isaiah. "The mass man," Nock said,

> is one who has neither the force of intellect to apprehend the principles issuing in what we know as the humane life, nor the force of character to adhere to those principles steadily and

strictly as laws of conduct; and because such people make up the great, the overwhelming majority of society, they are collectively called the masses. The line of differentiation between the masses and the Remnant is set invariably by quality, not by circumstance. The Remnant are those who by force of intellect are able to apprehend those principles, and by force of character are able, at least measurably, to cleave to them; the masses are those who are unable to do either.

Nock's position with regard to the Remnant is of a piece with his distinction between intelligence and sagacity—the Remnant are those who make social life possible; they represent the element of any society which maintains standards and thereby keeps civilization going. But as Nock points out, and knew by experience, a writer who directs himself to this group is not going to be overwhelmed by financial rewards—the publishers and editors of the *Playboys* of this world are far better paid than those who put out such journals as Nock's *Freeman*. One can be sure, however, as Nock was careful to point out, that the Remnant is there and is listening; besides, there are other compensations. In his own career Nock was rewarded in the way to which he no doubt attached the greatest value—by the recognition of people whose opinions he could respect.

From the selections from Nock's work quoted in the foregoing, and the emphasis placed on his views on education, a false impression may have been given of the sort of man he was. While he had no illusions about his fellow man, he viewed him with charity and understanding. Nock's view of man, it seems clear, was far more Christian, more tolerant, and more humane than that of the liberal intellectual with his talk of welfare, civil rights, equality and all the rest, who wants everyone to be integrated, adjusted, tested, analyzed, and educated to fit a preconceived liberal image of what man should be—if we are not equal, the liberal will make us so, whether we like it or not. Nock's choice of heroes—Jefferson, Rabelais, Artemus Ward, and Henry George, all men who viewed their fellow man with tolerance and affection, and without illusion of any kind—says much about Nock himself. In his book on Rabelais there is an observation which may help to give balance to some of the Nockisms quoted before:

> Men do about the best they can, as a rule, and it is mere delirium of egotism to expect more from them. One may smile at their inconsistencies and stupidities, one may make a diverting study of their absurd faults and failures, and yet be quite aware that the essential humanity underlying these untoward manifestations is pretty sound and by no means unlovely.

In the history of thought, Nock will probably not be considered a major figure. He had, for example, none of the driving creativity of his contemporary Wyndham Lewis, whose general position was not unlike that of Nock. He made common cause with no one, and made no effort to work out a consistent, systematic body of ideas. He was, however, a wise, highly cultured man. He wrote a book, the *Memoirs*, which is an American classic, and he was an important, perceptive social critic. He saw what was going on and where we were going, and understood the trend and direction of his time as did few others. And, finally, what he had to say he put into "eighteen carat, impeccable, idiomatic English," and it is still, a generation later, as it will be for generations to come, pertinent and well worth reading.

3

Richard M. Weaver:
Advocating Right Reason

To identify Richard Weaver with the University of Chicago and Southern Agrarianism provides a reasonably accurate approximation of the influences that determined his view of the world and the character of his work. He was born in 1910 in Weaverville, North Carolina, of a closely knit, substantial family, the first Weaver ancestor having come into the region in the 1790s when it was still wilderness. A family history published in 1962 includes two talks given in 1950 and 1954 at the annual family gatherings by the member of the family who had become a professor at the University of Chicago. In his 1950 talk he "looks at Weaverville and the Weaver community," as he puts it, "through a perspective of Chicago." He goes on to say:

I have been condemned for the past six years to earn my living in that most brutal of cities, a place where all the vices of urban and industrial society break forth in a kind of evil flower. I sometimes think of the university to which I am attached as a missionary outpost in darkest Chicago. There we labor as we can to convert the heathen, without much reward of success.

His 1954 talk, by way of contrast, is a tribute to his uncle, Ethan Douglas Weaver, who had died a few months before at the age of ninety-seven, the father of ten children and the acknowledged patriarch of the Weaver family.

In the whole course and tenor of his life, Uncle Doug suggests strongly the ideal citizen as he was contemplated, near the founding of this republic, by Thomas Jefferson. He was an agrarian, living on the soil; a primary producer creating things, not trafficking in the things that other men made.... In a world where so much is superficial, aimless and even hysterical, he kept a grasp upon those values which are neither old-fashioned or new-fashioned, but are central, permanent and certain in their reward. That is why we think of him as an outstanding example of the sturdy yeomanry which, though modest and self-effacing, has contributed so much to the fibre of this state.

Richard Weaver came to the University of Chicago in 1944 to teach English and rhetoric in the college; he became professor in 1957 and stayed at the university until his death in 1964 at the age of fifty-three. Before he died he had accepted a visiting professorship at Vanderbilt University which he hoped might become a permanent appointment; but for all his dislike of the city, I do not think that he was unhappy at the University of Chicago. He was a demanding but successful teacher, much respected by his students, and he enjoyed the stimulating, challenging, if not always compatible atmosphere of the University. In 1949 he was awarded the Quantrell Prize for excellence in teaching.

Weaver was of medium height, solidly built, had strongly held opinions which his rather heavy, clearly marked features reflected. He was pleasant to be with, always courteous, never forcing his opinions on others; but he was a man, I think, who found it difficult to establish close relations with others, which doubtless contributed to his loneliness at the University of Chicago. Eliseo Vivas, who was a colleague of Weaver's before becoming a professor at Northwestern University writes of him, "One impression that grew stronger the longer I knew him was that I would never get to know him intimately.... He did not put you off..., but somehow you did not breach the reserve that kept his inwardness inviolate and inviolable."

As soon as the teaching term ended in the spring he abandoned his rather dingy, unkempt bachelor apartment in Hyde Park and set off for Weaverville, always travelling by train, difficult as it became as rail travel deteriorated—he would never fly unless there was no other choice. "You have to draw the line somewhere," he once remarked to me. Distrustful of "progress" and industrialism in general, he regarded the airplane with particular repugnance. He always insisted that his garden be plowed by horse or mule, which became increasingly difficult for his mother to arrange prior to his arrival. As far as it was possible for him to be so in our modern world, Weaver was consistent.

Weaver entered the University of Kentucky at the age of seventeen. The professors, he tells us in his honest and characteristically modest autobiographical essay, "Up from Liberalism," were mostly "earnest souls from Middle Western universities, and many of them—especially those in economics, political science, and philosophy—were, with or without knowing it, social democrats." The university was given to the elective system, which meant that seventeen-year-old students, in effect, told the faculty what they ought to be taught. Having been given no defense against the doctrinaire position of his teachers, by the time he graduated in 1932, Weaver himself had been persuaded, as he said, "that the future was with science, liberalism, and equalitarianism, and that all opposed to these trends were people of ignorance or malevolence." In his third year he joined the Socialist Party and became secretary of the local unit, and while the socialist program had a certain appeal to him—it was then the bottom of the great depression—he soon found that he could not like the party members he met as persons: "they seemed dry, insistent people of shallow objectives."

Subsequent graduate study at Vanderbilt, where he came under the influence of the Southern Agrarians (who had published their manifesto, *I'll Take My Stand*, in 1930) and particularly of John Crowe Ransom, with whom he studied, marked a decisive turn in his life and ended his flirtation with socialism. While he did not, at first, fully agree with these men, he liked them as persons: "They seemed to me more humane, more generous, and considerably less dogmatic than those with whom I had been associated under the opposing banner..., the intellectual maturity and personal charm of the Agrarians were very unsettling to my then-professed allegiance."

The graduate degree in English he earned at Vanderbilt led to a teaching post at a large technical college in Texas where, as he described it, he "encountered a rampant philistinism, abetted by a complacent acceptance of success as the goal of life." While driving back at the beginning of his third year "across the monotonous prairies of Texas," it suddenly dawned on him that he was under no compulsion to go back to a job that had become distasteful to him or to go on professing the clichés of liberalism. At the end of the year he gave up his job and "went off," as he put it, "to start my education over, being now arrived at the age of thirty."

He had used his time in Texas to read extensively in the history of the Civil War, which he continued to do during the three years he spent at Louisiana State, giving special attention to the losing side: "It is good for everyone," he wrote in justification of his decision, "to ally himself at one time with the defeated and to look at the 'progress' of history through the eyes of those who were left behind....The people who emerged were human, all-too-human, but there was still the mystery of the encompassing passion which held them together, and this I have not yet penetrated. But in a dozen various ways I have come to recognize myself in the past, which is at least an important piece of self-knowledge."

In the biographical essay I have referred to, Weaver speaks of two convictions which took possession of him as a result of his studies of the Civil War: that "we live in a universe which was given to us, in a sense that we did not create it"; and that "we don't understand very much of it." Following the further experience of a world war and its consequences, he came to the conclusion, after having rejected it as a ridiculous superstition when he was a young man, that there is no concept that expresses a deeper insight into the enigma of man than that of original sin, which he defines as "a parabolical expression of the immemorial tendency of man to do the wrong thing when he knows the right thing," and finally that we must recognize evil "as a subtle, pervasive, protean force." Armed with such convictions and a firmly held view of the world arrived at after careful study and long reflection, he came to the University of Chicago in 1944 well prepared to teach English and rhetoric in the college and to hold his own in what must, at times, have seemed a rather hostile environment.

It is ironical that this Southern Agrarian, with his distrust of progress and materialism and of science as the source of truth, his rejection of liberalism and socialism, and his preference for the old, backward South to the progressive, industrial North, should have spent the productive years of his life at a university founded by John D. Rockefeller, where, not long before Weaver arrived, the first chain reaction had taken place, the event that launched the age of the atomic bomb, and in the city where fifteen years before there had been a great exposition, "A Century of Progress," celebrating the achievements of science and technology. Out of place as Weaver may have been in Chicago, the challenge and intellectual stimulation of the university undoubtedly contributed to his creative achievement.

One day in the fall of 1945, after the shooting and bombing had finally stopped and the appalling consequences of the war were becoming apparent, Weaver tells us in "Up From Liberalism," he was contemplating, from the vantage point of his office in Ingleside Hall, the actual course of events as compared with the glib promises of our wartime leaders, and wondering what it was that had gone wrong. How could it have happened, for example, that the medieval idea of chivalry, which recognized even the enemy as a man with an immortal soul and thus kept war within the bounds of civilization, could have been supplanted by total war which knows no limits and is subject to no restraint, to be followed by the demand for unconditional surrender that places the defeated at the mercy of the victor, and that, as Weaver says, "impiously puts man in the place of God by usurping unlimited right to dispose of the lives of others."

Believing as he did that the world is intelligible and that history is not accidental, nor determined by biological or economic forces, but is the result of conscious choice, he wondered if "it would not be possible to deduce from fundamental causes, the fallacies of modern life and thinking that had produced this holocaust and would insure others." To discover what went wrong and to describe its consequences is the purpose and the achievement of Weaver's first book, the beginning of which goes back to those ruminations in Ingleside Hall in the fall of 1945.

By fortunate coincidence, the director of the University of Chicago Press when Weaver submitted his manuscript, William T. Couch, was a man who by temperament and background would have been sympathetic to Weaver's unabashed attack on the accepted positions of the post-war period. Mr. Couch's enthusiasm for the book, from the standpoint of his own career, may have been ill-advised, but however that may be, the manuscript was accepted. The publisher insisted on a different title, *Ideas Have Consequences*, on the assumption that it better represented the thesis of the book than the author's *Fearful Descent*. In the fall of 1948 the book was published by the University of Chicago Press with the strong backing of its director, who used all the resources available to him to bring the book into the center of discussion.

The thesis of the book is far-reaching and can be said to question the basic assumptions of modern life. This thesis can be easily stated: It is the triumph of the doctrine of nominalism as propounded by William of Ockham in the latter part of the fourteenth century that put Western man on the wrong path. The practical result of such a doctrine was, Weaver argues,

> to banish the reality that is perceived by the intellect and to posit as reality that which is perceived by the sense. With this change in the

affirmation of what is real, the whole orientation
of culture takes a turn, and we are on the road to
modern empiricism....The denial of everything
transcending experience means inevitably—
though ways are found to hedge on this—the
denial of truth. With the denial of objective truth
there is no escape from the relativism of "man the
measure of all things"....Thus began the "abomi-
nation of desolation" appearing today as a feeling
of alienation from all fixed truth.... Man created
in the divine image, the protagonist of a great
drama in which his soul was at stake, was replaced
by man the wealth-seeking and -consuming animal.

Having described the changes in the perception of reality
and truth which he believed began the process of dissolu-
tion, Weaver goes on to describe its specific consequences:
The doctrine of original sin makes way for belief in the
innate goodness of man, hierarchy succumbs to equalitarianism, religion and faith to rationalism and science, discipline to comfort, the acceptance of the human condition as
a given to belief that man is master of his own fate. Because
society depends on distinction, Weaver asserts, "the most
insidious idea to break down society is an undefined equalitarianism," which, among other things, puts into question
the relationship between effort and reward. In a chapter
called "The Great Stereopticon" Weaver expresses his
strong feelings about the destructive influence of the press,
radio, and movies (TV was then still in its infancy):

What person taking the affirmative view of life can deny that the world served up daily by press, movie, and radio is a world of evil and negation? There is iron in our nature sufficient to withstand any fact that is present in a context of affirmation, but we cannot remain unaffected by the continued assertion of cynicism and brutality. Yet these are what the materialists in control of publicity gave us.

Dismal as all this sounds—and let us not forget that it was written shortly after the end of World War II when the prospects for the Western world seemed to be dismal in the extreme—Weaver "propounds," as he says, if not a whole solution, at least the beginnings of one. The last three chapters, therefore, are devoted to an account of the measures which he thinks would contribute to a recovery of sound values: the restoration of respect for private property, the restoration of the integrity of language, and the restoration of piety and justice as the cardinal elements of social life, piety understood in the classical sense as respect for the order of being.

Property, Weaver unequivocally states, is "the last metaphysical right," metaphysical "because it does not depend on any test of social usefulness." Is it not, he goes on to ask, "quite comforting to feel that we can enjoy one right which does not have to answer to the sophistries of the world or rise and fall with the tide of opinion?" Weaver's concept of property is specific and concrete; it involves not merely claiming the right to something, but bearing the responsibility for it. For him, however, Southern Agrarian that he was, the "last metaphysical right" does not include "the kind of property brought into being by finance capitalism," which, as an abstraction, lends itself to control by the state. I will conclude Weaver's observations on property with one last challenge to the utilitarians, levelers, liberals, or whatever their name may be: "In private property there survives the last domain of privacy of any kind. Every other wall has been overthrown. Here a unique privacy remains because property has not been compelled to give a justification of the kind demanded by rationalists and calculators."

Having determined a sanctuary in private property, Weaver goes on to speak about the nature of language and its relation to order. To demonstrate the ancient belief that there is a divine element in language, Weaver speaks of "the potency ascribed to incantations, interdictions, and curses. We see it in the legal force given to an oath or a word...which can only mean that words in common human practice express something transcending the moment." What Weaver sought to restore, with all the eloquence at his command, was an appreciation of language as something uniquely human, as something given to man to express his highest aspirations, not as a means to deceive others, but as the binding element in society, as "a great storehouse of universal memory" and as a way "to get at a meaning beyond present meaning."

Weaver begins the chapter "Piety and Justice," the last in the book, by extending the meaning of Plato's *Euthyphro* from the impiety of a son toward his father to the impiety of modern man, through technology, toward nature. This impiety takes the form of believing that the demands of man take precedence over the order of nature, as we see, for example, in the destruction of the environment. But the contempt for natural order can also take other forms, one of which, Weaver believes, is "the foolish and destructive notion of the 'equality' of the sexes." He concludes his observation on this subject with the remark, "After the gentlemen went, the lady had to go too. No longer protected, the woman now has her career, in which she makes a drab pilgrimage from two-room apartment to job to divorce court." Besides learning to regard the order of nature with piety, we must also learn to regard our neighbors with piety, and, finally, the past, by which he meant history and tradition.

It is instructive, from the distance of forty years, to consider the reception given to Weaver's first book when it appeared. While there were cries of outrage from the expected sources, on the whole it must be said that the book was given the serious attention it deserved. Howard Mumford Jones in the *New York Times*, as one would have anticipated, labeled it "a sincere, fanatical, and, for my money, irresponsible piece of writing"; George R. Geiger, in the *Antioch Review*, used such terms as "pompous fraud," "essentially evil," and "notorious"; Charles Frankel, in The *Nation*, criticized Weaver's "absolutist defense of the humanistic tradition"; and both the *Annals of the American Academy* and the *Christian Century* were critical of what they considered Weaver's nostalgia for the Middle Ages. The book was warmly welcomed by William A. Orton in *Commonweal* and by Charner Perry in *Ethics*—the latter remarking: "That the author's prejudices run counter to much of modern taste is helpful." Reinhold Niebuhr judged it "a profound analysis of the sickness of our culture," and Paul Tillich pronounced it "brilliantly written, daring and radical.... It will shock, and philosophical shock is the beginning of wisdom."

Only one other book of Weaver's was published during his lifetime, *The Ethics of Rhetoric* in 1953, which he once remarked to me was his best and which Eliseo Vivas, whose judgment Weaver greatly respected, considered "from a scholar's point of view...[his] most important contribution." The austere quality of the book may be surmised from the following observation at the beginning of the opening chapter, "The *Phaedrus* and the Nature of Rhetoric":

> Our difficulty with the *Phaedrus* may be that our interpretation has been too literal and too topical. If we will bring to the reading of it even a portion of that imagination which Plato habitually exercised, we should perceive surely enough that it is consistently, and from beginning to end, about one thing, which is the nature of rhetoric.

Weaver derives his definition of rhetoric from his discussion of the *Phaedrus*: "Rhetoric...consists of truth plus its artful presentation." He later remarks that "neuter discourse is a false idol" because the purpose of all, or most, discourse is to convince us of something, good or bad: The essential thing is to be aware of the rhetorical device being used.

In order to demonstrate the difference between dialectical and rhetorical argumentation, Weaver devotes the second chapter of the book to a discussion of the Scopes trial in Dayton, Tennessee, where in 1925 John T. Scopes, a high school teacher, was tried for having violated a law recently passed by the State of Tennessee making it illegal in any state-supported educational institution "to teach any theory that denies the story of the Divine creation of man as taught in the Bible." With Clarence Darrow for the defense and William Jennings Bryan for the prosecution, the case attracted national attention, the issue being represented as science and enlightenment arrayed against fundamentalism and superstition. Weaver, however, is not concerned here with the merits of evolution or the wisdom of the law forbidding its teaching in the public schools, but rather with the manner in which the case was argued. The defense, Weaver shows, "pleading the cause of science, was forced into the role of rhetorician; whereas the prosecution, pleading the cause of the state, clung stubbornly to a dialectical position." The defense brought in expert witnesses to prove the scientific truth of evolution; but a scientific theory cannot be proved or disproved in a court of law, and this, in any case, was not the issue. It was clear that the law had been enacted by the State of Tennessee and that John T. Scopes was guilty of having violated it, and so the court decided.

The law, as Weaver said, won a victory; but the defense accomplished what it set out to do: it made the law and the point of view it represented look foolish. No matter how much this victory may have been welcomed by the forces of modernism, it was a disservice to the understanding of what the true issue really was. In his discussion of the Southern heritage in his doctoral dissertation, *The Southern Tradition at Bay*, Weaver points out that the anti-evolution laws reflected the belief that "science has not usurped the seats of the prophets," and however foolish Clarence Darrow made such a belief appear to be, it is, as Weaver said, a "continuum of history" and thus deserving of respect.

In his discussion of the various forms of argumentation—the argument from genus or definition, the argument from circumstance, the argument from consequence—Weaver uses Edmund Burke, to the distress of some of his conservative admirers, to illustrate the argument from circumstance, and, in spite of his Southern heritage and Confederate sympathies, Abraham Lincoln to illustrate the argument from definition. The argument from circumstance, in Weaver's opinion, is the least philosophical form of argument because it only attempts to measure current conditions and pressures. It is, therefore, an argument philosophically appropriate to the liberal. Weaver gives numerous examples of what he calls Burke's "strong addiction to the argument from circumstance": his great speech on "Conciliation with the American Colonies," Weaver says, "is from beginning to end...an argument about policy as dictated by circumstances."

In contrast to Burke, Lincoln in his state papers and speeches habitually used the argument from definition, which Weaver believed is the higher form of argument. He gives many striking examples of Lincoln's reasoning in arriving at a position and of his method of argumentation, beginning with his stand against slavery in his debates with Douglas, which he based on the nature of man and the irrefutable fact that the Negro is a man. Weaver concludes his discussion of Lincoln with the following observation:

> The heart of Lincoln's statesmanship, indeed, lay in his perception that on some matters one has to say "Yes" or "No," that one has to accept an alternative to the total exclusion of the other, and that any weakness in being thus bold is a betrayal.

This may be true, but like every other rigid position it is true only within limits. If Lincoln had been less unbending in his conduct of the war, had been willing to consider the circumstances of Southern society, some of the worse excesses could have been avoided and eventual reconciliation made less difficult. A rigidly logical position is all very well, but we live in the world as it is. Edmund Burke states the issue with wonderful clarity:

> A statesman, never losing sight of principles, is to be guided by circumstances; and judging contrary to the exigencies of the moment he may ruin his country forever.

Having defined his subject, Weaver devotes the rest of *The Ethics of Rhetoric* to a masterful study of the nature of rhetoric and its relation to civilized discourse. In the chapter "Grammatical Categories" he describes the characteristics of the various parts of speech and demonstrates how the proper use of words and of sentence structure adds to the effectiveness of writing. He compares, for instance, the use of the adverb by Thomas Carlyle with that of Henry James. And to show how effective the proper use of the word "and" can be, Weaver refers to its use in the King James Bible to join long sequences of verses, giving one "the feeling that the story is confirmed and inevitable.... When this pattern is dropped, as it is in a recent 'American' version of the Bible, the text collapses into a kind of news story." There is a demanding but rewarding chapter, "Milton's Heroic Prose," which makes a sharp contrast to the chapter that follows, "The Rhetoric of the Social Sciences," a rhetoric, it becomes clear, which is neither heroic nor effective.

The last chapter, "Ultimate Terms in Contemporary Rhetoric," includes Weaver's description of "God terms" and "Devil terms," words or phrases which through use or association have acquired, or have been given, a force which goes beyond their original meaning. As examples of God terms he cites "progress," "fact," "science," "modern." An example of a "Devil term" is "prejudice," which, Weaver says, is an "uncontested term"—and who in public life would admit to being prejudiced?—that "disarms the opposition by making all positional judgments reprehensible." The present use of "racist" serves the same purpose. God terms, Weaver asserts, still have some relationship to their original meaning, to what he calls their "referent"; but there is another term, to which he gives the name "charismatic," whose referents are virtually impossible to discover because "it is the nature of the charismatic term to have a power which is not derived but which is in some mysterious way given." Weaver's rhetorical sensibility led him to believe that one of the principal charismatic terms of our time is "freedom." Our political leaders, he goes on to say, make the greatest demands in the name of freedom, in the form of military service, higher taxes, abridgement of rights—one need only think of Franklin D. Roosevelt's "Four Freedoms"—while carefully avoiding any attempt to clarify what it refers to. Another major charismatic term, in his opinion, is "democracy," which people seem to resist any effort to define for fear that the definition would deprive it of its charisma.

Except for a textbook, *A Rhetoric and Handbook*, *Ideas Have Consequences* and *The Ethics of Rhetoric* were the only books of Weaver published during his lifetime. A third book, *Visions of Order*, was in manuscript when he died and appeared the following year; although he had made arrangements for its publication, he had no opportunity to make final corrections. As in his previous books, his concern is with the disintegration of society, and in making his case he further develops many of the themes he had alluded to in these earlier works. In considering the prospect of the total destructiveness of war made possible by the development of modern science, Weaver refers again to the example of chivalry, by means of which, in a period of comparable moral chaos, it was possible to put a limit on destructive impulses. All this, it is clear, is another aspect of what he considers to be the destructive nature of the idea of equality, about which he has more to say in the chapters "The Image of Culture" and "Status and Function." By its very nature, he believed, culture is exclusive. There can be no such thing as a "democratic" culture. "Without the power to reject that which does not understand or acknowledge its center of force, it would disintegrate."

One of the strongest chapters in the book is "The Cultural Role of Rhetoric." Just as he used the Scopes trial in his earlier book to demonstrate the differences between rhetorical and dialectical argumentation, in *Visions of Order* he goes back to the trial of Socrates to illustrate his contention that dialectic, when used in disregard of accepted beliefs and traditions, can be destructive:

> By turning his great dialectical skill upon persons and institutions, Socrates could well have produced the feeling that he was an enemy of the culture which the Greeks had produced....The trial itself can be viewed as a supremely dramatic incident in the far longer and broader struggle between rationalism on the one hand and poetry and rhetoric (and belief) on the other.

And to demonstrate further the place of rhetoric he adds:

> The triumph and continuance of Christian culture attests the power of rhetoric in holding men together and maintaining institutions. It is generally admitted that there is a strong element of Platonism in Christianity. But if Plato provided the reasoning, Paul and Augustine provided the persuasion. What emerged from this could not be withstood even by the power of Rome.

The subject of the final chapter of *Visions of Order* is the imminence of "such a dark night of the mind" as man has experienced in those periods in the past when he seemed to lose sight of the knowledge of his own nature he had previously won. One of the things man has learned about himself, Weaver says, is that he is a creature of choice, which realization gives him a sense of his own worth and dignity. These two qualities, he concludes, give man the capability to create a rational civilization. Now Weaver was strongly of the opinion, and this is the theme of his concluding chapter, that the most serious threat to the concept of man as a creature enjoying the privilege of making choices, and therefore of freedom, is science, in various guises. From the realization that the earth is not the center of the universe, but a minuscule part of it, it has concluded that the fate of man is of little moment. The consequence of evolution, as Weaver puts it, is "to place man squarely in the animal kingdom." Finally, having gone this far, the next step was to make man entirely subject to material causality. "If his being and shape were due to natural law, which could be studied as phenomena, why not account for the whole of him, including his famous free will, in the same way?" The effect of this diminishing of man in his own estimation can be clearly seen, Weaver believed, in his representation in literature and religion: "If the story of man was but the story of an animal, was it really deserving of the sublime treatment it had been given in religion and literature?"

Weaver's answer to all this is to question the validity of the Darwinian hypothesis, which he does in a number of ways, the most convincing of which in his mind, apparently, is the mystery of language, which cannot be explained, Weaver believed, in any other way than as a gift. His criticism of the theory of evolution must have been convincing to him, but it did not convince his old friend and colleague Eliseo Vivas who, in an otherwise very positive review, called his attack on evolution "an embarrassing performance...it would have taken far more science and philosophy than he had at his command to undermine successfully the work of Darwin and his heirs."

From the standpoint of the strict philosopher, Vivas may well be correct. But it should also be said that the basis of Weaver's attack on evolution is not philosophy but instinct, and as Vivas remarks in the same review: "...back of his judgment there is something for which I have no other term than 'instinct'.... His arguments were not always the best, but the attitudes from which his rejections and acceptances issued were for the most part unerring." For the attitude from which his rejection of evolution issued we have not far to seek: it is clearly stated in Weaver's first published essay, "The Older Religiousness in the South," which is included in *The Southern Essays of Richard M. Weaver*:

> Nature is a vast unknown; in the science of nature
> there are constantly appearing emergents which,
> if allowed to affect spiritual and moral verities,
> would destroy them by rendering them dubious,
> tentative, and conflicting. It is therefore impera-
> tive in the eyes of the older religionists that man
> have for guidance in this life a body of knowledge
> to which the "facts" of natural discovery are either
> subordinate or irrelevant. This body is the "rock

of ages," firm in the vast sea of human passion and error.

While Weaver was not a churchgoer, I have no doubt that the "body of knowledge" he referred to was one of the givens of his view of the world.

For all his foreboding about the imminence of "a dark night of the mind," Weaver believed that our best hope lies not in science or politics but in culture, and that "literature is the keystone of culture." This is so, he said, not only because literature is the most various, searching, and complete of the forms of culture, but because "it is the form in which an intellectual culture stores the ideas from which society derives its rhetoric of cohesion and compulsion."

Besides his doctoral dissertation, *The Southern Tradition at Bay*, three other books were published after Weaver's death, all collections of essays: *Life Without Prejudice* in 1965, *Language is Sermonic* in 1970, and *The Southern Essays of Richard M. Weaver* in 1987. The eight essays included in *Life Without Prejudice* include many of Weaver's most strongly held convictions, which, presented in the concise form of the essay, are sharply and succinctly expressed. "Life without prejudice," he says in the title essay, "were it ever to be tried, would soon reveal itself to be a life without principle.... For prejudices...are often built-in principles. They are the extract which the mind has made of experience." In the essay, "Education and the Individual," he makes the following observation, which reflection will show to be completely in opposition to the position of "progressive" education:

Education thus has a major responsibility to what we think of as objectively true. But it also has a major responsibility to the person. We may press this even further and say that education must regard two things as sacred: the truth and the personality that is to be brought into contact with it. No education can be civilizing and humane unless it is a respecter of person.

In another essay, "Two Types of American Individualism," he compares what he considers to be the socially irresponsible individualism of the New Englander Henry David Thoreau with the more realistic, principled individualism of the irascible Southern eccentric John Randolph. It is not surprising that Russell Kirk considers this to be the "liveliest essay" in this collection, or that Eliseo Vivas, in his introduction, remarks that it contains "some essays that fully and completely express the man and his thought... [and] may rank as his best book."

The four books of which I have tried to give some idea reflect the rhetorician and the University of Chicago professor who had thought deeply about the social crisis of our time, its causes, and what might be done about it. *The Southern Essays of Richard M. Weaver* reflect the Southerner whose attitude and loyalty to the South are most clearly represented perhaps by the position of Southern Agrarianism, which, he said in the chapter "The Tennessee Agrarians," was "one of the few effective challenges to a monolithic culture of unredeemed materialism." With the mechanization of cotton farming and its industrial devel-

opment, the South, it must be said, is far more industrial-
ized now and, doubtless, more materialistic than it was
when the Southern Agrarians issued their manifesto in
1930. Even if he had lived to see what has happened since
then, Weaver could not have given up the belief that the
sort of change the Agrarians strove for was possible. At the
end of the same chapter he writes:

> There have been revolutions in human affairs
> which appear miraculous in the light of the
> conditions which preceded them. Ultimately it is
> the human psyche which determines the kind of
> world we live in, and history is marked by radical
> changes of phase which could undermine even so
> seemingly impregnable a thing as our modern
> scientific-technological order.

The truth of the matter was that in making a case for the
kind of life the Agrarians espoused, as Weaver himself
realized, they had become intellectuals, and in so doing, had
isolated themselves. "The South no longer had a place for
them, and the flight to the North completed an alienation
long in process." In writing this he may well have been
thinking of the boy from Weaverville, North Carolina,
who, after the University of Kentucky, Vanderbilt, and
Louisiana State, ended up condemned to earn his living, as
he said, "in the most brutal of cities," even though Chicago
gave him the intellectual stimulus and the platform he may
not have found in the South.

The doctoral dissertation that resulted from Weaver's
thorough study of the "losing side" was discovered several

years after his death and published in 1968 as *The Southern Tradition at Bay*. George Core of the University of Georgia and M. E. Bradford of the University of Dallas carefully, and I am sure, lovingly, edited the manuscript; and to make its Southern origin unmistakable, Donald Davidson wrote an appreciative foreword for what he called his former student's "wise, good-tempered book." It was Weaver's purpose to discover what it was about the South that sets it apart and makes it a distinct region, what it fought for in the war which Weaver thought of as its War of Independence, and then in his study of the postwar period, the time euphemistically called "Reconstruction," how it was that the South, despite defeat and the humiliation of military occupation, was able to resist spiritual disintegration. It is not a book about events, but rather an attempt to discover what people believed, what the "encompassing passion" was, as Weaver called it, that held the South together through four long years of war. For one brought up in a Northern community, where the righteousness of the Civil War as a war to free the slaves and save the Union was accepted as an article of faith, where, in school, to commemorate Lincoln's birthday, one sang "The Battle Hymn of the Republic" and "Marching through Georgia," it is an illuminating and rewarding experience to read Weaver's account of how it appeared from the other side.

Richard Weaver was not the sort of professor whose picture appears on the cover of *Time* or whose books receive rave reviews in the *New York Times*, but his work has had a profound influence which will continue. *Ideas Have Consequences* is one of three books, with F. A. Hayek's *Road to*

Serfdom (1944) and Russell Kirk's *The Conservative Mind* (1953), which provide the intellectual basis for the modern conservative movement. A program of scholarships sponsored by the Intercollegiate Studies Institute bears Weaver's name, and his continuing influence is evidenced by the quality and achievement of the students the program has sponsored; and the Rockford Institute has named one of the two Ingersoll Prizes it gives annually for contributions to literature and scholarly letters for Richard Weaver, the other for T. S. Eliot.

How much he was recognized or how highly regarded he may have been at the University of Chicago I have no way of knowing, but he was much respected as a teacher. In a letter written in 1959 to Russell Kirk he mentions that he was Chairman of the English course in the college and had been invited to teach the course the next year in the history of Western civilization. On the other hand, an old friend and former colleague of Weaver's told me that when the Dean gave him the Quantrell Prize for excellence in teaching he remarked, "Weaver, I hope you will take the money and go some place else."

Although *Ideas Have Consequences* was a commercial success and, however much it may have disturbed some people, was recognized as a book of intellectual distinction, the University of Chicago Press never published another book by Weaver. The head of the press who published Weaver's first book, William T. Couch, was rudely dismissed several years later; but the press has kept his book in print. When Weaver died, Robert E. Streeter, Professor in the Department of English and Dean of the Division of the

Humanities said of him: "Richard M. Weaver for two decades gave the University of Chicago undergraduates an understanding of what it means to think, speak, and to write with full responsibility."

The Richard Weaver I knew as a friend, not as a professor, was an unassuming man of great integrity. He was rather reticent, but always good company and pleasant to be with. During the last winter or two of his life several of us who were involved with the quarterly *Modern Age*, which was then published in Chicago, would meet on Friday afternoons in the modest office of the magazine to look over the manuscripts that had come in and to talk about the problems associated with such a venture—what might be done to make it more appealing to the readers we wanted to reach, whether we should try to obtain advertising, which books we should review; in short, what we should do to give it substance. Weaver always seemed to enjoy such occasions, took a lively part in the conversation, and added to the pleasure we all took in each other's company. It was on a Monday following such an occasion that I received the sad news of his death.

As his life and work make clear, Weaver had strongly held convictions and made no concession to the intellectual fashions of the day, however much his position in the academic community might have been helped by his doing so. He gave freely of himself in his teaching and in his willingness to write for publications he respected and to lecture to groups he felt were serious, irrespective of the honorarium or prestige involved. In his essay "Agrarianism in Exile," he remarks that no man saves himself alone: "He saves himself, if at all, by bringing the community around to right reason." This Richard Weaver tried manfully to do, and with more success, it seems fair to say, than he himself realized.

II

Russell Kirk: Making of the Conservative Mind

Emerging Conservatism: Kilpatrick, Morley, and Burnham

The Responsibility of the Educated: A Graduation Address

James Burnham   James J. Kilpatrick

Russell Kirk

4

Russell Kirk:
Making of the Conservative Mind

The critic of his time must accept the risk of being accused of negativism, but he can console himself with the knowledge that serious criticism has its source in a definite position with its own standards, values and objectives. By the 1950s, with the work of such men as Albert J. Nock, T.S. Eliot, Richard Weaver and Eliseo Vivas, among many others, the criticism of liberalism had grown into a substantial literature; what was lacking was a point of view, or attitude, perhaps better, which would bring the movement together and give it coherence and identity. It was the great achievement—one can say historic achievement—of Russell Kirk's *The Conservative Mind*, which was published in 1953, to provide such a unifying concept. Kirk not only offered convincing evidence that conservatism was an honorable and intellectually respectable position, but that it was an integral part of the American tradition. It would be too much to say that the postwar conservative movement began with the publication of Russell Kirk's *The Conservative Mind*; but it was this book that gave it its name, and more importantly, coherence.

When we published the book that made his reputation, Kirk was an instructor in history at Michigan State College. He had published one book, *John Randolph of Roanoke*, and numerous essays, many of them in English magazines. Canon Bernard Iddings Bell had spoken to me of Kirk; but I came to know him and became his publisher through a mutual friend, Sidney Gair, who had been a textbook traveler for many years for one of the large Eastern publishers, and after his retirement had become associated with our firm. Sidney was a delightful man—a good conversationalist. He had read widely and well, was courtly in his manner, and, as a confirmed conservative, greatly admired Paul Elmer More and Irving Babbitt. What it all comes down to, he used to say, is that a conservative knows that two plus two always, invariably, equal four, a fact of life that a liberal, on the other hand, is not quite willing to accept; it was through him that I met Russell Kirk and published *The Conservative Mind*, for which I will always remember Sidney Gair with gratitude.

Returning in the early part of 1952 from a trip to some of the colleges in Michigan, Sidney told me that a friend of his, a young instructor at Michigan State, had written a manuscript he thought I would be interested in. I remember his description of Russell Kirk very clearly: "...the son of a

locomotive engineer, but a formidable intelligence—a biological accident. He doesn't say much, about as communicative as a turtle, but when he gets behind a typewriter the
results are *most* impressive." Soon after, Sidney asked me
to read a letter Kirk had written him from St. Andrews in
Scotland, in which he described a ninety-mile walk he had
just made from "Edinburgh to Alnwich, in Northumberland,
over the desolate Lammermuirs and along the Northumbrian
coast." After describing various adventures, he continued,
"Appropriately enough, that evening, as I descended the
hills toward the douce old country town of Duns, I beheld
a bogle sitting motionless and malevolent by a fence-post,
in the misty gloaming—or what indubitably would have
been taken for a bogle, not many years syne." He expressed
the hope in this letter that he and I might meet during the
summer, and from this beginning a correspondence soon
developed. In reply to my expression of interest in his
manuscript, he told me that it was on offer to Knopf, but if
they declined it, he would send it to me. "There has never
been a book like it," he remarked in this letter, "so far as
breadth of subject is concerned, whatever its vices may be.
The subtitle is 'An Account of Conservative Ideas from
Burke to Santayana.'" In the same letter, he urged me to
bring out a collection of letters of his friend Albert J. Nock.
This was followed by a postcard from Trier showing a
photograph of the Roman Porta Nigra, which was my
publishing insignia. On July 31, 1952, he wrote from St.
Andrews that Knopf was willing to publish his manuscript
only if he would reduce it to about one quarter of its original
length, and that he was sending it to me. His manuscript,

he said,

> ...is my contribution to our endeavor to conserve
> the spiritual and intellectual and political tradi-
> tion of our civilization; and if we are to rescue the
> modern mind, we must do it very soon. What
> Matthew Arnold called "an epoch of concentra-
> tion" is impending, in any case. If we are to make
> that approaching era a time of enlightened con-
> servatism, rather than an era of stagnant repres-
> sion, we need to move with decision. The struggle
> will be decided in the minds of the rising genera-
> tion—and within that generation, substantially
> by the minority who have the gift of reason. I do
> not think we need much fear the decaying "liber-
> alism" of the retiring generation; as Disraeli said,
> "Prevailing opinions are generally the opinions of
> the generation that is passing." But we need to
> state some certitudes for the benefit of the grop-
> ing new masters of society. More than anyone
> else in America you have been doing just this in
> the books you publish.

On August 21st I acknowledged this letter and the
receipt of the manuscript, which after his description, I was
most anxious to read. My judgment of manuscripts has
often been faulty; but with this one I knew that I had an
important, perhaps a great book, and although I had some
doubts about its commercial possibilities—which proved to
be unfounded—I was determined to publish it. In reply to
my letter to this effect, Kirk, after urging me "not to forsake

our Lake States for the East," had this to say about the battle we both felt we were engaged in:

> It may well be that we shall be trampled into the mire, despite all that we can do. But Cato conquered. And we shall, in any event, be playing the part which providence designed for us. Even the failure of Charles I, after all, was in the long view of history a considerable success. By opposing what seems inevitable, often enough we find that its force is not irresistible; and at the worst, we have the satisfaction of the heroic attitude of the Sassenach confronting Roderick Dhu's crew
>
> *Come one, come all; this rock shall fly*
> *From its firm base as soon as I!*

The manuscript was in beautiful shape, and could have been sent out for typesetting as it came in, except for the original title, which none of us thought would do—"The Conservative Rout." Sidney Gair suggested "The Long Retreat," which was worse (he thought "rout," I mentioned in a letter to Kirk, "sounded 'too hasty'"), and Russell replied, not too helpfully, that "there is a rather fife-and-drum sound to 'rout.'" We kept trying, until someone finally suggested "The Conservative Mind," which Kirk readily accepted. We gave great care to the design of the book, which I wanted to be appropriate to the dignity of its language and the importance of what it had to say. The jacket confidently and, as it turned out, correctly predicted that this was a book which "will become a landmark in contemporary thinking," and on the back of the jacket, to make it evident that *The Conservative Mind* was not a solitary effort on our part, we listed four recently published books: *The Republic and the Person*, by Gordon Keith Chalmers; *The Return to Reason*, essays in rejection of naturalism by thirteen American philosophers and Charles Malik of Lebanon; *The Forlorn Demon: Didactic and Critical Essays*, by Allen Tate; and Wyndham Lewis' *Revenge for Love*. In March or April 1953, we sent out review copies; and with some fear and trepidation, since this book represented a major commitment on our part, we awaited the response, which was not long in coming, and far exceeded our most optimistic expectations.

Kirk approached the difficult task of presenting conservatism as a tradition relevant to our time with two enormous advantages: great skill in organizing a vast body of knowledge with which he was thoroughly familiar, and a superb literary style. "To review conservative ideas, examining their validity for this perplexed age," he tells us in the introductory chapter, "is the purpose of this book." It is not, he goes on to say, "a history of conservative parties...[but] a prolonged essay in definition. What is the essence of British and American conservatism? What system of ideas, common to England and the United States, has sustained men of conservative instincts in their resistance against radical theories and social transformation ever since the French Revolution?"[1] Any informed conservative, he continues, "is reluctant to condense profound and intricate intellectual systems to a few pretentious phrases.... Conservatism is not a fixed and immutable body of dogma, and conservatives inherit from Burke a talent for re-expressing their convictions to fit the times. As a working premise, nevertheless, one can observe here that the essence of social conservatism is preservation of the ancient moral traditions of humanity."[2] Kirk then lists "six canons" of conservative thought, which, in somewhat condensed form, are as follows:

1. Belief that a divine intent rules society as well as conscience, forging an eternal chain of right and duty which links great and obscure, living and dead.... Politics are the art of apprehending and applying Justice which is above nature.

2. Affection for the proliferating variety and mystery of traditional life, as distinguished from the narrowing uniformity and equalitarianism and utilitarian aims of most radical systems.

3. Conviction that civilized society requires order and classes. The only true equality is moral equality; all other attempts at levelling lead to despair, if enforced by positive legislation. Society longs for leadership, and if a people destroy moral distinctions among men, presently Bonaparte fills the vacuum.

4. Persuasion that property and freedom are inseparably connected, and that economic levelling is not economic progress. Separate property from private possession, and liberty is erased.

5. Faith in prescription and distrust of "sophisters and calculators." Man must put a control upon his will and his appetite, for conservatives know man to be governed more by emotion than by reason. Tradition and sound prejudice provide checks upon man's anarchic impulse.

6. Recognition that change and reform are not identical, and that innovation is a devouring conflagration more often than it is a torch of progress. Society must alter, for slow change is the means of its conservation, like the human body's perpetual renewal; but Providence is the proper instrument for change, and the test of a statesman is his cognizance of the real tendency of Providential social forces.[3]

For Russell Kirk, conservatism begins with Edmund Burke; one can say, in fact, that for him the teachings of Burke comprise the basic principles of conservatism. "In any practical sense," Kirk asserts, "Burke is the founder of our conservatism." The opening chapter of *The Conservative Mind*, "Burke and the Politics of Prescription," is quite appropriately devoted, therefore, to the thought of Kirk's teacher; and with the eloquence of language worthy of the great Whig himself, under such headings as Providence and humility, Prejudice and prescription, Equality and aristocracy, The principle of order, Kirk sets before us the principles of conservatism as developed by Edmund Burke. "Edmund Burke's conservative philosophy was a reply to three separate radical schools: the rationalism of the *philosophes*; the romantic sentimentalism of Rousseau and his disciples; and the nascent utilitarianism of Bentham,"[4] but it was a philosophy derived from a deep sense of piety and a profound understanding of the sources of order. "Now and again," Kirk tells us, "Burke praises two great virtues, the keys to private contentment and public peace: they are prudence and humility, the first preeminently an attainment of classical philosophy, the second preeminently a triumph of Christian discipline. Without them, man must be miserable; and man destitute of piety hardly can perceive either of these rare and blessed qualities."[5]

Russell Kirk sees Burke's accomplishment, "taken as a whole," as "the definition of a principle of order." He states Burke's position, "in the simplest terms," as he says, in the following paragraph:

> Revelation, reason, and an assurance beyond the senses tell us that the Author of our being exists, and that He is omniscient; and man and the state are creations of God's beneficence. This Christian orthodoxy is the kernel of Burke's philosophy. God's purpose among men is revealed through the unrolling of history. How are we to know God's mind and will? Through the prejudices and traditions which millenniums of human experience with Divine means and judgments have implanted in the mind of the species. And what is our purpose in this world? Not to indulge our appetites, but to render obedience to Divine ordinance.[6]

Russell Kirk was a young man when he wrote *The Conservative Mind;* he was in his late twenties when, still a graduate student at St. Andrews University in Scotland, he began the book and in his early thirties when finished it. One senses the freshness of discovery, particularly in the chapter on Burke, and the immense pleasure of a young man, searching for his way in a confused and confusing age, who had discovered a view of life that satisfied him, gave him direction, and seemed to answer his most pressing questions. For all its maturity and sound scholarship, Kirk is able to maintain the quality of discovery throughout the entire book that is evident in the first chapter; he may have been, as a young man, "about as communicative as a turtle," as his good friend Sidney Gair described him, but he wrote not only with profound knowledge of his subject but with the passion of a man who has discovered a great truth and wishes to communicate his discovery to others. It is this quality of freshness of discovery as much as its scholarship, perhaps, which carried the day for *The Conservative Mind* and made it one of the most influential books of the postwar period.

Having laid down, in his chapter on Burke, the basic principles of conservatism, Kirk proceeds to follow the development of conservative ideas and their influence through such men as John Adams, Alexander Hamilton, Walter Scott, John Randolph of Roanoke, John Calhoun, Macaulay, James Fenimore Cooper, Tocqueville, Disraeli, Cardinal Newman, down to Paul Elmer More, George Santayana, Irving Babbitt, and T.S. Eliot. To read the book again after almost twenty-five years was as rewarding as when I read it the first time in manuscript. It maintains its high level from beginning to end, but a chapter which especially impresses me at this late date of my life (more, perhaps, than when I first read it) is "Conservatism Frustrated: America, 1865-1918," which, it seems to me, brings out with particular clarity and perception the still unresolved contradictions, tensions, and conflicts which the rise of industrial society has created.

Kirk begins the chapter on America between the Civil War and the First World War with an account of the moral confusion of the country in the decades immediately after the collapse of the Confederacy: the South prostrate, desperately trying "to make a dismembered economy stir again," too much concerned with the exigencies of life to think about anything else; the Northern intellect, which, he says, "practically was the New England intellect," ill-equipped for the task of restoring values, for "splicing the ragged ends." New England conservatism, Kirk says, had always been, "in essence, a conservatism of negation"; and its recent "self-righteous flirtation with radicalism, political abstraction, and that kind of fanatic equalitarianism which Garrison represented,"[7] made it even less able to meet the needs of the day than it might otherwise have been. It was an age of "relentless economic centralization, of dull standardization, of an insatiable devastation of natural resources";[8]—"Jefferson's America," Kirk remarks, "is as much eclipsed as John Adams'...American character, individualistic, covetous, contemptuous of restraint, always had been stubborn clay for the keepers of tradition to mould into civilization. Now it threatened to become nearly anarchic, to slip into a ditch of spiritual atomism. What can be done? Lowell speculates uneasily; Godkin scourges the age in the *Nation*; the four sons of Charles Francis Adams try to fight their way into the thick of political affairs, but are repulsed, and Henry and Brooks Adams pry bitterly into the probabilities of social destiny."[9]

In the rest of the chapter Kirk describes the thought and influence of these four "keepers of tradition," and their attempt to fathom the currents of their time. Kirk's treatment of James Russell Lowell and of E.L. Godkin, the English-born editor of the *Nation,* gets to the heart of the matter, and by showing the manner of their confrontation with their time helps us to understand its nature. But it is in his presentation of the response of Brooks and Henry Adams to their age, and particularly of the enigmatic Henry Adams, that Kirk rises to the challenge and gives us a virtuoso demonstration of his skill in synthesizing and ordering a complex body of ideas and showing their sources and influence.

"A case might be made," Kirk asserts, "that Henry Adams represents the zenith of American civilization. Unmistakably and almost belligerently American, the embodiment of four generations of exceptional rectitude and intelligence, [he was] very likely the best educated man American society has produced.... But the product of these grand gifts was a pessimism deep and unsparing as Schopenhauer's, intensified by Adams' long examination and complete rejection of American aspirations." His conservatism, Kirk continues, "is the view of a man who sees before him a steep and terrible declivity, from which there can be no returning: one may have leisure to recollect past nobility, now and then one may perform the duty of delaying mankind for a moment in this descent; but the end is not to be averted."[10] By the discoveries of modern science man had released a jinni from the bottle, Adams thought, a jinni who would become his master. The laws of thermodynamics—which teach that while the total sum of energy remains constant, its usefulness is constantly dissipated— only increased his pessimism. As Kirk summarizes Adams's conclusions, "Once man turned from the ideal of spiritual power, the Virgin, to the ideal of physical power, the Dynamo, his doom was sure. The faith and beauty of the thirteenth century, this descendant of the Puritans declared, made that age the noblest epoch of mankind; he could imagine only one state of society worse than the rule of capitalists in the nineteenth century—the coming rule of the trade unions in the twentieth century."[11]

What had happened in the short span of three generations to change the robust confidence of John Adams, who risked hanging for freedom and was a founder of a new nation, to the despair of his enormously gifted great-grandson? If the law of dissipation of energy is valid, it has been valid since creation. Kirk's explanation of Henry Adams's pessimism is worth repeating, not only for what it says about Adams, but also for what it says about Kirk and his conception of conservatism:

> Christian orthodoxy believes in an eternity which, as it is superhuman, is supra-terrestrial; and the real world being a world of spirit, man's fate is not dependent upon the vicissitudes of this planet,

but may be translated by Divine purpose into a
realm apart from our present world of space and
time. In this certitude, Christians escape from
the problem of degradation of energy; but Adams,
however much he might revere the Virgin of
Chartres as incarnation of the idea and as a
symbol of eternal beauty, could not put credence
in the idea of Providence. He was determined
that history must be "scientific".... The phase of
religion was far nobler, to Adams' mind, than the
phase of electricity; but he felt himself borne
irresistibly along the wave of progress. One might
reverence the Virgin, in the Electric phase; but
one could not really worship. The blunt non-
conformist piety of John Adams gave way to the
doubts of John Quincy Adams, the humanitarianism of Charles Francis Adams, the despair of
Henry Adams. Belief in Providence, so endur-
ingly rooted in Burke's conservatism, was lost in
the vicissitudes of New England's conservative
thought.[12]

It was, as Kirk says, a "swaggering half-century," and
"even if conservatives had been able to command any
substantial body of public opinion, they scarcely would have
known what way to lead the nation.... By the time the First
World War had ended, true conservatism was nearly extinct
in the United States—existing only in little circles of
stubborn men who refused to be caught up in the expansive
lust of their epoch, or in the vague resistance to change still
prevalent among the rural population, or, in a muddled and

half-hearted fashion, within certain churches and colleges. Everywhere else, change was preferred to continuity."[13]

In the last three chapters of his book, Kirk considers the situation of conservatism in the twentieth century: the last chapter, in the first edition, is called "The Recrudescence of Conservatism"; in the most recent edition, that of 1995, this has become "Conservatives' Promise." His treatment of Irving Babbitt and Paul Elmer More, in whom "the dismayed aloofness of Henry Adams was succeeded by a dogged endeavor to achieve conservative moral reform,"[14] is written with particular understanding and sympathy. In Irving Babbitt, Kirk says, "American conservatism attains maturity."[15] With his emphasis on self-discipline, on the need of the active will to rise above the lethargy of the senses, and in his rejection of humanitarianism, Babbitt arrived at a conception of work which shows how great the gap was between him and his time: "It is in fact the quality of a man's work that should determine his place in the hierarchy that every civilized society requires."[16] For Babbitt, according to Kirk, "The only true freedom is the freedom to work."[17] Babbitt and More had much in common, but with More there is a different emphasis; through all his work, Kirk believes, "runs a stern continuity; the insistence that for our salvation in this world and the other, we must look to the things of the spirit, accept the duality of human nature, remind ourselves that the present moment is of small consequence in the mysterious system of being."[18] Kirk goes on to say, "For him, sin and redemption, justice and grace, were realities which the naturalists can ignore only at the cost of brutalizing society; and after half a century of controversy, the tide appears to be turning sharply in More's favor."[19] Kirk concludes this discussion with the observation, "With Babbitt and More, American conservative ideas experienced a reinvigoration attesting to the coquetry of History and the mystery of Providence."[20]

Kirk is a thorough-going realist, and has no illusions about the destructive forces at work in our time and country. But believing that "a divine intent rules society," and with Burke that "God's purpose among men is revealed through the unrolling of history," he does not succumb to despair. He is well aware that "conservatives have been routed," as he puts it, but equally so that they had not been conquered; and while much has been lost, much remains, and the enemies of conservatism, whether they call themselves liberals, socialists, fascists or communists, stand discredited by history. "The Federal Constitution," Kirk points out, "has endured as the most sagacious conservative document in political history"; and "[d]espite the disruptive forces of mass-communication, rapid transportation, industrial standardization, a cheap press, and other mass media, and Gresham's Law working in the affairs of the mind, despite the radical effects of a vulgarized scientific speculation and weakened private morality, despite the decay of family economy and family bonds, most men and women in the twentieth century still feel veneration for what their ancestors affirmed and built, and they express a pathetic eagerness to find stability in a time of flux."[21] Kirk ends his book with "Cupid's curse against the hubris of the ruthless innovator":

They that do change old love for new,
Pray gods they change for worse.

The first indication that the response to *The Conservative Mind* might be favorable was an advance notice from the somewhat unpredictable Kirkus Book Review Service on March 15th, which was all we could have asked for, and certainly more than I had expected: "A fine study of conservative thought in politics, religion, philosophy and literature from 1790 to 1952." This was followed by a recommendation in the *Library Journal* on May 1st that "since the book is sure to provoke heated controversy...libraries should have copies available." On May 17th, the day before publication, the *New York Times* Sunday Book Review section raised our hopes and spirits immeasurably with an excellent, half-page review in a prominent position by Gordon Keith Chalmers. The book was beginning to show signs of life, and in a letter to Kirk I reported that we were selling about one hundred copies a week, but what really put it into the center of discussion was a long, intelligent review in the July 4th issue of *Time* (dated July 6th). The whole book review section was devoted to one book, *The Conservative Mind*, with George Washington on the cover, and the Kirk book taking up the entire book review section—it was also mentioned in the news pages—the theme of the issue could be taken to be the continuity of the American conservative tradition. The review, which I am told was written by Max Ways, was not only favorable, it was the kind of review which stimulates the interest and curiosity of the reader, which is not true of

every review, favorable or not. All this, and the circumstances of the review having appeared in this particular issue
and being featured as it was, made the publication of *The
Conservative Mind* a significant event. Sales increased immediately—as I wrote to Kirk, to four hundred a week—
and the first printing was sold out before the end of July. A
second printing of five thousand was delivered in August
and a third before the end of the year. Russell Kirk, from
having been a rather obscure instructor at what he was later
to call Behemoth U, had become a national figure.

The impact of *The Conservative Mind* when it first
appeared in 1953 is hard to imagine now. After the long
domination of liberalism, with its adulation of the "common man," its faith in mechanistic political solutions to all
human problems, its rejection of the tragic and heroic
aspects of life, and the not exactly inspired prose in which
its ideas were usually expressed, after all this, I repeat, such
sentiments as "the unbought grace of life," the "eternal
chain of right and duty which links great and obscure, living
and dead," a view of politics as "the art of apprehending and
applying the Justice which is above nature," came like rain
after a long drought. August Heckscher began his review in
the *New York Herald-Tribune* (August 2, 1953): "To be a
conservative in the United States has for so long been
considered identical with being backward, and even faintly
alien, that Mr. Kirk's proud justification of the term is to be
welcomed." Harrison Smith, in a syndicated review which
appeared in many papers including the *Washington Post*,
welcomed the book with the words, "Thoughtful Americans concerned with the rapidity with which totalitarian

theories and revolutions are spreading over a large part of the world should read Russell Kirk's landmark in contemporary thinking." Peter Viereck reviewed the book in the *Saturday Review*. There was a most favorable and effective review in *Fortune*, and *Partisan Review* discussed the book at length in two separate issues. A long essay about *The Conservative Mind* appeared in the *Kenyon Review* by John Crowe Ransom (later reprinted in a collection of his essays), and another, in part a reply to Ransom, by Brainard Cheney in the *Sewanee Review*. It was reviewed in the *Times* (London) *Literary Supplement*, and both Golo Mann and Wilhelm Roepke wrote extensive essays about *The Conservative Mind* in German publications. The post-World War II conservative movement had attained intellectual respectability and an identity, and was on its way.

For the review in *Time* we are indebted to Whittaker Chambers. I had first met Chambers in 1952, when he was given an honorary degree by Mount Mary College in Milwaukee. Hearing that he was in Milwaukee, I called to ask if I might see him. I did this, I must say, with some hesitation, since I was reluctant to intrude on his privacy, and was therefore all the more pleased when he told me that he would be delighted to see me, and to come along at once. He was with his wife, Esther, who had made her own contribution to his achievement and firmness under fire, and for all her gentleness and charm of manner, had character and resolution of steel. The admiration I had felt for him ever since reading *Witness* quickly developed into warm friendship. I visited the Chambers a number of times at their Maryland farm, visits of which I have the most pleasant memory, and corresponded with him to the end of his life. To have known Whittaker Chambers, and to have been able to regard him as a friend, was a great privilege. Feeling as I did about the manuscript, I spoke to Chambers about *The Conservative Mind* soon after I had read it, and sent him a set of proofs as soon as they became available. His response was the following letter, dated June 26, 1953:

> I wrote to Roy Alexander, the editor of *Time*, recently, to say that I thought that Russell Kirk's book was one of the most important that was likely to appear in some time, and to suggest that *Time* might well devote its entire Books section to a review of it.... I also told *Time* why I thought *The Conservative Mind* important, what it was and did.
>
> Yesterday, Roy telephoned to say that *Time* agreed and that its whole forthcoming Books section will be devoted to Kirk's book. It will be the July 4 issue with G. Washington on the cover. So I am able at last to do something, in a small way, for you who have done so much for us—and to do something for Kirk's book, which you and I both would agree is the big thing. Incidentally, this shows that simply by picking up a pen, things can be done if we have the will to overcome inertia.

I can make no claim that I ever did anything for Whittaker Chambers beyond offering him my friendship; I felt more than repaid by the return of his. He was one of the great men of our time; and by his assuming the terrible burden of being, as he put it, "an involuntary witness to God's grace and to the fortifying power of faith," all of us are immeasurably in his debt.

The sense of exultation we all felt when the advance copies of *Time* came in is still very clear in my memory. Sidney Gair, who had recommended the book to me in the first place, was in a state bordering on ecstasy. "Just look," he said, striking the magazine with his hand for emphasis, "pictures of Paul Elmer More and Irving Babbitt in *Time* magazine, and all because you decided to go into the publishing business. If you had gone into oil instead, and had struck four or five gushers in a row, it wouldn't have given you a fraction of the satisfaction you feel now." I readily admitted that this was true, but mentally observed that the proceeds from only one oil well would have been most welcome at the moment to pay some bills, which, as always, were rather pressing, a circumstance which helped to keep my pride and sense of achievement within bounds.

Not all the reviews, needless to say, were favorable, and neither *Harper's* nor the *Atlantic* could find space to review the book at all. The diehard liberals of the academy, in particular, were unwilling to concede anything to Kirk. Peter Gay of Columbia University, for example, ended his review in the *Political Science Quarterly* (December 1953) with the observation: "In trying to refute Lionel Trilling's position (that American conservatives have no philosophy and express themselves only "in action or irritable mental gestures"), Kirk has 'only confirmed it.'" Stuart Garry Brown reviewed the book in *Ethics* (October 1953), a quarterly published by the University of Chicago, and was not at all impressed. He reviewed Scott Buchanan's *Essays in Politics* at the same time, which, he said, "is much the better book." (Brown quotes with apparent approval a remark of Buchanan's to the effect that the Soviet Union is a "province of the democratic empire.") Brown is "tempted to say that Mr. Kirk has translated Babbitt's *Democracy and Leadership* into his own, inferior idiom and reissued it to nourish the complacency of the neoconservative coterie. But this would be in some measure unfair both to Mr. Kirk and the neoconservatives." Before going on to the more congenial task of considering Scott Buchanan's book, Brown observes, "Since...Kirk's despised American majority allows him to cultivate such tastes and virtues as he pleases, it is not, by the same token, required to take him seriously." Each to his own taste, and to his own manner of going from premise to conclusion. Norman Thomas, in the *United Nations World* (August 1953), concluded a long and wordy review, which gives the impression that his reading of the book was rather spotty, with the remark, "What he has given us is an eloquent bit of special pleading which is, in part, a false, and, in sum total, a dangerously inadequate, philosophy for our time."

In contrast to the opinions of Peter Gay and Stuart Garry Brown, Clinton Rossiter, in the *American Political Science Review* (September 1953), states flatly that Kirk's "scholarship is manifestly of the highest order," and concludes his review: "Certainly the so-called 'new conservatism' of the postwar period takes on new substance and meaning with the publication of this splendid book." L.P. Curtis reviewed

The Conservative Mind together with Richard Pares' *King George II and the Politicians* in *Yale Review* (Autumn 1953), and expressed the opinion, "This eloquent and confident book should hearten present conservatives and open the eyes of many of them to the splendor of their moral heritage. It should give pause to those scientistic planners and sentimentalists who dismiss the forebodings of Shakespeare's Ulysses as old hat...in spite of shortcomings Kirk fulfills one of the higher aims of the historian: he teaches us a way of life, and one, moreover, that is tried in experience and sprung from our condition."

The acceptance of "conservatism" as the description of the growing movement in opposition to the rule of liberalism was not automatic or without strenuous opposition. Both Frank S. Meyer, who eventually became one of the acknowledged leaders of the conservative movement, and F.A. Hayek, who did as much as any other single person to give direction and a sound footing to the movement in opposition to the planned economy, wrote vigorously against conservatism as a description of their position. Although recognized as one of the founding fathers of the conservative movement, Hayek has never been willing to describe himself as a conservative; he prefers to be known as an "Old Whig," a label which requires several pages of explanation, an explanation which probably convinces everyone who reads it except Professor Hayek himself that he really is, at heart, a conservative. All of which provides us with a fine example of "the proliferating variety and mystery of traditional life," which, Kirk tells us, conservatives particularly cherish.

Frank Meyer's attack on the "New Conservatism," as he called it, appeared in the July 1955, issue of the *Freeman* and had the ominous title, "Collectivism Rebaptized." He begins by acknowledging that "the emergence of the New Conservatism, which has for some time filled the quarterlies and magazines of opinion and is now spilling over into the larger world, can be accurately correlated with the appearance of that book...it was *The Conservative Mind* which precipitated the New Conservatism." Kirk's position, and that of the new conservatives in general, Meyer argues with his usual vehemence and confidence, is rhetorical, and "without clear and distinct principle." Since, he says, Kirk "presents himself and his beliefs always rhetorically, never on a reasoned basis, he can succeed in establishing the impression that he has a strong and coherent outlook without ever taking a systematic and consistent position...to make tradition, 'prejudice and prescription,' not along with reason but against reason, the sole foundation of one's position is to enshrine the maxim 'Whatever is, is right,' as the first principle of thought about politics and society."

Meyer is particularly sharp in his criticism of Kirk's rejection of individualism; for Meyer, "all value resides in the individual; all social institutions derive their value and, in fact, their very being from individuals and are justified only to the extent that they serve the need of individuals." While he did eventually call himself a conservative, Meyer always differentiated his position from what he called the "New Conservatism," and primarily on the basis of his conception of the individual and what he took to be Kirk's position in this respect to be. Meyer concludes his *Freeman* article with a stern, and in my opinion, completely erroneous judgment, and a judgment I have every reason to believe he himself later came to regret, "The New Conservatism, stripped of its pretension, is, sad to say, but another guise of the collectivist spirit of the age."

Hayek's rejection of conservatism was first given in the form of a paper at a meeting of the Mont Pèlerin Society, an international organization of liberal—in the traditional sense—economists and others who share their concern for the free society. The first meeting of the society took place in Switzerland in April 1947; its annual meetings ever since, held usually in September, have provided opportunity for the consideration on the highest level of contemporary problems and issues. Hayek is the founder of the society and was still its president when he gave his paper, later printed as the postscript, to his monumental book, *The Constitution of Liberty*, which was first published in 1968. While neither *The Conservative Mind* nor Russell Kirk were specifically mentioned in the paper, it was obviously inspired by the success of Kirk's book and the influential position the ideas it set forth had attained—which is attested by the fact that Kirk was invited to defend his position immediately afterward, which he did extemporaneously, without notes of any kind, and with great brilliance and effect. This encounter in an elegant Swiss hotel before a distinguished international audience between one of the most respected economists of his time, who had been honored by professorships at the universities of Vienna, London and Chicago, and the young writer from Mecosta, Michigan, was a dramatic and memorable occasion; as a rather biased witness, I would not be prepared to say that the young man from Mecosta came out second best.

Hayek's rejection of conservatism, as a noun rather than a concept, may well have been unconsciously influenced by the fact that in the Austria, in which he reached maturity, conservatism was identified with the House of Habsburg and clerical Catholicism. In his explanation of why he is not a conservative, however, Hayek undertakes to base his argument on strictly rational grounds, but it is an argument carried through without the coherence or unremitting logic one associates with Professor Hayek. Conservatism, he argues, is reactionary; while it may be against what all of us are against—collectivism or socialism—"by its very nature it cannot offer an alternative."[22] Guided as they are, he says, "by the belief that the truth must lie somewhere between extremes," conservatives "have shifted their position every time a more extreme position appears on either wing." In consequence, "the conservative lacks principle," and "is essentially an opportunist."[23] In saying that the conservative lacks principle, Hayek does "not mean to suggest that he lacks moral conviction"; what he means, he says, "is that he (the conservative) has no political principles which enable him to work with people whose moral values differ from his own for a political order in which both can obey their convictions."[24] From this assertion, Hayek goes on to say, "to the liberal neither moral nor religious ideals are proper objects of coercion, while both conservatives and socialists recognize no such limits."[25] Finally, Hayek tells us, "one of the fundamental traits of the conservative attitude is a fear of change, a timid distrust of the new as such, while the liberal position is based on courage and confidence, on a preparedness to let change run its course even if we cannot predict where it will lead."[26]

Conservatism, as Kirk has repeatedly pointed out, is not an ideology or a fixed body of dogma; it can much better be described as an attitude, as a way of viewing the world, which includes the willingness to come to terms with the realities of the human condition and to accept and pass on the order of being as it has come down to us; it begins, as Kirk puts it, "with the premise that we must be obedient to a transcendent order." As for the assertion that conservatives lack principle, are mere opportunists, one need only point to some of the great representative conservatives—to Edmund Burke, to John Adams and the others who framed the Constitution, the "most sagacious conservative document in political history," as Kirk describes it—can one say that they were men without principle? Hayek takes conservatives to task for their "fear of change"; if we have learned nothing else from the history of the last hundred years, we should have learned that a skeptical view of change is highly desirable, that "innovation is a devouring conflagration," as Russell Kirk puts it, "more often than it is a torch of progress." As ironical as it may sound, it is quite possible that Hayek's resistance to conservatism is nothing more than resistance to change; the conservatism described by Russell Kirk comes to Hayek, with the heritage of the Austro-Hungarian monarchy behind him, as a new concept, and, conservative at heart that he really is, he is not willing to accept it without a struggle.

Conservatism, Professor Hayek argues, by its very nature "cannot offer an alternative to socialism." But why should it? Why should an American conservative, with the free and incredibly successful society behind him made possible by the American tradition and the U.S. Constitution, feel any compulsion to offer an alternative to socialism, a concept of government and society not only completely contrary to human nature, but utterly discredited by experience? As for the criticism that conservatism fails to recognize that moral and religious ideas are not proper objects of coercion, has not the present age of licentiousness taught us the contrary? A society has the right to protect itself from those who would destroy it, from those who would destroy it physically as well as from those who would destroy the moral principles on which it rests, John Stuart Mill to the contrary notwithstanding. Or as Willmoore Kendall would put it, a society embodies "a public truth, which it defends against barbarians outside its confines and heretics within them."[27]

By his tireless, unselfish, and effective devotion to the cause of the free society, Frank Meyer earned the right to nourish an aberration or two, one of which was his infatuation with individualism. In a very broad sense, so broad as to become meaningless, it is true that "all social institutions derive their value from individuals," but which individuals? A society is more than the individuals who momentarily make it up; its character and quality are also determined, and determined very largely, by its history, its traditions, its symbols, its myths and all the other things that comprise that "eternal chain of right and duty which links great and obscure, living and dead." The South is different from the

North not so much because those now living in the South are different, but because it has had a different experience, just as German or Austrian society is different from French or English society. To say these things, to talk about the primacy of "prejudice and prescription" in the preservation of order, is not "enshrining the maxim 'What is, is right,' as the first principle of thought about politics and society," but viewing reality as it is, and its consequences as they must be.

However much our respected late friend Frank Meyer may have tilted against what he called the New Conservatism, when the first issue of *National Review* appeared in November 1955, with Frank S. Meyer on the masthead as one of the editors, and only a few months after the appearance of the article which called the New Conservatism "but another guise of the collectivist spirit of the age," the new magazine was described as "a conservative journal of opinion," and Russell Kirk was a regular contributor. It would seem, therefore, that Kirk had won.

We published five further books by Russell Kirk. One on *John Randolph of Roanoke*, was a revised edition of a book first published in 1951 by the University of Chicago Press; and another, *Beyond the Dreams of Avarice* most of which in somewhat different form, had appeared, was a collection of essays, in various English and American periodicals. The other three books were original works, and to some extent at least, were written with encouragement and stimulation by our firm, in which act and secondary creativity we performed one of the proper functions of the publisher.

The author describes his *John Randolph of Roanoke* as "an account of a radical man who became the most eloquent of

American conservatives."[28] It was not the purpose of the book to give an account of Randolph's life, except summarily, "but rather to describe his opinions and to suggest their influence." Our edition differed from the original chiefly by the inclusion of an appendix containing several of Randolph's speeches which had not been accessible before to the general reader, and a number of representative letters, some published in our book for the first time. To recall the thought and influence of John Randolph, that passionate, eccentric, wonderfully eloquent Virginia aristocrat, was for Russell Kirk, as he says, "a pious act"; to publish such a book in 1964, the year of the great triumph of Lyndon Baines Johnson, was for me a particularly satisfying act of defiance.

The reader of *Beyond the Dreams of Avarice* will soon discover that Russell Kirk is a master of the essay form. Whether writing on censorship, on social boredom, liberalism, the island of Eigg in the Hebrides or on Wyndham Lewis, Kirk's sense of history, his skill in illuminating a contemporary subject from the perspective of the past, and his spacious style give his essays a quality all their own. A most appreciative review in the *New Yorker* (August 4, 1956) ended with the comment, "As a critical tool in the hands of a writer as adept as Russell Kirk, conservatism has a sharp cutting edge indeed."

The three books by Russell Kirk following *The Conservative Mind* which were entirely original with us were *A Program for Conservatives, Academic Freedom,* and *The American Cause,* the first two published in 1955, and the last in 1957. *A Program for Conservatives,* in a way, was a continuation of *The Conservative Mind*; in it, Kirk undertook to apply to the contemporary situation the principles he had described in his earlier book. The critical response was almost as extensive as that brought forth by *The Conservative Mind*, but somewhat more varied. By some it was as warmly welcomed as the first book. James Burnham, for example, in the *Annals of the American Academy* (March 1955) concluded a most favorable review with the words, "He is not only reviving the conservative tradition, but he is rescuing it: both from sterile reactionaries who have degraded it, and from verbalists who...are trying to hitch a ride on the shifting Zeitgeist." While not entirely uncritical, Raymond English pronounced the book, in the *New York Times* (November 21, 1954) "necessary and most welcome." Perhaps the most remarkable review was that of James Rorty in the socialist *New Leader* (October 25, 1954) who ended a two-page, serious discussion of the issues Kirk raises with the conclusion, "What he has done is to give us the most systematic, eloquent and persuasive general statement of the conservative position that has appeared in print."

There were also, needless to say, voices of dissent. The review in *Partisan Review* was headed "The Conservatism of Despair"; the *Progressive* (July 1955) predictably felt that the book represented "the worst aspects of the 'conservative recrudescence,'" and *Commonweal* (December 31, 1954) called it a "sterile book." A long review in *Harper's* (January 1955) was headed "Backward, Turn Backward," and accused Kirk of "utopianism," but had to admit, reluctantly, it would seem, that he "raises the gravest questions; he has real moral fervor; he is far better educated, more literate,

than most contemporary writers on politics and society."
From all this it is evident that, having started the discussion,
Kirk was well able to keep it going and on his own terms.

Of the three books, the one that represented the most
original contribution to thoughtful opinion and had the
greatest influence was probably *Academic Freedom*. The
book was written in response to what the author felt was a
widespread misuse and misunderstanding of a concept he
considered vital to the well-being of the university and
therefore of society as a whole. The somewhat flamboyant
rhetoric of the late Senator from Wisconsin, Joseph R.
McCarthy, and even more, a sense of guilt and inadequacy
on the part of certain members of the academic community,
had led to a state of mind bordering on hysteria. We were
solemnly assured that a professor who dared to drive a
foreign car or assign a work of Thomas Jefferson to his
classes was in danger of instant dismissal. When the senator
recommended that certain books critical of American institutions in the libraries maintained in foreign countries by
the U.S. Government be removed, the cry of "book burning" was heard throughout the land; and the American
Library Association, with great fanfare, responded with a
manifesto, "The Freedom to Read." In all this, "academic
freedom" was invoked like an incantation. The situation
was further confused by the appearance in 1951 of a book,
God and Man at Yale, by a recent Yale graduate, William F.
Buckley, Jr., whose argument culminated in a paragraph, at
the end of a chapter headed "The Superstitions of 'Academic Freedom'":

One thing is clear: it is time that honest and
discerning scholars cease to manipulate the term
academic freedom for their own ends and in such
fashion as to deny the rights of individuals. For in
the last analysis, academic freedom must mean
the freedom of men and women to supervise the
educational activities and aims of the schools
they oversee and support.[29]

In this welter of claim and counter-claim, of accusation
and counter-accusation, Kirk felt that the real meaning of
academic freedom, both "as a security against hazards to the
pursuit of truth by those persons whose lives are dedicated
to conserving the intellectual heritage of the ages and to
extending the realm of knowledge"[30] and as an obligation on
the part of those it is intended to protect to act in a manner
appropriate to their profession, was in danger of being lost.
Academic freedom, Kirk points out, "belongs to that cat-
egory of rights called 'natural rights,' and is expressed in
custom, not in statute,"[31] which makes its proper understanding, particularly by those who claim its privilege, all
the more necessary. Academic freedom, Kirk emphasizes,
does not mean "complete autonomy for teachers, or the
licentious toleration of a bewildering congeries of private
fancies"; nor is it "freedom simply for the masters of
educational institutions to enforce their opinions upon the
teachers." It is a special kind of freedom which arose from
the realization that the protection it afforded was necessary
if the university was to fulfill its high moral and intellectual
purpose, and will survive only so long as the university
remains true to its purpose.

The critical response to *Academic Freedom* was extensive, and, for the most part, of the kind one hopes for but does not often experience for a serious discussion of an important subject. For once, also, the response to the book was not rigidly ideological, as is so often, unfortunately, the case with a book which takes a strong position on a controversial issue. The book was reviewed at considerable length, and although not without some difference of opinion, most positively in the *New York Times* (March 20, 1955), by Roswell G. Ham, who called it a "brilliant and exciting study," while William F. Buckley, Jr., found himself joining hands with the *Nation* in a complete rejection of the book. Buckley's review (the *Freeman*, July 1955) is headed "Essay in Confusion," and asserts "...Dr. Kirk's book on academic freedom has something in it for everybody.... But no one could conceivably refer to this book for a reasoned statement of a coherent position on academic freedom."

One of the most useful, conscientious, and thoughtful reviews was that of Paul Pickrel in *Commentary* (July 1955). Pickrel, in places, is sharply critical and strongly disagrees with Kirk's position, but writes:

> Yet for all that I remain unconvinced of Mr. Kirk's historical account of academic freedom, for all that I regard his philosophical position as too narrow and (as he would say) too doctrinaire, for all that I am annoyed by occasional inaccuracies, when I called his book valuable at the beginning of this review I meant it. I think the book makes a major contribution to the discussion of academic freedom in this country.

The last book we published in our firm's early years by Russell Kirk, *The American Cause*, was written following the disclosure of the dismal performance of many Americans while prisoners of the Communists in North Korea. The lack of any sense of loyalty, or awareness of what their country stands for, of its traditions, history and achievement, even of the will to survive on the part of a substantial number of American soldiers taken prisoner during the Korean War, came as a great shock and demonstrated that something was seriously wrong with the American system of education. To correct this situation, insofar as one small book can do so, was the purpose of *The American Cause*, and that it served its purpose is demonstrated by the fact that it has been widely read, and, after twenty years, is still in print. Reviewing it in *Commonweal* (December 6, 1957), Thomas Molnar remarked that it combined the "great qualities" of "the philosopher's grasp of ideas and the pamphleteer's singleness of purpose."

As I mentioned earlier, Russell Kirk was an instructor of history at Michigan State College (now University, of course) when we published *The Conservative Mind.* Michigan State is one of those vast educational conglomerates which have developed in consequence of the widely held belief that if a college education is useful and helpful to some, justice and the principles of democracy demand that it be made available to all. Courses are offered, as Kirk has often remarked, in everything from medieval philosophy to elementary and advanced fly casting. The school's chief function, in his opinion, is to deprive the young people who pour through its gates of whatever prejudices and moral principles they bring with them, and to send them out into the world again having given them nothing in return in the way of principles or understanding to help them to come to terms with the realities of life.

Not long after the publication of *The Conservative Mind* Kirk resigned his position at Michigan State, using the occasion to get off a great blast at the President, John Hanna—"bachelor of poultry husbandry and honorary doctor of laws at his own institution" as he was later to describe him—and at the whole conception of such an institution as Michigan State. When he told me of his intention to do this, I urged him to reconsider, pointing out the advantages of a relatively secure academic position with its monthly check as opposed to the uncertainties of living as a writer and lecturer, to say nothing of the retribution to be expected from the academic establishment. To this he replied in his characteristic fashion in a letter dated October 12, 1953:

> Poverty never bothered me; I can live on four hundred dollars cash per annum, if I must; time to think, and freedom of action, are much more important to me at present than any possible economic advantage. I have always had to make my own way, opposed rather than aided by the times and the men who run matters for us; and I don't mind continuing to do so.

Make his own way he did; Russell Kirk, one can truthfully say, has become one of the most influential men of our time. We listen to him because he speaks with authority, not with the outward authority of the tax collector or the public official, but with the inner authority of a man who has thought deeply about what he says, means it, and is willing to put himself on the line for it. Our lasting publishing association was the founding in 1957, with David S. Collier, of *Modern Age*. He resigned as editor after only two years, but gave the publication direction and quality which, after twenty years, it still has. "By the time Kirk resigned in 1959," George Nash remarks in his *The Conservative Intellectual Movement in America*, "he had established what he wanted: a dignified forum for reflective, traditionalist conservatism. *Modern Age* had fulfilled a desperate need; even after Kirk's departure it remained the principal quarterly of the intellectual right."

Russell Kirk has chosen to live in a small town in northern Michigan, Mecosta, where he spent many happy summers as a boy with various relatives, in a region of small lakes, sand hills, and the stumps of the great pines that once covered the area. The house of his great-grandfather, where he lived as a bachelor, burned to the ground, ghosts and all, on Ash Wednesday, 1975, but the large, solid, square brick house, surmounted by a cupola rescued from a demolished public building (which was nearly finished at the time of the fire) provides ample room for his charming, down-to-earth, energetic wife—the perfect wife for Russell—and their four daughters and for numerous visitors. Appropriately, as the home of its most prominent citizen, the house dominates the village. A former woodworking shop some quarter of a mile away has been converted into a study, and there, surrounded by the books accumulated during thirty years of disciplined study, he does his work. A student or protégé is usually in residence, and groups of students come during holidays for study and discussion. The rather remote, obscure village of Mecosta has become an important intellectual center, and doubtless has more positive influence in the world of ideas than the huge "university" Kirk abandoned in its favor.

One of the most remarkable aspects of Kirk's career has been its uninterrupted consistency. In a disorderly age he has tirelessly and eloquently made clear the necessity and sources of order; against the false prophets who proclaim that all values are relative and derive from will and desire, he shows their immutability; and to those who believe that man is capable of all things, he teaches humility and that the beginning of wisdom is respect for creation and the order of being.

5

Emerging Conservatism:
Kilpatrick, Morley, and Burnham

The postwar conservative movement, it can be said without too much simplification, grew out of two impulses: the attempt to strengthen traditional institutions and attitudes as forces in modern life; and a reaction against those "new modes and orders," to use a phrase beloved by Willmoore Kendall, which had already changed and threatened to alter beyond recognition the structure of American society. Both aspects of modern conservatism are clearly evident in three remarkable books on American government which appeared within two years of one another in the late fifties: Felix Morley's *Freedom and Federalism* (1959), James Jackson Kilpatrick's *The Sovereign State*s (1957), and James Burnham's *Congress and the American Tradition* (1959). These books are rather different in style and in their

approach to the problem of government—a problem,
Burnham says in his book, which "is insoluble yet is
solved"—but all three were written by men of strong
convictions whose respect for the traditional American
method of reconciling order with freedom derives from a
profound knowledge of its history. That these three books
were written almost at the same time and not long after the
administration of Franklin D. Roosevelt and Harry S.
Truman is evidence not only of the vitality of the American
governmental tradition, but the depth of the realization
that it was gravely threatened.

When he wrote *The Sovereign States*, James Jackson
Kilpatrick was editor of the *Richmond* (Virginia) *News-
Leader*. This book may properly be considered, I think, the
Southern reply to *Brown* vs. *Board of Education*, the Supreme Court decision of May 17, 1954, which undertook
to put an end to racial separation in the public schools.
While the school decision was the immediate stimulus to
the writing of the book, its concern is with the much larger
issue of the usurpation by Washington of the authority of
the states. In his introduction Kilpatrick sets his position
with complete frankness:

> May it please the court, this is not a work of
> history; it is a work of advocacy. The intention is
> not primarily to inform, but to exhort. The aim
> is not to be objective; it is to be partisan.
>
> I plead the cause of States' rights.
>
> My thesis is that our Union is a Union of
> States; that the meaning of this Union has been

obscured, that its inherent value has been de-
based and all but lost.

I hold this truth to be self-evident: That
government is least evil when it is closest to the
people. I submit that when effective control of
government moves away from the people, it
becomes a greater evil, a greater restraint upon
liberty.

Kilpatrick is a fine stylist, and in the pages of his book
develops his thesis with the eloquence of the great Virginia
orators he so much admires. His book, as he says, may not
be a work of history; but there is much history in it,
primarily of the means, sometimes successful, sometimes
not, by which the various states ever since 1789 have tried
to protect themselves from the encroachment of the national government in Washington. Our government,
Kilpatrick argues, was "constitutionally intended to be...a
federation of sovereign States jointly controlling their
mutual agent, the Federal government." It is true, he goes
on to say, that the sovereign States "...jointly had delegated
some of their powers, but they did not become less sovereign thereafter. They remained separate, respective States."
While the Fourteenth Amendment—Kilpatrick devotes a
fascinating chapter to the means by which this amendment
became a part of the Constitution, if it ever properly did—
has greatly weakened the power of the individual states, as
has the income tax amendment, the states still have the
means to protect themselves, if they use it. This is the "right
of interposition," as developed by James Madison in his

report of 1799 to the Virginia House of Delegates during the great controversy that resulted from the Alien and Sedition Acts. Kilpatrick quotes the following sentence from Madison's report:

> That, in case of deliberate, palpable, and danger-ous exercise of other powers, not granted by the said compact, the States, who are parties thereto, have the right and are in duty bound, to interpose for arresting the progress of evil, and for main-taining their respective limits, and authorities, rights and liberties appertaining to them.

"This," Kilpatrick adds, "is the heart and soul of the 'right to interpose.' The language was to be reaffirmed, substan-tially verbatim, by the Hartford Convention in 1814; by the Wisconsin Legislature in 1859; and by the Virginia Assem-bly in 1956. When men talk of the 'Doctrine of '98,' this is the paragraph they are talking of."

Kilpatrick gives many examples of the use of interposi-tion by individual states, examples which are not only of the greatest interest in themselves, but clearly show how much we have lost of the independence Americans once regarded as their most treasured and characteristic possession. When, in 1793, the Supreme Court, in the Chisolm case, held against the State of Georgia, commanding the state to appear in court or suffer judgment in default, the Sovereign State of Georgia, as it then considered itself to be, re-sponded in no uncertain terms. As Kilpatrick describes the incident: "The Georgia House of Representatives passed a bill providing that any Federal marshall who attempted to levy upon the property of Georgia in executing the court's order 'shall be...guilty of felony, and shall suffer death, without the benefit of clergy, by being hanged.'" There were the Kentucky and Virginia Resolutions, in the preparation of which both Jefferson and Madison had a leading part, in answer to the Alien and Sedition Acts of 1798; the response of the governor of Pennsylvania in the Olmstead case, who, in 1809, ordered out the state militia to prevent a United States marshall from serving a writ against two ladies who had inherited a sum of money from a disputed prize case; and, of course, the revolt of the New England states against the Embargo Acts of 1807 and 1809. Kilpatrick describes all this in fascinating detail and in great style, all of which makes the supine acceptance by present-day Americans of any order emanating from a federal court or agency, no matter how outrageous, all the more depressing. The threat by some bureaucrat to withhold "federal" money—it comes, after all, from the taxpayers—is sufficient to bring any recalcitrant state, city, school board, or, for that matter, university promptly into line.

It is the purpose of Felix Morley's *Freedom and Federalism* to define the principles and circumstances which have made the American form of government eminently successful, to determine why it was, as Morley puts it, that "the political system of this representative Republic has done more for its people as a whole than any other ever devised." In addition, he undertakes to describe the influences which presently endanger the continuance of the American form of government as it has developed since the Philadelphia Convention. Like Kilpatrick, Morley lays great stress on the federal structure of the American system: "The United States, as the name implies, are a union of sovereign states, federal in nature," he tells us on the first page of his book. The immediate issue which motivated him to begin his book was not, however, a Supreme Court decision, as was the case with Kilpatrick's *The Sovereign States*, but the threat to the independence of the Court implied in President Roosevelt's bill of February 5, 1937, to reorganize the court—the "court packing bill," as it was called. It was the president's "Fireside Chat" on the following 9th of March, in which he undertook to allay the mounting criticism of the bill by, among other things, asserting that his only purpose was "to make democracy succeed," which, Morley says, "for the first time brought home to me...the demonstrable fact that uncritical praise and practice of political democracy can readily be the highway to dictatorship, even in the United States. The collection of material for this book was begun that evening."

American society, Morley is willing to grant, is democratic, but society must be distinguished from government. The democratic nature of American society, in his opinion, is based on a religious conception, that "all are brothers under the Fatherhood of God." From this, he says, derives the idea of equality which underlies American society and makes it democratic; as Morley puts it, "All men are subject to the same natural laws and therefore should be treated equally by man-made laws." The American structure of government, however, is not democratic, and was never intended to be, although there are strong forces pushing it in that direction. Morley puts great emphasis on the destructive influence of Rousseau, and particularly his specious, but superficially appealing concept of the "general will." "A single, unified popular will," Morley points out, "implies a single, unified governmental direction to make the will effective." Hitler and Stalin both doubtless considered themselves to be the embodiment of the "national will," which was the basis of the claim that their systems were democratic, and that Franklin D. Roosevelt thought of himself in a somewhat similar fashion is not so far fetched as it might sound. In his "State of the Union" message of January 6, 1941, in which he outlined what he called the "four essential freedoms," Roosevelt proclaimed, "A free nation has the right to expect full cooperation from all groups," which, as Morley argues, "is exactly what Rousseau meant in stating that 'whosoever refuses to obey the general will must in that instance be restrained by the body politic, which actually means that he is forced to be free.'"

While Morley is well aware of the continuing vitality of the American system and tradition of government, he is equally aware of the forces behind the growing tendency to concentrate political power in Washington, to change the Federal Republic, as he would put it, into a centralized democracy. Two Amendments to the Constitution, in his opinion, have "operated subtly to undermine the federal structure of the United States as originally planned. The Fourteenth Amendment in effect reversed the emphasis of the first eight Amendments, all designed to limit the powers of the central government, so as to make these limitations applicable by the central government to the States. The Sixteenth Amendment supplemented this revolutionary change by giving the central government virtually unlimited power to tax the people without regard to State needs or boundaries." It was the Sixteenth Amendment, of course, which provided the means to implement the "service state" which, as we are constantly being made more aware, gradually becomes the bureaucratic state.

James Jackson Kilpatrick and Felix Morley are both journalists in the best tradition of that much maligned— largely by the conduct of some of its own members— profession. While both are serious students of American history and government, the particular strength of their approach to the problem of government is their intimate, firsthand knowledge of how it actually works and their unblinking realism. To go back to their books some twenty years after having published them was a rewarding and encouraging experience: rewarding because it made me realize again the substance and quality of the governmental traditions we have inherited, something that is easy to forget in a time seemingly dominated by the Internal Revenue Service, the Department of Health, Education and Welfare, and the Presidential Fireside Chat; and encouraging because they have stood up so well.

James Burnham can best be described, it seems to me, as a political philosopher in a tradition that goes back to Plato; but when I first met him, he was associated with the magazine *National Review*, and could, therefore, also be described as a journalist. He has thought deeply about government: how it comes about, the source of its legitimacy and its right to power, its purpose, its limitations, and the basis on which a particular government is to be judged.

When I first talked to him about a book, it was with the purpose that he write a study of the congressional investigating committee. In the aftermath of the McCarthy episode and particularly the irrational response of the liberal intellectuals to it, there was a danger, it seemed to me, that the importance and unique function of the congressional committee could be overlooked. There was a need, I thought, for a serious, solidly based book showing how the congressional investigation committee has developed and the enormously important role it has played, a role which was becoming all the more necessary as a counterweight to the constantly growing power of the executive department of government. Out of this suggestion came a much more inclusive study, not just of the place of the congressional committee in our system, but of Congress; reading it again makes me all the more convinced that *Congress and the American Tradition* will, with time, be recognized as one of the classic books on American government.

Political philosopher that he is, Burnham quite properly begins his book on Congress with a discussion of the source of government. To the question, by what right does one man rule another? There is, he says, no rational answer: "...the problem of government is, strictly speaking, insoluble; and yet it is solved." The ancients sought the answer in myth: "In ancient times," the first sentence of *Congress and the American Tradition* tells us, "before the illusions of science had corrupted traditional wisdom, the founders of Cities were known to be gods or demigods." While contemporary explanations of the sources of government, as Burnham says, use a less picturesque language, they tell us little more. He concludes these reflections with the observation: "Without acceptance by habit, tradition or faith of a principle which completes the justification for government, government dissolves, or falls back wholly on force—which is itself, of course, non-rational."

The principle which Americans have traditionally accepted as the justification of government, of rule by another, is embodied in the "We, the People" of the Preamble to the Constitution. This, of course, is also a myth: the Constitution was not ordained or established by "The People of the United States": it was drafted by the members of the Philadelphia Convention and ratified by the individual states. Like all myths, its acceptance makes it true, and it will remain true only so long as it lives as a part of the American tradition.

No one, I feel confident, has expressed the tradition of American government more eloquently or beautifully than James Burnham:

> Surely it must have been their faith in tradition as a living and continuous force that reconciled the Fathers to a document that, as the lawyers that many of them were, they would never have accepted as a valid contract: internally contradictory, with its assertions of dual and divided sovereignty; ambiguous as well as unfinished in its definition and assignment of rights, duties and power. Pure reason could not guarantee a good government, strong, just and free. But reasonable men, drawing on the wisdom of the

past shaped into institutions as well as principles, and relying on the future interplay between individuals and their inheritance of tradition, might devise an orienting directive, which would itself become an essential, even critical, part of the living tradition. So, of course, has the Constitution become, so that it seems the précis, the distillation of the entire American political tradition. Our governmental structure, whether good or not as a conceived rational system, becomes, is made, good and even the best through time and history. The Constitution is like a man's wife who, though to tell the truth that would be revealed by an objective scale, she is not the most beautiful and talented creature in the world, nevertheless through twenty or thirty or fifty years of successful marriage becomes, as a living and historical being, a good and indeed the best of all possible wives.... I accept it as right that Congress, the President and the courts shall govern me because they have been chosen by prescribed forms (however strange in themselves, and very strange they are) that have been honored by observance and prior acceptance.

Having described the place of Congress in the American system of government as it was intended by the Founders and as it developed during the nineteenth century—the "Golden Age" of parliamentary government, as Burnham calls it—Burnham goes on to consider "The Present Position of Congress," as the second part of his book is called. Article I of the Constitution, as we all should know but may be inclined to forget, grants "all legislative powers" to "a Congress of the United States." In addition, Congress was to exert a strong influence over those other two attributes of government, the sword and the purse; as Burnham puts it: "The size, temper and target of the sword are to be decided by Congress, just as Congress is to determine the amount, source and purpose of the monies. The President wields the sword, as he opens the purse, only as attorney, steward, agent for Congress, and only through Congress for the nation and the people." The Congress, of course, still goes through the formality of passing laws, levying taxes and appropriating money, of exercising its legislative prerogative; but more often than not, the initiative for legislation comes not from Congress itself but from the executive department. In actual practice, the judiciary and the bureaucracy in many ways now exert a far greater legislative power than Congress; in both legislation and fiscal control, Congress is in danger of becoming little more than a formality. As for the war-making power, once thought to be vested solely in Congress, here too the President has assumed the decisive voice. "Not only do the presidential acts, as in the case of Franklin Roosevelt's moves from 1939 to 1941, make a war inevitable, so that the Pearl Harbor occasion of its open start is, like the congressional declaration, a secondary incident; President Truman further demonstrated in Korea how one of the biggest wars in our history, in terms of casualties and cost, can now be entered and conducted without any legal authority from the legislature, simply by not calling it a 'war.'" In a process which began during the early days of the New Deal, Congress has more and more become accustomed to delegating its powers to the Executive and the various agencies it has established; but, as Burnham wisely points out, "To 'delegate' such powers as control over money, war and foreign affairs is, in reality, to renounce them, to abdicate."

It was not always so. "Throughout most of our history," Burnham tells us, "there has been congressional predominance within the central government." To illustrate his point, Burnham quotes the following from the *Diary of John Quincy Adams*, written after his first election to Congress in 1830: "My election as President of the United States was not half so gratifying to my innermost soul. No election or appointment conferred on me ever gave me so much pleasure." Can one imagine a former President making such an observation in our day, or even giving a moment's consideration to the possibility of becoming a Member of Congress? "To understand what is happening to the political structure of American society," Burnham continues, "we need to keep both facts in mind: that the legislature was, traditionally, predominant in theory and practice, and that is no longer so." In the modern, computerized, highly bureaucratic state, where every citizen must have his social security number and his every transaction is carefully monitored by the Internal Revenue Service, has Congress, with its debates, its committees, and its formalized procedures become an anachronism, a picturesque but wholly unnecessary vestige of the eighteenth century? Burnham most emphatically believes not, and he bases his justification of Congress on a rigorous discussion of government and the threat to liberty inherent in its nature.

Burnham distinguishes between two possible forms of government in the modern world: one based on the "general will," on "the theory that the will of the people is the ultimate sovereign," and the other on a "structure of government in which there obtains, or is thought to obtain, a 'rule of law,' certain 'rights' that are in some sense basic and inalienable, and a 'juridical defense' that protects the citizen through forms of 'due process' backed by the underlying rule of law." The first he calls the "democratic ideology," and the second the "constitutional principle"; between the two, he says, "there is no logical relation whatever."

The democratic formula, he goes on to say, necessarily ends in dictatorship, because only Caesar—whether his name be Bonaparte (who, as Burnham points out, was *elected* First Consul in a national plebiscite) Hitler, Stalin, Mussolini, or Peron—can embody the people's will. "Caesar," he says, "is the symbolic solution—and the only possible solution—for the problem of realizing the general will, that is, for the central problem of democratist ideology."

While there is, Burnham argues, no necessary connection between representative assemblies and liberty—constitutional government and liberty have existed without representative assemblies—the survival of constitutional government and liberty under the power relationship now existing between the citizen and the state depends on the survival of Congress. It is what Burnham calls "the intermediary institutions" which diffuse the power of the state and thereby protect the liberty of the individual citizen; and chief among these, with the decline of the influence of the several states and the subservience of local government and the judiciary to the executive and the bureaucracy, is Congress:

> Among the political institutions of the American system it is Congress that now remains the one major curb on the soaring executive and the unleashed bureaucracy. If Congress ceases to be an actively functioning political institution, then political liberty in the United States will soon come to an end. If Congress continues to have and to exercise a political function, then there will be at least a measure of political liberty—a workable minimum, and a chance for more.... No one can deny the accuracy and cogency of many of the adverse criticisms that have been made of Congress as an institution and of many individual Congressmen. But the hard relation remains: if liberty, then Congress; if no Congress, no liberty.

"For Congress to survive politically," he goes on to say,

> means that it shall be prepared to say Yes or No, on its own finding and responsibility, in answer to the questions of major policy; and this it cannot do unless the individual members of Congress have the courage to speak, to say No even against the tidal pressures from the execu-

tive and bureaucracy, and the opinion-molders
so often allied in our day with the executive and
bureaucracy, even against the threat that the
semi-Caesarian executive will rouse his masses
for reprisal at the polls—or in the streets.

During the course of his discussion of the American
system of government, Burnham develops, almost as a by-
product, one might say, a most illuminating syndrome, as
he calls it, to illustrate the contrasting characteristics of the
liberal and conservative positions. This includes such attitudes toward man as belief on the part of the conservative
that human nature is limited and corrupt and on the part of
the liberal in its unlimited potentiality. In the area of
government, Burnham finds a presumption on the part of
the conservative in favor of Congress as against the executive and the opposite position on the part of the liberal; he
believes that the liberal is inclined to view with favor the
concentration and centralization of government power in
the interest of social progress, while the conservative is
suspicious of government power in any form, and inclines,
therefore, toward states' rights and the diffusion of power.
In this connection, it is interesting to observe that the
response of the liberal reviewers to the Morley, Kilpatrick,
and Burnham books accurately reflects the attitudes
Burnham describes. It is possible that I ascribe more
importance to reviews than they deserve: while they are
often written hurriedly, without knowing much more about
the book than can be gained from the jacket and skimming
through a few pages, reviews of such books as these three,

which take a strong, definite position on a diverse issue, reflect rather accurately current tendencies and attitudes.

Reviewing the Kilpatrick book in the *Yale Review* (Autumn 1957), C.L. Black, for example, after dismissing it as "without serious merit," went on to say that it "strikingly exemplifies the South's intellectual desperation in the present crisis of its caste system." Cecil Johnson, in the *Annals of the American Academy* (September 1957) thought that Mr. Kilpatrick, "if he applied himself with the same energy and enthusiasm and selected his materials as carefully...might produce comparable treatises in defense of slavery or in condemnation of democracy." William S. White, in the *New York Times* (April 28, 1957), was more generous, and appeared actually to have read and enjoyed the book. He did not agree, needless to say, but found it "...an extraordinary essay by a gifted, if perhaps very wrong-headed man. A polemical tract, it nevertheless has grace and skill."

Two such distinguished scholars as Edith Hamilton and Roscoe Pound (the former Dean of the Harvard Law School) praised the Morley book in the highest terms: Dean Pound called it "a notable contribution to political science and indeed to juris-prudence." Cecil Miller, on the other hand, reviewing the book in *Ethics*, expressed the opinion that Morley "is essentially apologetic with respect to the question of states' rights," and concluded, "if such tongue-in-cheek philosophizing serves a useful purpose, this reviewer fails to discern what it is." He also, I am sure, failed to read the book.

The response to the Burnham book provides an even more striking example of the refusal, or inability, of the liberal intellectuals to confront the serious issues these three books raise. R.H. Salisbury, in the *American Political Science Review* (December 1959) expressed the opinion, which he makes no effort to substantiate, that "some difficult factual and theoretical contradictions are glided over simplistically." A.N. Holcombe in the *Annals of the American Academy* (September 1959) criticizes Burnham for not troubling himself "to consider the impact of the unplanned party system on the constitutional scheme of government," a "strange neglect," he says, "which may explain his failure to put together a more persuasive case for his pessimistic conclusions." Paul Simon, in the *Christian Century* (November 11, 1959) is willing to concede that the book is "well written" and makes "some valid points," but finally concludes that it "is an effective presentation of a weak case." R.K. Carr in the *New York Herald-Tribune* (August 30, 1959) finds that the book is "rooted in more than one factual error," without specifying what they might be, and that this is "fatal to the central thesis." It remained, however, for Professor Lindsay Rogers of Columbia University to demonstrate the greatest skill in the art of evading the issue: reviewing the book in the *New York Times* (May 31, 1959) he pontificated, "Occasionally in his book Mr. Burnham disclosed that if he is not an amateur in the matters he considers, he is plowing fields that have only recently become familiar to him."

If further evidence is needed of the liberal "presumption in favor of the executive as against Congress," as Burnham calls it, there is the current campaign, in books and articles, to represent Truman as one of our "great Presidents." It was

Harry Truman, let us not forget, who involved the nation in the Korean War without authorization of Congress, and who, when he ordered the seizure of the steel mills by the Federal Government, based his action on "the authority invested in me by the Constitution and the laws of the United States," although there was nothing in either the Constitution or the law authorizing such action. Burnham comments on this incident as follows:

> The sovereign executive claims to embody the will and interest of the people, by bypassing an intermediary institution [Congress]. The executive decides whether an emergency exists. If he so decides, he acts as he sees fit to solve the emergency. Such an action so taken becomes lawful, without regard to any previously existing law. It follows, therefore, that the executive can legally do whatever he decides to do, provided he states his decision in a proper formula.

By a six to three decision, the Supreme Court rejected Truman's claims and, upholding an injunction, invalidated his action in the steel seizure case. "Although Harry Truman," Burnham says, "reasoned like Caesar, he was one of Caesar's precursors, not Caesar."

When my firm published these three books, it was with the firm conviction that they were worth publishing, and for several reasons: they had, I thought, something important to say about the essential nature of American government, and in making this clear, might help to stem the tide toward the concentration of power in the Washington bureaucracy. In addition, I hoped that they might make a little money for the men who had devoted their time, scholarship and skill to producing them as well as for our struggling firm. As it worked out, all were moderately successful. The Morley book enjoyed a fairly good bookstore sale, the subscribers to *Human Events* loyally bought the book of the man who had brought them many carefully written and thoughtful pieces over the years, and several thousand copies were used in the high school debate program, the subject of which, in the year after publication, happened to be related to the federal system. James Burnham's book also did quite well in the bookstores, and was given wide distribution as a selection of the Conservative Book Club, by which means it was kept in print several years longer than might otherwise have been the case. The sale of the Kilpatrick book was undoubtedly hurt in the North, where most books are sold, by its position in opposition to the Supreme Court decision on the school integration case; but this was compensated, in some degree, by orders from various groups which had been organized in the South to do battle against the invaders from Washington but have since, seemingly, been seduced into inaction, either by "government" money or the promise of the same. As books of high quality they were certainly worth writing and publishing, and all of us in any way involved with them need make no apologies but great money-makers they were certainly not. Let us not forget, however, that Elvis Presley probably made more money in one year than Beethoven, Schubert, Mozart and Bach, all together, in their entire lives: "It all depends," as Professor Schumpeter used to tell us in Economics I, "on what you want."

As for the impact of these three books, what can we say? *Brown vs. Board of Education*, which set our much admired and brilliant stylist Jack Kilpatrick to work, seems mild in comparison to what the federal courts are doing to the public schools now; we are still awaiting for that resounding "No!" from Congress that James Burnham pled for with such knowledge and eloquence; and as for Felix Morley and Rousseau's "general will," what more appropriate embodiment for it could we have than Jimmy Carter? The impact of a book, and more especially a book of integrity, can never be measured; such books, as bearers of the truth, are worthwhile for their own sake. If we believe in the work of the Founding Fathers, in the way Americans have traditionally reconciled the perennial problem of maintaining a government which gives its citizens a decent degree of freedom while maintaining the order without which society cannot exist, they were worth writing and publishing.

6

The Responsibility of the Educated:
A Graduation Address

There are certain subjects which everyone, whether he knows anything about them or not, feels free to discuss—education and responsibility being two conspicuous examples. Only a physicist would dare to talk publicly about physics and only a person with specialized knowledge in the field about mathematics; but almost anyone feels he has something important to say about such a broad subject as education. You will find, if you ever go into the business of publishing books, that almost everyone feels competent to write a book. As a publisher, I am one of those people without specialized knowledge of any kind; and so I have chosen one of those subjects today which, as I say, people who don't know much about anything in particular feel perfectly free to talk about. You will, I hope, extend the customary indulgence to me.

Oswald Spengler remarks some place that we are all, each one of us, born in a certain time, a certain society, a certain family; that we arrive in the world with a certain cultural tradition; that this is our fate, and with this fact, everything else is pretty much determined. To a certain extent, of course, this is true. The time, place, and circumstances of our birth are the given facts of our specific situation—how we meet them, what we make out of these and of ourselves, however, are the measure of our achievement and of our worth.

Most of you who are students now were born during the early part of World War II. The fact of World War II, and the consequences of the decisions which followed it, have profoundly influenced the world in which you will live. We are thrust into a world not of our making; and we must bear the consequences, good and bad, of decisions over which we had no control, just as those who follow us will have to bear the consequences of the decisions we make, and will have to live in whatever world we leave them.

As Americans, you have had the great advantage of being born into a free society. You will inherit the free institutions which wise and brave men established and preserved for us, and you benefit by educational institutions other people have provided. Furthermore, we live in a century, though no fault of our own, where there is not only unequalled wealth, but opportunity available as to few others in the world, to develop our abilities and to lead our own lives.

On the other hand, we belong to the nation that created the atomic bomb and first used it against helpless civilians.

It was an American president who needlessly prolonged the war by demanding unconditional surrender of our national enemies, something unprecedented in modern history among civilized societies; who thoughtlessly and heedlessly consigned millions of people to virtual slavery and despair; who brought Communist Russia to the middle of Europe; and who laid the basis for another World War. These are some of the elements of the world in which you must live and which you, as educated men and women, must understand.

Something else to which you, as educated people, must give some thought is how it could happen that a country that produced such a document as the American Constitution could also produce leaders who in the Yalta, Teheran, and Potsdam agreements lost for the world's free people what we were told had been won by terrible cost and sacrifice in the two world wars. What went wrong?

How much it went wrong, and how completely it went wrong, was brought very vividly to my mind one evening not long ago when I heard the ambassador of an Arab country talk at a small dinner. He began by saying that he belonged to one of the countries which are at the edge of the great events of history, which suffer the consequences of those events, but which have little or no influence on the decisions which bring them about. He then recounted, as he saw it, the procession of European-American history since 1914: the slogans of World War I—Peace without Victory, Self-determination of Peoples, the Fourteen Points, which were followed by the Versailles Treaty; the promises of independence to the Arab nations, followed by the disclosure of the Sykes-Picot Agreement and the Balfour Declaration, which had been made at approximately the same time, and by which the Arab countries were to be divided among the victorious powers and the Jews promised a homeland in Palestine. He spoke of the interminable wrangles over boundaries and reparations, the Ruhr invasion, the rise of Hitler, World War II, and then more slogans. This time it was the Four Freedoms and the Atlantic Charter which were followed by unconditional surrender, Yalta, Teheran, and Potsdam. The dismal story went on; there is no use going into further details. The point I wish to make is not only that these decisions were made by educated men, but what is, perhaps, even worse, that those who should have known better almost without exception approved, or did little or nothing to raise their voices in protest. We quite rightly reproach the German universities and intellectual leaders for not doing more to oppose Hitler, but how conspicuously did the intellectual and moral leaders of our country speak out against the monstrosities and incredible immoralities of Yalta? I know of one college president who did; he soon lost his job, and received no support for his position from the academic profession.

The ordinary man, the soldier, the famous "man in the street," could hardly have been expected to object when Soviet Russia was called "our noble ally," when one of the bloodiest tyrants of history was called "good old Uncle Joe," when half of Europe was turned over to Communist Russia because, it was thought, this would assure peace, at least for us. The educated should have objected, however. The intellectual and moral leaders of the country should have spoken out. That was their responsibility!

By their silence, they failed their country. By their silence, they failed the generations to come. Silence is the temptation of the educated man or woman who finds himself or herself in the minority. The bitter results of the last decade should be a warning to every educated person. When you see truths which others do not see, that is the time to speak. Education without courage is useless. The conformity expressed by silence is a betrayal of your own soul, and of your own mind.

Courage is a virtue whose value cannot be overestimated. Education without the courage to form convictions from the knowledge a student acquires becomes meaningless and purposeless. This is an age which has great need of courage. We hear much talk in praise of individualism, but how many actually have the courage to practice it? Modern history is literally filled with the individualists who were not there—who conformed, who kept quiet. We seem to have turned individualism over to the non-ethical people, while the ethical people drop into silence.

Hitler and Stalin were notable individualists. Where were the individualists on the other side with the voice and the stature to stop them before they rose to such power that only the whole world in arms could withstand their tyranny? Years of agony for the human race came because of the people who were needed and were simply not there at the time when they could still have been effective.

America shows grave signs of having great numbers of people who as far as effective action is concerned simply are not there. As educated people you already know these terrible lessons of our recent history. You must also have the acumen to form convictions from what you know, and then the courage to act upon your convictions.

What has gone wrong with America? As the poet Roy Campbell once suggested, "Until the idea once more predominates over the thing, and the thought over the action, there can be no faith, nothing but helplessness and paralysis."

What went wrong between the time when we could produce a man who could speak with the courage and intelligence Washington showed in his Farewell Address and the fuzzy-mindedness and utter cynicism which resulted in Yalta and Teheran? What did the Founding Fathers possess that people and their leaders in the twentieth century have so far failed to show? What did America lose between the Farewell Address and the Quarantine Speech of President Franklin D. Roosevelt?

It seems to me that one attribute the men who wrote the Constitution possessed to a high degree was the ability and moral strength to face things as they are. They were not inclined to self-deception. They wanted to give us free institutions, a government strong enough to govern but not centralized enough to tyrannize; and while they wished their fellow man well, they had few illusions about him or themselves. They knew that man is capable of great achievement but also of great mendacity, and they were well aware of the truth later to be expressed by Lord Acton as "All power tends to corrupt." They knew that history was not a struggle of "good guys against bad guys," a truth which we

Americans of the twentieth century, in spite of some rather ludicrous experiences, still seem to find difficult to grasp.

They knew, on the contrary, that history was a struggle for power, for existence, for advantage, that life itself is struggle, and that to see it otherwise is rank self-deception. But they also knew that the task of civilization is to bring, in so far as it is possible, order and justice out of the chaos of the struggle for existence. They knew that man is imperfect, that human institutions are equally imperfect, and that to expect perfection from the one was as futile and deceptive as to demand perfection from the other.

They were men who also knew something about the nature of society. They were deeply aware of the fact that, as Edmund Burke expressed it, society is a partnership, not only of the living, but of the dead, and the yet unborn. They did not think of themselves as the end result, as the culmination, of time and of history, but as tiny particles in a mighty stream. They wished to live not at the expense of the future, but so that the future might be better. Most of all, I think, these men, by their actions, demonstrated their belief in an orderly universe. They believed not only that the life of the individual has a purpose, but that all creation has meaning, and that by attempting to establish a more orderly society they were, in a small way, and to the extent of their ability, contributing something to the larger design of creation.

If the political arrangements and national decisions of a people are an expression of their moral worth, as I believe to be the case, then it is the responsibility of the educated to concern themselves about them, and to take a stand. If the educated do not fulfill their responsibility, the civilization which has nourished them cannot long survive. Perhaps I can give you some idea of how great this responsibility is if I point out that all the knowledge that humanity has acquired in its long history must be reacquired by each generation. Much can be preserved in books, of course, but this becomes a living force, a part of our lives, only as it is acquired and made vital by living people.

You, therefore, are a part of the rather small group on which the future of our civilization rests because you belong to the group which has as its responsibility the transmission and vitality of the ideas and values which will determine the future. The course of human history is determined by what people believe, by the values they hold, and most of all by whether or not they will act upon them.

It is because I believe in the power and influence of ideas that I publish books and that I am here today. If we did not believe in ideas and values, education would be nothing more than training in skills. Because man can think, and has been given the freedom to choose, he is necessarily governed by ideas.

We live in a revolutionary time, in a time when all values are under attack. The fabric of our civilization has been seriously weakened. There are many who would like to do away with respect and confidence and the voluntary relationships which are the essence of our society, and replace them by compulsion; who prefer a society of mass men organized in a mechanistic totality toward the achievement of specific materialistic goals, to a society of free men making their own decisions. We have long taken for granted a society in which the freedom and happiness of the individual are regarded as legitimate goals. The extent to which society based on the individual and upon values is threatened is well illustrated by the current discussion in which "Gross National Product" is regarded as an end rather than a means, and in which the only goals even considered are material and quantitative. It will be your responsibility, as educated people, not only to transmit ideas and values to the next generation, but to select those values which ought to be passed on. Above all, you must speak.

Coleridge is quoted as having said, "In every state, not wholly barbarous, a philosophy, good or bad, there must be." While most people may not even be aware of such things as philosophy or speculation, or conscious of the ideas which dominate their time, it is the educated who give them voice and currency and make them a part of the life of the time. And unless they are made part of the life of the time, unless the ideas which dominate a time are in harmony with basic moral values and traditions of a nation, society is in grave danger.

When I speak about the responsibility of our national leaders for what seems to me to be a series of appalling decisions, I should probably have said that they only reflected the opinions and attitudes which many leaders supposed was American "public opinion" at the time. But what is "public opinion" if not the opinion of those in a position and with the necessary convictions to express themselves? Was the "common man" responsible for the illusion that we could trust "good old Uncle Joe," that Mao

Tse-tung and his friends were just simple "agrarian reform-ers," that to eliminate Prussian and Japanese militarism was all that was necessary to inaugurate an era of perpetual peace? The common man or the forgotten man, whatever the politician courting his favor and his vote may call him, is common and forgotten precisely to the extent that he either has no opinions, or has no way of making his opinions felt.

Public opinion is the opinion of the publicists, teachers, writers, publishers, diplomats, politicians, wire pullers, and all those persons who are in a position to make their opinions and ideas public, and thereby to influence the course of events. It is for this reason that the ultimate influence of a book, or magazine, or newspaper cannot be measured by how *many* people buy or read it, but by *which* people.

Das Kapital was one of the most influential books published in the nineteenth century, not because it ever attained a large sale—it did not—but because some very strong-minded, strong-willed men, among them Nicolai Lenin, read it and took it to heart. This was an evil idea put to an evil use. But it does show what can be done with an idea. Held in the beginning by a mere handful of men, it spread to cover the world.

You belong to the new generation of the educated. From your ranks will come the decisions which will shape the future, and determine the philosophy, ideas and values on which the decisions will be based. This is a sobering prospect, all the more so when you understand the nature of the world you face. You live in a world divided into two hostile camps, more bitterly divided, perhaps, than ever before in history. Not only your country, but also civilization itself, faces an implacable, resourceful and determined enemy which is intent upon complete destruction of all who stand in the way. You will be called upon to face great challenges.

I would urge you courageously to take a position, and with endless courage to be willing to stand by it. You will need to know not only where you stand, but how to think clearly. There are many who will try to confuse you, and you will need to see things as they are, and in the proper relationship to each other.

If our free society as we have known it is to continue, you will need to understand and to appreciate it, to know not only the nature and value of freedom, but something about the nature of man. As Ezra Pound put it succinctly and precisely, you will need to "regain the habit of thinking of things in general as set in an orderly universe."

If I have given you a rather somber picture of the responsibilities ahead of you, and of the nature of the world you will have to face, I can only say that I do not think I have overstated the case. You should remember that if there are great challenges, it is precisely great challenges which invoke great responses, and you will indeed face a great challenge.

The greatness of the response of your generation will depend on you—I can only hope that you will do better than the last several generations have done. In closing, let me quote a few sentences which Roy Campbell wrote shortly before he was killed. Campbell wrote some of the most beautiful lyric poetry of our century. He was a man of great courage and vitality, who truly understood the challenge of our time, and yet he wrote: "At no other time was it ever more thrilling and enjoyable to be a poet, and to be alive, than it is today, when the life of the whole planet is triggered by a hair, when every moment is as precious as bread and wine, and when the rumble and roar of chaos is challenging us for every atom of faith, hope and courage, in a measure which our Maker has never before done us the honour of expecting from His creatures."

III

Historical Revisionism and World War II: Part I

Historical Revisionism and World War II: Part II

Winston Churchill: A Question of Leadership

Joseph Stalin   *Winston Churchill*

Franklin D. Roosevelt

7

Historical Revisionism and World War II:
Part I

The Japanese attack on Pearl Harbor on December 7, 1941, put an abrupt and final end of the great debate that had raged in Congress, in the press, and on public forums from one end of the country to the other on whether the United States should become involved in what had begun as a European war. The America First Committee, which had been the largest and most effective organization opposing American intervention, was formally dissolved two days after war was declared; and its leaders, General Robert E. Wood, Colonel Charles A. Lindbergh, and Robert D. Stuart, among others, loyally and unstintingly served their country at war. But when the war ended, the great question of American involvement—its necessity, how it had come about, and its results—again became a burning issue. The form the developing debate was to take between, on the one hand, the "orthodox" historians, who supported the official version of events, and, on the other, the "revisionists," who questioned the accepted account, was clearly foreseen by Charles A. Beard, the distinguished historian and one-time president of the American Historical Association, in a short article on the editorial page of the *Saturday Evening Post* in the issue dated October 4, 1947.

The immediate reason for Dr. Beard's article was the announcement by the Rockefeller Foundation in its annual report for the year 1946 that in order to forestall a repetition of "the debunking journalistic campaign following World War I" the sum of $139,000 had been granted to the Council on Foreign Relations, which the Council had agreed to use to support the preparation of a "clear and competent" history of World War II from 1939 to "the peace settlements," a project which was to be entrusted to Professor William Langer of Harvard. The report of the Foundation went on to say that Professor Langer had been granted "exceptional access to materials bearing on foreign relations." Dr. Beard pointed out that in a previous book concerned with foreign policy, *Our Vichy Gamble*, Professor Langer in the introduction acknowledged that he had been furnished secret documents, or digests of such documents, by President Roosevelt, Secretary Hull, Admiral Leahy, and the War Department. In addition, the first draft of the book had been read by Secretary Hull, who had suggested the project to Professor Langer in the first place, and by other government officials, who had made suggestions for revision, and, finally, had approved publication. To all this

Dr. Beard commented:

> Duly blessed by Secretary Hull, the War Depart-
> ment and Admiral Leahy, the professor's book
> was issued by a private publisher with an official
> fanfare valuable to all parties of interest. Presum-
> ably, in carrying out the new Rockefeller com-
> mission, Professor Langer will again enjoy spe-
> cial favors denied to others—favors from the
> State Department, the War Department, Admi-
> ral Leahy, President Truman and the guardians
> of the Roosevelt and other papers.

In conclusion Dr. Beard wrote:

> Who is to write the history of World War II?
> Some person or persons well-subsidized and
> enjoying access, under Government patronage,
> to secret archives? Or is the opportunity of in-
> quiring and writing the story of this critical
> period to be open to all talents on the same terms,
> without official interference or favoritism? There
> is the choice before us, and if tested methods of
> truth-seeking are to be followed in the business
> of history writing, the answer seems rather obvi-
> ous.

What might be called the intellectual establishment of
the country—the prestige universities, the great foundations, the established publishers and the influential press—
was predominantly on the official, the "orthodox" side of
the controversy, as Dr. Beard's article indicates; but those

not afraid to look behind the accepted version of events and to take an independent position were by no means reduced to silence. What they lacked in foundation grants, academic prestige, official support and recognition by the influential press, they made up for in conviction, resourcefulness, and energy.

The first revisionist book on World War II was George Morgenstern's *Pearl Harbor: The Story of the Secret War*, published in 1947 by a small New York firm, the Devin-Adair Company. It was the thesis of the Morgenstern book that the Roosevelt administration had deliberately and intentionally provoked the Japanese attack as a means of getting into the European war; that the fleet had been kept at Pearl Harbor against the advice of the admirals directly involved; and that information concerning the probability of a Japanese attack had been withheld from the military commanders for fear that if the proper moves to protect the fleet were taken, the plans of the Japanese might have been changed. Morgenstern's thesis was succinctly stated for him by Secretary of War Henry L. Stimson in a passage in his diary describing a meeting of the war cabinet in the White House on November 25, 1941, thirteen days before Pearl Harbor: "The question was how we should maneuver them into the position of firing the first shot without allowing too much danger to ourselves."

The Morgenstern book presented the defenders of the Roosevelt foreign policy with a formidable challenge: it was skillfully written, meticulously documented, and its jacket carried the endorsement of two highly respected men, Charles A. Beard and Norman Thomas. In his endorsement Dr. Beard wrote:

> Having scrutinized the more than ten thousand
> pages of sworn testimony and official papers
> bearing on this disaster before I read the proof
> sheets of Mr. Morgenstern's book, I can say out
> of some knowledge of the subject that his volume
> is a powerful work based on primary and irreduc-
> ible facts in the case, carefully gathered and
> buttressed by exact citations of the sources. For
> his own inferences and conclusions, he gives
> documentary contexts.

Norman Thomas called the book "a well written, well
organized, and well documented story of the events of
which the Pearl Harbor attack was the climax." In view of
the foregoing, and the irrefragable nature of the facts of the
case, the intellectual establishment found it necessary, in its
response to the Morgenstern book, to take refuge in either
one or several of the following evasions: to ignore it
completely; to treat it as the work of an anti-Roosevelt
crank and therefore not worthy of serious consideration; to
question the propriety of writing such a book at all; or,
finally, to admit that there might be something, in a very
limited way, in the author's presentation of facts, but to
deny its significance with the assertion that he was incapable of grasping the larger issue.

Such publications as the *Atlantic, Harper's, Saturday
Review* chose the first alternative and ignored the book
completely. The *New Yorker* ended a brief paragraph with
the neither relevant nor witty remark, "Mr. Morgenstern is

a Chicago newspaperman, and you have only one guess as
to which paper he works for." The *New York Times* review,
which appeared on a back page and was headed "Mythology
for the Critics of F.D.R.," was written by Gordon A. Craig,
a young assistant at Princeton who, after pointing out that
Dr. Morgenstern was "an editorial writer for the *Chicago
Tribune*," contented himself with the assertion that
Morgenstern is propagating "mythology" and "nowhere
seriously considers the possible consequences to the United
States of an Axis victory." That may be true, but there is
good reason to doubt that an Axis victory was possible, with
or without American intervention; nor do Mr. Craig, the
New York Times, or President Roosevelt appear to have
given much, if any, consideration to the far more serious
consequences to the United States of the victory of Communist Russia. Craig argues that a "*modus vivendi*" with
Japan in 1941 would have represented the "complete aban-
donment of the principles underlying American policy in
the Far East." After two further wars—Korea and Viet-
nam—where, it is fair to ask, are the "principles underlying
American policy in the Far East" now?

In his review in the *New York Herald-Tribune*, which was
headed "Twisting the Pearl Harbor Story," Walter Millis,
after the usual references to the *Chicago Tribune*, argues
that in all his actions supporting Britain and Russia, President Roosevelt was "repeatedly sustained...by Congress as
well as by public opinion." If this is true, why were so many
of the President's actions done in secret—the joint staff
talks with the British and the Dutch, the North Atlantic
naval patrol, for example; why were such measures as the

destroyer deal and "Lend-Lease" represented as means to "keep us out of war"; and why, if public opinion favored the war, did President Roosevelt, on October 30, 1940, during an election campaign, assure the mothers and fathers of Boston—"again-and-again-and-again"—that "your sons are not going to be sent to any foreign wars"?*

The longest, most serious, and probably most significant critical review of the Morgenstern book was that of Samuel Flagg Bemis, professor of diplomatic history at Yale, in the *Journal of Modern History*. Professor Bemis begins his review with a condemnation of the revisionism that followed World War I:

> This disillusionist historiography resulted in the complete repudiation of Woodrow Wilson's foreign policy and in the neutrality legislation of 1935-37. As everybody now can see, that legislation assisted the rise of Hitler's power and his onslaught on Western civilization.

Then, after inferring the dire consequences of a "new campaign of revisionism," he carefully warns the reader "not to be prejudiced against the author because he is not a professional historian or because he is a journalist and on the editorial staff of what is considered by many to be a notoriously isolationist newspaper, the *Chicago Tribune*."

Bemis accepts Morgenstern's carefully documented thesis that it was the officials in Washington who were responsible for the disaster at Pearl Harbor, not the military commanders, General Short and Admiral Kimmel, who were made the scapegoats:

The numerous and serious failures of these high officials (Roosevelt, Stimson, Knox and Marshall) to keep the commanders in Hawaii adequately informed of the crisis and fully alerted, at a time when they knew from their breakdown of Japan's secret code that war was a matter of days only, are detailed at great length scrupulously from the record and to the reviewer are entirely convincing.

Bemis, however, is not willing to agree with the second thesis of Morgenstern's book, that the failure to alert the commanders at Pearl Harbor was deliberate and the final act of a plan to provoke a Japanese attack in order to give the President the *casus belli* he needed. Bemis, rather, asserts that with Lend-Lease we had "deserted American neutrality in the Atlantic," and were, therefore—in fact, if not in name—already at war. This is doubtless true, but after such election promises as "Your boys are not going to be sent into any foreign wars" (which as he remarked at the time, he had said "again, and again, and again"), President Roosevelt needed such an incident as Pearl Harbor to get a formal declaration of war and to mobilize the country behind him. Although unwilling specifically to admit this, Bemis argues that confronted by "the most awful danger ever faced by our country," which in his opinion the German-Japanese-Italian alliance represented, Roosevelt's actions were justified.

The most remarkable, and significant, aspect of the Bemis review is not so much his defense of the Roosevelt foreign policy, which from a Yale professor could almost be taken for granted, but his attack on "revisionist historiog-raphy." In the opinion of this professor of diplomatic history at a great American university, as expressed in this review, the mission of the historian is not to discover truth, to tell what actually happened, "to winnow fact from fiction," as Beard put it, but to justify the foreign policy of the nation.

The Morgenstern book was followed by Charles A. Beard's *President Roosevelt and the Coming of the War, 1941*, which was published in 1948 by Yale University Press. This was a sequel to Beard's *American Foreign Policy in the Making, 1932-1940*, which the Yale Press had published two years before. The first book was a documentary account of the foreign policy of the first two Roosevelt administra-tions, a policy which marked a distinct break from that of previous administrations, and of which three wars were the immediate consequence. Dr. Beard, in the second book, which carries the subtitle "A Study in Appearances and Realities," uses his unequalled mastery of the documentary material and his long experience in the writing of history to bring those to account who were responsible for the deci-sions that led to war with Japan and intervention in the European war. In the first chapter, which is entitled "Moral Commitments to the American People for the Conduct of Foreign Policy," Dr. Beard argues that President Roosevelt, in his public statements and in his acceptance of the 1940 Platform of the Democratic Party, had made an unequivo-cal covenant "with the American people to keep this nation out of war—so to conduct foreign affairs as to avoid war."[1] In the following chapter, "Representations of Lend-Lease

Aid to the Allies," he points out that while, "under international law, as long and generally recognized, it was an act of war for a neutral government to supply munitions, arms and implements of war to one of the belligerents,"[2] as many opponents of the bill made clear at the time, Lend-Lease was represented by the President as "just a precautionary measure for continuing American defense,"[3] as "not a war policy but the contrary."[4] The following chapters are a similar contrast of "appearances" with "realities," with the successful "maneuvering of the Japanese into firing the first shot" the ultimate consequence.

Charles A. Beard was a man of great independence of mind and of strong convictions, character traits he had demonstrated by resigning his professorship at Columbia to protest the dismissal of two professors during the hysteria of World War I and supporting himself and his family for some years thereafter as a dairy farmer. Such a man is capable of moral indignation, not to say outrage, of a high order, as the epilogue of the present book makes clear. Beard felt, and felt strongly, that President Roosevelt had not only deceived the American people, but by arrogating unto himself complete control of foreign policy, including the power to make war, had subverted the Constitution and the orderly process of government. In addition, he strongly objected to the habit of certain American presidents, and President Roosevelt in particular, of moralizing on an international scale, of proclaiming that "it is the duty of the United States to assume and maintain 'the moral leadership of the world.'"[5] As a rather old-fashioned American, Beard felt that moral leadership began at home, and was best exerted by example.

Such a book, coming from a man who had been president of both the American Historical Association and the American Political Science Association, and had long been regarded as the dean of American historians, reduced the academic establishment to a state of utter irrationality. Arthur Schlesinger, Jr., after characterizing the book in the *New York Times* (April 11, 1948) as a "Philippic against Franklin D. Roosevelt," loftily suggested that it "cannot fail to provoke criticism on grounds of historical method," without specifying what such grounds might be, and finally remarked, "as a devotee of reality against appearance, he should have inquired into the realities of alternatives." The alternative to going to war, obviously, is not going to war, an alternative Dr. Beard was quite willing to accept, and had unhesitatingly recommended. There were equally strong, and sometimes more unrestrained, objections to the book from Harry D. Gideonse, Max Lerner, Quincy Wright, Percy Miller, and Peter Levin, among others. Commenting on the reviews in the professional journals of *President Roosevelt and the Coming of the War* Howard K. Beale, in an article in the *Pacific Historical Review,* observed:

> There are in the profession people of standing who agree with Beard's interpretation, and others who disagree but feel the book has much of the impressive quality of the early works on the Constitution and Jeffersonian democracy that made Beard's great reputation. Curiously, no editor could find any of these people to review the book.[6]

It remained for Samuel Eliot Morison, professor of history at Harvard and official historian of the United States Navy in World War II, to return the final verdict of the orthodox historians on the Beard thesis.

Professor Morison's review appeared in the *Atlantic Monthly* (August 1948), is seven full pages in length, is entitled "Did President Roosevelt Start the War?" and subtitled, "History Through A Beard." The *Atlantic* review, it must be said, for all its urbanity, is no credit to its author. The review begins with a tribute to Dr. Beard's generosity and independence, as well as to his great achievements in the writing of history—*The Rise of American Civilization* is described as "the most brilliant historical survey of the American scene ever written"—but soon degenerates into a personal attack. Morison makes much of Beard's belief, which had been expressed in articles and particularly in his presidential address to the American Historical Association,[7] that no historian can write truly "objective" history; that he must make choices from the vast mass of historical evidence, and in so doing, consciously or unconsciously, acts in accordance with some frame of reference. As Professor Beale put it in the article just referred to:

> What Beard contended was that, since all historians, being human, write subjectively, they would come nearer to the truth if they would recognize their points of view and try to write fairly within them instead of pretending they do not have any.[8]

On the basis of this quite logical, straightforward, and honest conception of objectivity in historical writing, Morison asserts that Beard's "standards of truth and objectivity differ from those of any other professional historian," and that this is the source of his "inconsistencies and tergiversations." Morison furthermore asserts, without offering any evidence whatever for such an assertion, that in Beard's view the "object of history is to influence the present and the future, in a direction that the historian considers socially desirable."

Morison is "astonished" that Beard should have used "so solemn a word" as "covenant" for "flimsies like party platforms and campaign promises," but he had no reason to be astonished. Morison needed only to remember that Beard was the sort of man who took pledges seriously. While Morison admits that President Roosevelt did, perhaps, mislead the American people and "utter soothing phrases in 1940 in order to be re-elected," he believes that this was justified in view of the "isolationist" campaign against intervention; the President, as he put it, was compelled "to do good by stealth."

The extent to which Professor Morison felt obligated to go to justify the Roosevelt foreign policy is well illustrated by his bland explanation of Secretary Stimson's "unfortunate use" of the word "maneuver." This, we are told, was due to his imperfect knowledge of semantics—what he might have meant to say, however, we are not told. Professor Morison furthermore asserts: "Throughout modern history Western nations in danger of war choose to await the first blow rather than to give it," and that maneuvering

the Japanese into firing the first shot was entirely comparable to Captain Parker's command at Lexington: "Stand
your ground. Don't fire unless fired upon, but if they mean
to have a war, let it begin here." All this may not be an
example of the "tergiversation" of which Morison accuses
Beard, but to compare all that was involved at Pearl
Harbor—the breaking of the Japanese code, the withhold-
ing of information from the commanders, the secret under-
standings with the British, General Marshall's mysterious
disappearance at a critical moment—with the command of
an honest captain at Lexington Green is pure sophistry. Is
it any wonder, then, that in a letter to George Morgenstern
about the reviews of the latter's book Dr. Beard remarked,
"Such, my young friend, is life in the 'intellectual world'"?

It was into this intellectual world, in the Fall of 1950, that
the Henry Regnery Company launched its first revisionist
book, William Henry Chamberlin's *America's Second Crusade*. Chamberlin was a distinguished and respected writer—
he had been Moscow correspondent of the *Christian Science
Monitor* from 1922 until 1934, after which he served as a
correspondent in the Far East and in France, and was the
author of eleven previous books. His *The Russian Revolution, 1917-1921*, published by Macmillan in 1935, is recognized as one of the authoritative books on the subject. His
former publishers, however, which included, besides
Macmillan, Scribner's, Knopf, and Little, Brown, were not
interested in his new book, and on March 10, 1950, he
wrote the following letter to me:

I recently completed a book entitled "America's Second Crusade," dealing with the origins, course and final results of our involvement in the last war. It runs to about 400 typewritten pages and the enclosures will give you an idea of its character and outlook....

Through the mediation of Harry Elmer Barnes I contracted for the publication of this work with the University of Oklahoma Press. However, they seem rather lukewarm about going ahead with it because of the vigorous criticisms of Roosevelt's foreign policy. They have intimated that the contract will not stand in the way if I can find a more sympathetic publisher.

The book is based on a careful examination of the more important books about the diplomatic and political side of the war which have appeared in this country and England and also on private talks with a number of men who were active in the making of policy. Among these were former Ambassadors Bullitt, Lane and Grew; George Kennan, Charles Bohlen and Philip Mosely, of the State Department, former Assistant State Secretary A.A. Berle, General Donovan, and Allen Dulles, of the OSS, and others. Former President Hoover was most helpful in making available to me a kind of secret diary of the war containing much interesting unpublished material. This must be regarded as quite confidential.

I am convinced that the book is unique in its field, as there has been a strong justification complex in most of the published works on the subject. It drives home steadily, with a final summing up in the last chapter, an idea that must be appealing to more thoughtful people all the time: that the late victorious war was a colossal political and moral failure. Its net result has been to strengthen an equally vicious and more dangerous form of totalitarianism as a substitute for those we destroyed.

Although I feel there is an irresistible factual logic behind this idea (how ironical to think that we went on a crusade for China, Poland, Czechoslovakia, in view of their present regimes!) I can fully appreciate that a book which frankly upholds this view is strong meat for the average publisher.

In view of your own courage in publishing books like Freda Utley's and Montgomery Belgion's I hope this work may appeal to you. I should be glad to know whether you would like to see the manuscript and whether, if it appeals to you, there would be a good prospect of early publication.

The letter from Chamberlin, as I have said, was dated March 10, 1950; before the end of that month we had agreed to publish the book and on the terms of the contract. Much work was involved in getting the manuscript ready for publication—checking quotations, straightening out matters of style and presentation, etc.—which was complicated by the fact that the original copy was lost in the mail on one of its trips between Cambridge and Chicago, but we were able to send page proofs to reviewers in July and finished books in late August, and to publish the book in October. Chamberlin was well known, of course, through his years as a correspondent and his previous books, and had built up a following, particularly among conservatively inclined businessmen, through his regular columns in the *Wall Street Journal.* In addition, he was a regular contributor, and listed as "associate editor," of the socialist, but strongly anti-communist, *New Leader.* In launching the book, therefore, we had the great advantage of an established and respected author—an author the reviewers, however strongly they may have disagreed with him, would have to take seriously.

Like Charles A. Beard, Chamberlin was a man of strong convictions, and his years in Soviet Russia had made him, if possible, even more critical of the manner in which the war and its objectives were represented to the American people by the administration and the liberal press. Chamberlin had seen both forms of totalitarianism in action and had himself experienced the fall of France and its consequences. He had no illusions whatever, therefore, about Nazi Germany. But the claim, which was made on the highest levels of government, that peace, freedom, and the brotherhood of man were to be secured by an alliance with Communist Russia was for him, knowing what he did about Communism in practice, the rankest form of misrepresentation. The Beard book was the work of an experienced, highly skilled historian who, by the nature of his profession, relied heavily on official documents. Chamberlin was also an historian, but his approach was broader: he was able to supplement the ample documentation of his book by information and knowledge acquired from his many years of experience as a correspondent.

The Chamberlin book begins with a brief account of the circumstances of America's First Crusade: of the manner, that is, of our intervention in the first Great War, the glowing promises, the hysteria aroused in its behalf, and the disillusionment that followed. He wrote:

> By no standard of judgment could America's First Crusade be considered a success. It was not even an effective warning. For all the illusions, misjudgments, and errors of the First Crusade were to be repeated, in exaggerated form, in a Second Crusade that was to be a still more resounding and unmistakable political and moral failure, despite the repetition of military success.[9]

Chamberlin, after so disposing of Mr. Wilson's war, concludes his book with the following unequivocal judgment on Mr. Roosevelt's:

> It is scarcely possible...to avoid the conclusion that the Roosevelt Administration sought the war which began at Pearl Harbor. The steps which made armed conflict inevitable were taken months before the conflict broke out. Some of

Roosevelt's apologists contend that, if he deceived the American people, it was for their own
good. But the argument that the end justifies the
means rests on the assumption that the end has
been achieved. Whether America's end in its
Second Crusade was assurance of national security or the establishment of a world of peace and
order or the realization of the Four Freedoms
"everywhere in the world," this end was most
certainly not achieved. America's Second Crusade was a product of illusions which are already
bankrupt.[10]

Such statements, more than a generation after the end of
World War II and with all that has happened since, may not
appear either particularly startling or to say anything that is
not fairly obvious and generally accepted in 1950, only five
years after an overwhelming military victory, when American power and influence seemed to dominate the world,
and when the memory of Franklin D. Roosevelt—the
sound of his soothing voice and the feeling of security
engendered by the magnetism of his personality—was still
cherished, such assertions were regarded as a particularly
repulsive form of blasphemy. In spite of his years of
experience in the "intellectual world," even Chamberlin was
taken aback by the violence of the attacks on his book, from
which he was also not spared.

The *New York Post* based its case against the book not on
what it said, but on the device of guilt by association
Colonel McCormick's *Chicago Tribune* and the *New York*

Daily News liked the book, which was enough to condemn it. The reviewer called Chamberlin a "totalitarian conservative," and implied that he justified or apologized for things that were done in Germany and Japan which he found execrable in Russia. J.M. Minifie in the *Saturday Review of Literature*, November 18, 1959, commented, "To anyone who had to endure over a number of years the daily dose of Virgilio Gayda or Dr. Goebbels, it comes as a shock to find Mr. Chamberlin ladling out of the same dish." Harry D. Gideonse, then president of Brooklyn College, in the *New Leader*, November 27, 1950, called the book "another rehash of the 'Chicago Tribune history of World War II,'" and was "not surprised to discover" that Robert M. Hutchins was "Chairman of the Editorial Board of the publishers of the volume"—a discovery, I must say, which came as a great surprise to me.

The *New York Post* failed to print Chamberlin's reply to their slanderous suggestion that he had justified or apologized for Nazi behavior. In this letter, he reminded the *Post* that he had been "one of the first American writers who pointed out the many common traits of Communism and Fascism," and in his book had listed ten "deadly parallels between Fascism and Communism." The *New Leader,* to its everlasting credit, did print a long "Reply to my Critics" from Mr. Chamberlin. In this letter, he remarked that he was not discouraged by the fact that the reception accorded the book was largely critical—"there is endless room for difference of opinion"—but that "all but a small minority of the reviewers (failed) to face the challenge of the book head-on, to debate specific points of fact and opinion instead of flying into fits of stratospheric emotionalism or lapsing into vague generalities."

We published two further books by William Henry Chamberlin. For all his strong convictions, he was a thoroughly reasonable man, and, unlike some authors I came to deal with, easy to get along with. He was by no means the swashbuckling, trench-coated foreign correspondent sometimes depicted in novels, but quiet, reserved, completely without pretensions of any kind, and of uncompromising integrity, as he demonstrated many times during his career. An account of William Henry Chamberlin would be incomplete without some mention of his love of chocolate, of which he ate quantities, always of the best quality—no five cent candy bars for him; he was also a good tennis player, and in spite of his rather innocent appearance, an expert at poker, as a correspondent who had known him in China once told me he had learned to his regret.

In 1953, three years after *America's Second Crusade*, we published William Henry Chamberlin's *Beyond Containment*, in which, based on his long experience in Russia, he set forth his conception of a positive foreign policy for the United States. While not willing to forgive him for his "revisionism," the reviewers, for the most part, treated the new book with respect. The following from the *New York Times* review by Samuel Flagg Bemis (October 11, 1953), who had been sharply critical of Chamberlin's earlier book, is a good example of the way in which the new book was received:

Mr. Chamberlin's present book echoes the revisionist school of writers including himself who believe that it was a mistake for the United States to have embarked on "America's Second Crusade."...It would be so much healthier and helpful for the nation if writers like Mr. Chamberlin would bury their old bones and pour their talents into such excellent books as this one is in all other respects. Nowhere will you find a better primer on the threat of Communist power abroad and Communist conspiracy within our midst, and the terrifying objective of enslaving the whole world.

Following the publication in 1947 of the editorial in the *Saturday Evening Post* referred to at the beginning of this essay, in which Charles A. Beard objected to the policy of granting access to official papers only to those who supported government policy, the historian responsible for the State Department archives, I was told, informed Dr. Beard that if he would submit a list of historians he considered competent and independent, one would be given permission to work in the State Department papers. From this list, to complete the story as it was told to me, Charles C. Tansill, professor of diplomatic history at Georgetown University, was selected. Professor Tansill later told me that he was given complete freedom to see and copy anything he wanted in the State Department archives. He did not gain access to the Roosevelt papers at Hyde Park, and had no idea if certain papers had been removed from the archives, but he felt that he saw enough, with what he knew and could learn from other sources, to put together a fully documented diplomatic history of the events that led to World War II and of American participation in it.

Tansill had first become seriously interested in the causes of World War I and of American intervention when he prepared a special study on the subject in the early twenties for the Foreign Policy Committee of the U.S. Senate. One result of this study was his book, *America Goes to War*, published by Little, Brown in 1938, which Allan Nevins, in the *Atlantic Monthly* (August 1938), called "absolutely indispensable to an understanding of three critical years in our history," and no less a figure than Henry Steele Commager, in the *Yale Review* (Summer 1938), described as "...the most valuable contribution to the history of the pre-war years in our literature, and one of the notable achievements of historical scholarship of this generation." However, when Professor Tansill finished his book manuscript on World War II, which represented a detailed, carefully documented study of years that were even more critical in our history, and was an achievement of historical scholarship on the same level of quality as his much-praised earlier book, none of the large Eastern publishers were interested, and the manuscript came to our firm. We brought it out in 1952 under the title *Back Door to War*. It made a book of nearly 700 pages, and in every respect is a formidable work of historical scholarship. After twenty-five years it was still in print, and still stands as the most thoroughly documented and complete account of American participation in World War II by a revisionist historian.

Back Door to War begins with the provocative sentence, which is characteristically Tansill: "The main object in American foreign policy since 1900 has been the preservation of the British Empire."[11] A few pages later, so that there might be no mistake about where he stood, he adds:

> American intervention in World War I established a pattern that led America into a second World War in 1941.... Our intervention [in World War I] completely shattered the old balance of power and sowed the seeds of inevitable conflict in the dark soil of Versailles. We had a deep interest in maintaining the political structure of 1919. Thousands of American lives and a vast American treasure had been spent in its erection.... The bungling handiwork of 1919 had to be preserved at all costs, and America went to war again in 1941 to save a political edifice whose main supports had already rotted in the damp atmosphere of disillusion.[12]

Professor Tansill gives us a detailed account of the decisions—in which stupidity, arrogance, pride, selfishness, and lack of vision played their customary role—that led to the outbreak of war in Europe in September 1939. In telling all this, he displays his mastery of the documentary material and skill in putting the pieces together, but the greatest original contribution of his book, perhaps, is his account of Japanese-American relations, of the long chain of events which culminated in an unnecessary, brutal war, of which Hiroshima and Nagasaki are the most appropriate symbols, and the rise of Communist China the most conspicuous result. While Tansill shows that the history of American economic and diplomatic pressure against Japan goes back at least to the Wilson administration, he ascribes a major role in this tragic episode to Henry L. Stimson. "Some scholars like Charles A. Beard," Tansill writes in the Preface to *Back Door to War*:

> have pointed out that presidential pronounce-
> ments from 1933 to 1937 gave scant encourage-
> ment to ardent one-worlders, but they underes-
> timated the importance of the Chief Executive's
> conversion to the explosive non-recognition doc-
> trine so strenuously advocated by Henry L.
> Stimson. This was the bomb whose long fuse
> sputtered dangerously for several years and fi-
> nally burst into the flame of World War II. It was
> entirely fitting that Stimson became Secretary of
> War in 1940; no one better deserved the title
> quite as well as he.

Later in the book Tansill remarks, "The main barrier across the road to friendly relations [with Japan] was the Stimson doctrine itself."

The last chapter of *Back Door to War* is devoted to Pearl Harbor. Tansill's conclusions concerning the causes of this disaster are generally the same as those of Morgenstern and Beard, as the title of the chapter indicates—"Japan is Maneuvered into War"—but he was able to add some important details in confirmation of his thesis from official sources which were not available to his predecessors. He ends his book as provocatively as he began, with the following paragraph:

> But the President and Harry Hopkins viewed these dread contingencies with amazing equanimity. In the quiet atmosphere of the oval study of the White House, with all incoming calls shut off, the Chief Executive calmly studied his well-filled stamp albums while Hopkins fondled Fala, the White House scottie. At one o'clock Death stood in the doorway. The Japanese had bombed Pearl Harbor. America had suddenly been thrust into a war she is still fighting.[13]

While the Tansill book was hardly greeted with open arms by the liberal reviewers, it did not arouse the violent, almost irrational condemnation evoked by the books by Morgenstern, Beard, and Chamberlin. It was given quite a fair review in the *New York Times* (May 11, 1952), for example, by Dexter Perkins: "When he is at his best, he is unfolding a diplomatic narrative with considerable skill, and with an excellent command of his sources. Unfortunately, however, Mr. Tansill is not always at his best.... Yet let it be cheerfully conceded that speculative though Mr. Tansill's judgments must be, the discussion which he will stimulate will be useful." The *Library Journal* (May 1, 1952), recommended "caution as to his conclusions...since he is sometimes as unjust as Charles A. Beard was in his last works," and suggested that the book "should be read in conjunction with William Langer's recent *Challenge to Isolation*, which does more justice to F.D.R. and his collaborators." In the *Yale Review* (Autumn 1952), *Back Door to War* was reviewed by Charles Griffin together with Langer and Gleason's *Challenge to Isolation*. Professor Tansill, in Mr. Griffin's judgment, "adds nothing convincing to those whose minds are not already so disposed to uphold his theory of Rooseveltian rash irresponsibility." After remarking that Langer and Gleason, "like most men of our age" were "awed" by Roosevelt's "towering personal force," Mr. Griffin goes on to say, "but beyond this, they chronicle events and policies with conscious and sober restraint...," which reminds me of Roy Campbell's famous quatrain:

> *You praise the firm restraint with which they write—*
> *I'm with you there, of course:*
> *They use the snaffle and the curb all right,*
> *But where's the bloody horse?*

One of the sillier reviews of *Back Door to War* was that of Michael Straight in the *New Republic* (June 16, 1952), who suspected a Jesuit conspiracy: "This book is part of the devious attack on American diplomacy directed by Dr. Edmund Walsh, S.J., from Georgetown University."

Professor Tansill doubtless opened himself unnecessarily to criticism by the rather strident tone his book sometimes assumes, but this must be considered together with the circumstances under which it was written. He wrote his book fully aware that the position he was taking was completely in opposition to the views of those who largely controlled opinion, and doubtless felt, therefore, that to make himself heard he would have to raise his voice.

Professor Langer, on the other hand, writing with the self-confidence of a Harvard professor, with the assurance of favorable treatment by the reviewers, and the comfort of a $139,000 grant from the Rockefeller Foundation, was in quite a different situation and could afford to be more restrained. Tansill's access to the archives had to be opened by a vigorous assault; Langer, on the other hand, was greeted as a friend and collaborator, and offered every possible official assistance. Tansill was not in a position even to hire a secretary; with his Rockefeller grant, Langer could employ a staff. In the case of the Tansill book, however, no one will ever have to ask Roy Campbell's question about the whereabouts of "the horse."

Charles C. Tansill, as his book makes clear, was a man of decided opinions which he never hesitated to express. He was born in Texas and the grandson of a Confederate general, a fact of which he was inordinately proud; he was also the proud possessor of Thomas Jefferson's rabbit foot. Through some hideous misunderstanding, he was invited, some time in the thirties, to give the Lincoln Day Address at the Lincoln Memorial in Washington. Facing "Arlington," General Lee's old mansion on the other side of the Potomac, Professor Tansill took full advantage of the situation to deliver a ringing defense of the Confederacy, with appropriate oratorical flourishes. In the ensuing scandal—people probably took such things more seriously then than now—Tansill, he told me, might well have lost his Georgetown professorship had it not been for the intervention of an influential southern bishop. In getting his manuscript ready for publication we tried hard, I remember, to induce him to remove some of the overblown metaphors with which he adorned his pages—the dark soil of Versailles, the exotic wench of collective security, for example—but to no avail; he loved his metaphors, and was quite proud of them. For all that, Charles Callan Tansill was his own man, and a man of courage and integrity. He was a tireless and resourceful searcher for historical truth, and wrote history as the facts led him.

8

Historical Revisionism and World War II:
Part II

While American involvement in World War II did not begin at Pearl Harbor, it was the attack at Pearl Harbor that led to the formal declaration of war; Pearl Harbor marked the transition from a nation legally and formalistically at peace to one mobilized for total war. It is for this reason that Pearl Harbor occupies a central place in any account of American involvement in World War II, and that two historians of the reputation and standing of Charles A. Beard and Samuel Eliot Morison could have such contrary opinions on what led up to it. Having published two books which went into the Pearl Harbor disaster in considerable detail, those by William Henry Chamberlin and Charles C. Tansill, I was pleased to have the opportunity to be able to give one of the central figures, and victims, of the great drama, Admiral Husband E. Kimmel, a chance to tell his side of the story. The Henry Regnery Company published his book, *Admiral Kimmel's Story*, in 1955. It is always a gratifying experience to publish a book one can feel is honest and has something to say that needs to be said: in the case of Admiral Kimmel's book there was the further compensation that it was successful—it even made some of the best-seller lists.

The two commanders at Pearl Harbor at the time of the Japanese attack, Admiral Husband E. Kimmel and General Walter C. Short, were both summarily relieved of their commands a few days later. A commission consisting of Owen J. Roberts of the Supreme Court as chairman and of two retired officers from the Navy and two from the Army was appointed immediately by President Roosevelt to make an investigation. The report of the Roberts Commission was released to the public on January 24, 1942, with the comment by Stephen Early, the White House Press Officer, that the President had spent two hours over it with Justice Roberts and had expressed "his gratitude for a most painstaking and thorough investigation."[14] The Roberts report charged Short and Kimmel with derelictions of duty and errors of judgment, and held that the latter were "the effective cause for the success of the attack." Their superiors in Washington were found blameless. A further element of guilt was implied by the announcement that both commanders would be tried by courts-martial. In spite of Admiral Kimmel's repeated request for such a trial, however, it was never held. Admiral Kimmel's account of all this is factual, straightforward, and without self-pity of any kind; it leaves the reader with the distinct impression that those in responsible positions in Washington were determined to use every means at their disposal to hide the true facts, and to make the two commanders, Short and Kimmel, appear responsible for a disaster that cost the lives of more than 2,000 men, for which later investigations held them to be blameless.

Admiral Kimmel's persistent requests for a trial, or, if that were inappropriate in wartime, for an extension of the statute of limitations so that it could not be invoked later to preclude a trial after the war, finally led to a joint resolution of the House and Senate on June 13, 1944, directing the Secretary of War and the Secretary of the Navy "to proceed forthwith with an investigation into the facts surrounding the catastrophe...and to commence such proceedings against such persons as the facts may justify." These investigations, in contrast to that of the Roberts Commission, were conducted in proper legal fashion, with cross-examination of witnesses, presentation of evidence, full reporting, etc., and led to the complete exoneration of both Short and Kimmel, and, as Charles A. Beard put it, "besides bringing Secretary Hull, General Marshall, General Gerow, the War Department, Admiral Stark, and the Navy Department into the network of responsibility, did more. They placed on the public record numerous facts about transactions in Washington relative to Pearl Harbor which were hitherto unknown to the American public."[15] Although the reports of the Army and Navy boards were filed with the Secretaries of the Army and Navy in October 1944, no information concerning their findings was made public

until after the November 1944 elections, and the full
reports were not published until after the 1946 elections,
and then only after persistent prodding by members of
Congress and the press.

The publication of Admiral Kimmel's book caused a
sensation. The various investigations and several previous
books had made the facts concerning Pearl Harbor generally available; but Admiral Kimmel's account, presented
within the compass of a slim book and with the conviction
of a brave man who had been unjustly treated by the highest
officials of the government, had an impact all its own. *U.S.
News and World Report* reprinted a large part of the book on
the thirteenth anniversary of Pearl Harbor, and the *Chicago
Tribune* ran a front page story with a banner headline—it
was still Col. McCormick's *Tribune*. There were news
stories, editorials, reviews, and letters to the editor in
literally hundreds of papers in all parts of the country. The
reviews, especially in the less "sophisticated" publications,
were generally favorable; the more "sophisticated," that is,
those more or less committed to administration policy,
were often sympathetic to Admiral Kimmel, but were not
willing to accept his contention that vital information had
been purposefully withheld from the commanders at Pearl
Harbor. The *Columbus Dispatch* called the book "convincing"; the *Wall Street Journal,* besides running a long and
favorable review, in an editorial suggested that it was time
for a full and honest investigation of Pearl Harbor. The
New York Times review ended with the remark that Kimmel's
allegations "must remain conjectural," while the review in
the *San Diego Union* ended with the sentence, "It is

impossible...to read the chapter 'Suppression of Evidence' in this book without a shudder and a blush of shame for the honor of our country." The *U.S. Quarterly Book Review* found the book "well written and well documented," while the *American Historical Review* found it "repetitious and badly organized." *Time*, in a long review, felt that "the admiral has presented his case with brevity, restraint and a quarter-deck command of facts," but was not willing "to go along with him when he concludes: 'I cannot excuse those in authority in Washington for what they did.... In my book they must answer on the Day of Judgment like any other criminal.'"

With the publication of the Roberts report in 1942, those in control of Washington doubtless felt that Pearl Harbor had been safely buried, and it seems probable that such facts as we know now—and we do not know them all—would still be hidden had it not been for the courageous and persistent demand by Admiral Kimmel for a fair trial. His book is a tribute to a brave man; a man who, in spite of the most shameless calumny, never lost his dignity nor confidence in his own integrity.

The Henry Regnery Company published many more books on foreign policy, but only one more, in addition to the three I have already described, was specifically concerned with American intervention in World War II. The author of this book, George N. Crocker, appeared in my office one spring day in 1959, told me that he had come from San Francisco to bring me a manuscript he thought might be of interest to me, and that he proposed to stay at the Drake Hotel, where he had taken a room, until I was prepared to tell him whether or not we would publish it. As it worked out, he only had to spend two or three days in Chicago. We published the book—the title was *Roosevelt's Road to Russia*—the following September; it was without doubt one of the most effective of all the revisionist books, and it was successful.

George Crocker received his education at Stanford University and the Harvard Law School and served as an officer in the army in World War II. After practicing law and experience as an assistant U.S. attorney and dean of a law school, he devoted several years to the study of the diplomatic history of the Second World War to discover, if possible, why, after overwhelming military victory, none of our professed war aims had been achieved. He was not willing to accept the argument that it had all been in accordance with the iron logic of events, as though it had been a gigantic Greek tragedy; he did not believe that the destruction of the geographical unity of Europe, the expulsion of millions of people from their homelands, and the expansion of Communist Russia to the Yalu River in Korea and in Europe to a line fifty miles from Frankfurt were necessary. These things had come about as the result of decisions made by powerful men. It was Crocker's purpose in writing his book to describe what went on at the meetings that brought them together—the first aboard a cruiser in Placentia Bay, attended only by President Roosevelt, Prime Minister Churchill, and their staffs; others at Casablanca, Quebec, Cairo, Teheran, again at Quebec; the last at Yalta—and to discover how the fate of millions was determined by a few men. It is not a pleasant story, nor one which can give us as Americans reason for pride in those who guided our country during those years or in us as a people for having chosen them, or in our educational institutions for preparing the way, nor in our sources of information and means of communication for having so thoroughly misrepresented not only what went on, but its fatal consequences.

For the participants, these great conferences were pleasant occasions, the surroundings luxurious and the general atmosphere relaxed and friendly. The weighty business of determining the future of the world, the fate of nations, the location of boundaries, the movements of armies of men and fleets of ships, was interspersed with sumptuous banquets, lengthy toasts, and hearty camaraderie. Following a dinner at the Casablanca Conference, to which "the President had invited the British and American chiefs to dine with him and Churchill and Averell," Hopkins reports, there was "much good talk of war."[16] Elliott Roosevelt, writing of the same occasion, remarks, "I busied myself filling glasses."[17] It was at the Teheran Conference that Stalin offered a toast as a salute to the execution of fifty-thousand German officers and technicians. Churchill was appalled and instantly protested "the cold-blooded execution of soldiers who had fought for their country."[18] Roosevelt, with his customary aplomb, suggested a compromise, that "we should settle on a smaller number. Shall we say forty-nine thousand and five hundred?"[19] The Russians and Americans present found this amusing; Churchill left the table, but by this time it was too late: British power no longer counted in this world.

It was also at the Teheran Conference that the division of Germany, the annexation of Eastern Poland by Russia and of Eastern Germany by Poland, and the complete expulsion of the populations involved were settled; and with these decisions, the fate of Eastern Europe. As Crocker describes it:

> History knows that on the afternoon of December 1, 1943, in the Russian Embassy at Teheran, the Polish Republic was secretly partitioned by a Russian, an Englishman, and an American. Forty-eight percent of the land of Poland was to be torn away and given to the Soviet Union. No Pole was present. There was no talk of plebiscites, of the will of the people, of justice, of compensation to the inhabitants, of legal rights, of moral rights. It was a naked power deal. Roosevelt did not lift a finger to prevent it and must be deemed to have acquiesced. Reading Churchill's memoirs, one is struck by the casualness—and the callousness—with which these Moguls of the twentieth century wielded the cleaver. Ancient cities were picked off like the wings of butterflies. "I was not prepared to make a squawk about Lvov," and "Stalin then said that the Russians would like to have the warm water port of Konigsberg."[20]

The State Department account of the Teheran Conference reports President Roosevelt's opening remarks as follows:

He said he wished to welcome the new members to the family circle and to tell them that meetings of this character were conducted as between friends with complete frankness on all sides with nothing that was said to be made public.[21]

(Robert Sherwood's account in *Roosevelt and Hopkins* omits the phrase "with nothing that was said to be made public.") With an election coming up the following year, and, as Roosevelt explained to Stalin, several million Polish-Americans among the voters, it was of the utmost importance that the details of the Polish agreements be kept secret. ("Open covenants openly arrived at" had been one of Woodrow Wilson's slogans in World War I.) Rumors, however, began to circulate, and there was the obvious fact of Russian behavior toward Poland. When, therefore, Congressman Joseph Mruk asked President Roosevelt whether any secret agreements regarding Poland had been made at Teheran, he received the following letter, dated March 6, 1944, from the President:

I am afraid I cannot make any further comments except what I have written to you before—there were no secret Commitments made by me at Teheran and I am quite sure that other members of my party made none either. This, of course, does not include military plans which, however, had nothing to do with Poland.[22]

A few weeks after the Teheran Conference, on a worldwide broadcast on Christmas Eve from Hyde Park, President Roosevelt characterized Stalin with these words:

> He is a man who combines a tremendous, relent-
> less determination with a stalwart good humor. I
> believe that he is truly representative of the heart
> and soul of Russia; and I believe that we are going
> to get along very well with him and the Russian
> people—very well indeed.[23]

The second Quebec Conference is memorable chiefly as the occasion when the Morgenthau Plan became official allied policy. Churchill vehemently objected, as did Secretaries Stimson and Hull, but the promise by Secretary of the Treasury Henry Morgenthau of six and one-half billion dollars in the form of postwar credits to Britain brought Churchill around. In describing his futile efforts to dissuade the President from accepting Morgenthau's proposal, Stimson quotes Morgenthau as having written, in a memorandum to the Cabinet Committee, that in the Ruhr and surrounding industrial area, comprising some 30,000 square miles, "All industrial plants and equipment not destroyed by military action shall either be completely dismantled or removed from the area, all equipment shall be removed from the mines and the mines shall be thoroughly wrecked."[24] This was bad enough, but events soon overtook the Morgenthau Plan and left it little more than an embarrassing memory; it was the Yalta Conference, when an American President went half-way around the world to meet the Russian dictator on Russian soil, which will be remembered as one of the most shameful episodes in modern history. The suffering and bitterness caused by the Morgenthau Plan are now largely forgotten and the dismantled industrial plants have long since been rebuilt; but the decisions made at Yalta, which resulted in the dislocation and death of millions and the enormous increase of the power and influence of Communist Russia, will plague mankind for generations. Yalta, as Crocker puts it, "was a moral debacle of unimaginable evil to the world."[25]

In the second chapter of his book, which he calls "The Secret in the Closet," Crocker argues that World War II was, in reality, not one war but three: the British, French, American, and Russian war against National Socialism in Germany; the American war against Japan; and the war of Communist Russia against the non-Communist world. The wars against Germany and Japan, from the Russian standpoint, were only the necessary prelude to the much bigger third war. Crocker further argues that while the American people may have been deceived about the nature of the war they were in, their president was not:

> In this third war, which was to be the longest and most crucial one of the twentieth century, we find Franklin D. Roosevelt almost invariably charging ahead on the side of Soviet Russia. In fact, his support was the *sine qua non* of its successful launching. His mission, which he performed implacably, was to put weapons in Stalin's hands and, with American military might, to demolish all the dikes that held back the pressing tides of Communist expansion in Europe and Asia. Meanwhile, everything was done to prevent the average American citizen from becoming conscious of this war; his mind was kept preoccupied hating Hitler and Tojo. And since

Roosevelt was concealing the war itself, *a fortiori* he did not reveal his own sympathies in it.[26]

That all this happened there can be no doubt—the present state of the world is ample evidence of the correctness of Crocker's presentation of the facts. There may be room for disagreement with Crocker's emphasis or interpretation, but the facts and their consequences speak for themselves, and no amount of glossing over with arguments of historical necessity or such pretty phrases as "doing good by stealth" will make them go away. The big question, however, remains: Why did it all happen? Why did the American president acquiesce to almost any Russian demand; why, to bring Russia into the war against Japan, when his military commanders had told him that Japan was beaten, did he make concessions to Stalin that betrayed a loyal ally, Chiang Kai-shek, and led inevitably to the loss of China? Crocker does not accept the argument that Roosevelt was deceived, that he was not aware of the true nature of Communism, of Stalin's rapacity and ruthlessness:

> The predatory government that had, in December, 1939, been expelled from the League of Nations for its cold-blooded attack on little Finland, had swallowed up Estonia, Latvia, and Lithuania and had, in concert with Hitler, carved up Poland and erased it from the map could not and did not undergo a metamorphosis. Its leaders were not miraculously purged of international banditry when another bandit, Adolph Hitler, turned on them. They never specifically recanted;

they never showed penitence. They never told
Roosevelt they would free the Balts and the
others, nor did he ever require them to say so. On
the contrary, they continued to whet their appe-
tites as war raged. He was aware of this, even if
the American people were not.[27]

If Crocker does not accept the theory that Roosevelt was
gullible, he does not accept the explanation either that he
was ideologically motivated. There were without doubt
many Communists and Communist sympathizers in the
Roosevelt Administration—Alger Hiss was an advisor at
Yalta; Owen Lattimore was deputy director of the Office of
War Information; and on a number of occasions, President
Roosevelt sought the advice of Earl Browder, the head of
the American Communist Party, but Crocker does not
believe that Roosevelt himself was "any more a Communist
than a Jeffersonian." As Jesse Jones put it, he was "a total
politician." The State Department report on the Teheran
Conference quotes Roosevelt as remarking to Stalin, on the
question of India, "that the best solution would be reform
from the bottom, somewhat along the Soviet line," [28] which
rather indicates admiration for the Soviet way of getting
things done, which, as he must have known, included mass
extermination. Yet, while Crocker believes that Roosevelt
was the consummate politician, that however much he may
have loved to exercise power and admired the ruthless
exercise of power by others, he was not himself ideologically
motivated. For Roosevelt, it was power for its own sake, not
for any ideological objective. It is with Roosevelt's complete

surrender to politics, Crocker believed, that the "psycho-biographers of the future will probably start in their quest for the 'Why?'"[29] Crocker himself, however, lets the matter rest there.

There are many unanswered questions: Roosevelt's sudden shift, for example, in his public attitude toward the situation of religion in Communist Russia. On February 10, 1940, Crocker points out, in a speech to the American Youth Conference, President Roosevelt remarked that he detested "the banishment of religion" from Russia.[30] This was a few months after Russia had been expelled from the League of Nations for the attack on Finland, which had begun with the bombing of Helsinki, all of which had had an adverse effect on public opinion, and 1940 was an election year. In a letter to Pius XII, however, dated September 3, 1941, Roosevelt told the Pope, "Insofar as I am informed, churches in Russia are open." He went on to say:

> There are in the United States many people in all churches who have the feeling that Russia is governed completely by a communist form of society. In my opinion, the fact is that Russia is governed by a dictatorship, as rigid in its manner of being as dictatorship in Germany. I believe, however, that this Russian dictatorship is less dangerous to the safety of other nations than is the German form of dictatorship.... I believe that the survival of Russia is less dangerous to religion, to the church as such, and to humanity in general than would be the survival of the German form of

dictatorship. Furthermore, it is my belief that the leaders of all churches in the United States should recognize these facts clearly and should not close their eyes to these basic questions and by their present attitude on this question directly assist Germany in its present objectives.[31]

Had the situation of the church in Russia changed for the better between the time of the speech before the American Youth Conference and the writing of the letter the following year to the Pope? Not in the slightest, neither was Roosevelt in the slightest concerned with the situation of the church under Communism; if he were, why would he have acquiesced, without a murmur of protest, to the occupation of half of Europe by Soviet Russia? It was not the purpose of his letter to inform the Pope concerning the situation of the church under Communism or National Socialism—the Pope knew more about such matters than he; the purpose of the letter was purely political—to get the American churches, and particularly the Catholic Church, behind him in his support of Communist Russia in the war—Pearl Harbor was still some months away. As Msgr. Tardini put it in a memorandum to the Pope concerning the letter, "It is clear that political preoccupations predominate."[32]

It is also worth remembering, as Crocker reminds us, that Palmiro Togliatti, the head of the Italian Communist Party, was brought to Naples from Russia on an American ship immediately after the American occupation and given every possible assistance. As Alicide de Gasperi, the non-Fascist premier of postwar Italy, told a press conference in

Rome on February 24, 1954, "the evil plant (of communism)...was born and prospered in the Roosevelt climate."[33]

The response to the Crocker book, not surprisingly, was of two kinds—warm approval from those who agreed with it, and stony silence from those who did not. The one exception to the latter was a brief review in the *New York Times* (December 6, 1959) which ended, "...neither history nor scholarship—it is sheer nonsense." By the time of the publication of the Crocker book, however, both *National Review* and *Modern Age* had come into existence, so that there were at least two serious publications where such a book could be given fair and adequate consideration. Forest Davis, in *National Review* (December 5, 1959), suggested that the then President, Dwight Eisenhower, "would do well to include *Roosevelt's Road to Russia* in his knapsack as he reconnoiters the Communist Empire's southern frontiers from New Delhi to Rome." Crocker, he said, "expertly marshals the familiar sources, driving in terse prose to his conclusion," but Davis felt that "he falters when it comes to motive." Davis, who had known Roosevelt well, and in the early days of the New Deal had been a White House insider, remarked that Crocker minimizes Roosevelt's "essential frivolity, his empiricism, his vindictiveness and his one-dimensional mind." Harry Elmer Barnes, in *Modern Age* (Spring 1960), expressed the opinion that *Roosevelt's Road to Russia* was "the most brilliantly written and felicitously expressed of all revisionist books yet published on the second World War." He also commended Crocker for "his extraordinary command of the relevant facts, which makes

his book so impressive and convincing as well as exciting."
Except for excellent reviews in the *Chicago Tribune* and the
Boston Herald—the latter was headed "How We Got into
Our Awful Mess"—there were a few other reviews, but two
widely syndicated and respected columnists, Lyle Wilson
and Holmes Alexander, each devoted a column to the book,
which brought it to the attention of people in all parts of the
country. Largely as a result of their interest, *Roosevelt's
Road to Russia* went through five large printings within a
year after publication, and in 1961 there was a revised
edition in the paperback Great Debate series. George
Crocker, unfortunately, did not live to write the second
book he had planned, but his one book is an appropriate
memorial to a man of conviction who searched for the truth
and did not shrink from telling what he found.

No account of revisionism would be complete without an
expression of gratitude and respect to Harry Elmer Barnes.
Barnes wrote the first fully documented revisionist book on
World War I, *The Genesis of the World War*, which was
published by Knopf in 1926, and following World War II
devoted much of his time and incredible energy to encouraging and helping those willing to try to penetrate what he
correctly called the "historical blackout," the well organized
practice of "ignoring or suppressing facts counter to wartime propaganda." It was Harry Elmer Barnes who found
the financial support which enabled William Henry
Chamberlin and Charles C. Tansill to take time from their
regular work to write their two revisionist books. He found
similar help for others, not all of whose proposed books
were ever finished; and in such pamphlets as *The Struggle*

Against the Historical Blackout and *A Select Bibliography of Revisionist Books*, which he published and distributed himself, he carried on a relentless campaign for the historical truth as he saw it. He believed that American intervention in the two world wars had been unmitigated disasters and that, if such disasters were to be avoided in the future, it was essential that the true facts be known. As he put the case for historical revisionism:

> The mythology which followed the outbreak of war in 1914 helped to produce the Treaty of Versailles and the second World War. If world policy today cannot be divorced from the mythology of the 1940s, a third world war is inevitable, and its impact will be many times more horrible and devastating than that of the second.[34]

Barnes was born and raised on a farm near Auburn, New York, in a house built by his great-great-grandfather. He wanted to study at Cornell, but his mother, fearing the influence on the orthodox religious beliefs he had grown up with, insisted that he go instead to Syracuse University. He graduated in 1913 with high honors, taught at Syracuse for two years, and in 1915 was given a scholarship for graduate work at Columbia, where he studied with such scholars as the historians James Harvey Robinson and James T. Shotwell, the sociologist Alvan A. Tenney and the anthropologist Alexander A. Goldenweiser, and quickly made a reputation for himself for his retentive mind, his industry, and his intellectual curiosity. While Barnes rejected his mother's religious convictions while still an undergraduate, he never got away, I think, from the humanistic faith which was characteristic of the time during which he reached maturity—a faith which manifested itself in belief in progress and the power of knowledge and science, in the service of reason, to solve all human and social problems. The historian Carl L. Becker once characterized Barnes as "that rare phenomenon, a learned crusader," which is exactly what he was. Revisionist historiography was doubtless the cause that absorbed the major part of his talents and energy, but was by no means the only one; he was completely in the tradition of the liberal reformer. As Justice D. Doenecke put it in an informative article on Barnes,

> He opposed prohibition and censorship, assailed capital punishment, pushed for prison and court reform,...liberalization of divorce laws, abolition of sexual taboos, planned parenthood, compulsory health insurance, revision of drug legislation, and far greater equality for women and blacks.[35]

Barnes's commitment to revisionism was in no way related to sympathy for Germany or German culture—by temperament, he said, he was more inclined toward the French than the German tradition—but derived entirely from his firmly held belief that if the truth concerning American involvement in the two world wars could be made generally known, such disasters would not recur. It may have been a naïve faith, but it was a sincere one, and Barnes unhesitatingly sacrificed a brilliant academic career in its behalf. His commitment to revisionism was a reflection of his belief in the primacy of reason: if "the American people" could only be correctly informed, they would act in a way which is in accordance with their own best interests.

It is interesting and instructive to reflect that Barnes's *Genesis of the World War*, which challenged the whole basis of American intervention in the First World War and of the punitive peace that followed it, was not only published by Alfred Knopf, but that Knopf himself had suggested that Barnes write it, Knopf having read and been impressed by the series of articles on the causes of World War I Barnes had written for the *Christian Century*. While not every reviewer agreed with Barnes's book, it was widely and seriously reviewed. Sidney B. Fay's monumental *The Origins of the World War* was published by Macmillan, C.H. Grattan's *Why We Fought* by Vanguard, C.C. Tansill's *America Goes to War* by Little, Brown, and Walter Millis' *Road to War* by Houghton Mifflin. The revisionist books on World War II, by way of contrast, were nearly all published by small publishers or, in the case of the two books by Charles A. Beard, by Yale University Press. For the most part, they were either ignored by influential reviewers, or treated as irresponsible assaults on public order. George Morgenstern's *Pearl Harbor*, Admiral R.A. Theobald's *The Final Secret of Pearl Harbor*, and F.R. Sanborn's *Design for War* were all published by Devin-Adair in New York. I have already mentioned the four revisionist books published by the Henry Regnery Company, and the authoritative collection of essays Harry Elmer Barnes put together, *Perpetual War for Perpetual*

Peace, was published by the Caxton Press in Caldwell, Idaho. On the other hand, the four revisionist books we published all sold well—more than 20,000 copies in each case, which is quite respectable—and several of the other revisionist books did considerably better, so that it cannot be said that the large New York publishers rejected them on the grounds of lack of public interest.

As the author of many successful books, including some widely used college texts—*The History of Western Civilization* (2 vols., 1935), *An Intellectual and Cultural History of the Western World* (1937), *An Economic History of the Western World* (1937), *A History of Historical Writing* (1937), *Social Thought from Lore to Science* (1938), and *Society in Transition* (1939), for example—Barnes was well acquainted with New York publishers and editors. One of the principal reasons, Barnes told me on several occasions, that the large New York publishers gave him for rejecting the revisionist books he suggested to them was fear of reprisals from the academic community. They all had reason to believe, so Barnes told me, that if they published such books as those by Tansill, Chamberlin, or Beard, their sales of text books in the colleges and universities would be adversely affected.

For all his strongly held convictions, Barnes was an amiable man, had an excellent sense of humor, and was good company. I enjoyed his friendship. We made a trip to Texas on one occasion to try to arouse interest on the part of some of the Texas oil tycoons in books which, in our opinion, undertook to "set the record straight." It was an enjoyable trip, but produced no tangible results—there was much good conversation, a number of pleasant lunches and dinners, but little else. The oil barons commended us for our efforts, but were not willing to risk a commitment. One of the Texans I met on another occasion had a fine library, of which he was justly proud, and had given substantial financial support to one of the left-liberal magazines of New York, and while he was temperamentally fully in agreement with the position of the books I was publishing, he was not willing to support them financially—a left-liberal magazine was more fashionable, offered greater recognition, and was certainly less controversial.

In his fight against the "historical blackout," Barnes became argumentative, strident, and at times, rather bitter. Having been an extremely successful and sought after teacher, author and lecturer, he now found himself literally stifled, reduced to writing for obscure publications or having to publish his writings himself. "Short of some monstrous crime," he once said, "I could have chosen no line of activity less likely to be of material benefit to myself." His stridency becomes understandable in view of all this, as does his enthusiasm for one or two books which were not worthy of his support. One of these enthusiasms led to a brief period of distinct coolness on his part toward me, an episode which also had its comic aspects. Barnes had become quite angry because I rejected a manuscript he had been most insistent that I publish, but he finally agreed that my reasons for rejecting it had been well founded. In one of the last of many letters on the subject he wrote that the author in question "appears to be breaking down mentally, and the only reason that one cannot truthfully say that he is breaking down ethically is that I have discovered far too late that he apparently never had any ethics at any time." Harry Elmer Barnes was an honest, generous, unselfish man, a distinguished scholar, was devoted to the best traditions of his country, and, as he demonstrated many times, willing to stand up for his convictions.

Was the fight for what we thought was the historical truth worthwhile? I find it difficult to believe, as much as I would like to believe it, that telling the true story of what happened when Roosevelt and Churchill met in the Bay of St. Lawrence on board the cruiser *Augusta*, the true story of Pearl Harbor, Teheran or Yalta will prevent such occurrences in the future—men and politics, ambition and power are what they are and will remain so to the end of history— nor will the consequences of the decisions made at Teheran and Yalta be in any way changed because that rather abstract collective, the "American people," are given the means to find out what actually happened. The vast literature which set the record straight concerning the lies, misconceptions, blunders, and misrepresentations involved with the First World War did not, obviously, prevent their recurrence on a much larger scale during the Second. One of the most effective revisionist books on the manner in which America was brought into World War I was *Road to War*, but this did not even prevent its author, Walter Millis, from becoming one of the most ardent interventionists the second time around.

Whether writing and publishing the historical truth brings any immediate practical results or not, if we believe in anything, we must believe that the truth is worthwhile for its own sake. If the free society is to survive, is to have any meaning, men must be made accountable for their actions, we must know what our leaders did, said, and agreed to in our name. The alternative is the society described in George Orwell's *1984*.

9

Winston Churchill:
A Question of Leadership

Martin Gilbert's massive, carefully documented book, *Winston S. Churchill, Road to Victory, 1941-1945*, the seventh volume of what one can assume to be the official biography of Churchill, gives the reader an almost day-by-day account of his decisions and actions in World War II.[1] The author makes no judgments, ascribes no motives, and makes no attempt to relate Churchill's role to the overall strategy of the war. It is not, therefore, history in the usual sense and can better be described as a chronicle. Since Gilbert had access to all the relevant documents, including private correspondence and diaries, and because of his meticulous scholarship, this work will remain an indispensable source for historians of World War II.

The book begins with Churchill's decision following the Japanese attack on Pearl Harbor on December 7, 1941, to go to Washington to confer with President Franklin D. Roosevelt; the purpose of his visit, as he said in his telegram to the President, was to review "the whole war plan" and to discuss problems of production and distribution. The meeting was set to take place just before Christmas, in Washington. Churchill concluded his telegram with these words: "I never felt so sure about final victory, but only concerted action will achieve it."[2] With his usual respect for the procedures and traditions of British parliamentary government, Churchill obtained the approval of the War Cabinet for his plans and informed King George VI. The American declaration of war against the Axis powers was a triumph for Churchill and the culmination of many months of careful effort, one of the more skillfully staged events in the process of bringing the United States into the war being the meeting aboard the cruiser *Augusta* in the Gulf of St. Lawrence on August 17, 1941, from which emanated the much-heralded Atlantic Charter, soon to be forgotten after it had served its purpose.

While crossing the stormy Atlantic in that fateful December, Churchill dictated a series of memoranda on the future conduct of the war. One of these, "The Atlantic Front," dated December 16, is of utmost relevance to an understanding of the future conduct of the war and its consequences. "It was essential," Churchill concluded, "for Britain and the United States to send Russia the supplies they had promised 'without fail and punctually.' In this way alone 'we shall hold our influence over Stalin and be able to weave the mighty Russian effort into the general texture of the war.'"[3] In April 1942, Churchill told the House of

Commons that the war could be ended "only through the defeat of the German armies."[4] Following Adolf Hitler's decision to turn against his former ally, Joseph Stalin, therefore, Churchill supported the Soviet Union in every possible way, making no conditions of any kind—"To help Russia there was nothing he would not do," as he told the House of Commons.

It must have given Stalin, that former Georgian bandit, immense satisfaction to have this British Prime Minister, a descendant of the Duke of Marlborough, no matter how pointed his insults, literally at his beck and call. When, for example, convoys bringing Soviet supplies to Murmansk were temporarily halted following the loss, from one convoy, of twenty-three merchant ships out of a total of thirty-four, Gilbert quotes Stalin as saying to Churchill at their August 1942 meeting in Moscow. "This is the first time in history that the British Navy has turned tail and fled from battle. The British are afraid of fighting."[5] Churchill concluded his stay in Moscow with an *aide-mémoire*, to Stalin, which ended: "We reaffirm our resolve to aid our Russian allies by every practicable means." No matter what the provocation by Stalin, which included the refusal to permit the British to maintain medical facilities in Murmansk for sailors suffering from frostbite and the use of Russian airfields by their British allies to supply the Poles fighting the Germans during the Warsaw uprising, Churchill continued to supply the Russians "without fail and punctually," still in the belief that by this means "we shall hold our influence over Stalin."

Churchill's conduct of the war can only be understood in view of his determination to win, whatever the cost and whatever the consequences. Two of the elements of his strategy were the unconditional support of the Soviets on the German eastern front, and "an absolutely devastating attack by very heavy bombers from this country upon the Nazi homeland."[6] Churchill sent numerous messages to Stalin describing the British air attacks on German cities that give the impression he was intimidated by Stalin and wished to impress him.

On January 17, 1943, he telegraphed Stalin: "We dropped 142 tons of high explosives and 218 tons of incendiaries on Berlin last night." On January 18 he telegraphed that it had been 117 tons of high explosives and 211 tons of incendiaries.[7] In May 1943 he proudly informed Stalin: "We gave Duisberg 1,450 tons, the heaviest yet launched in a single raid."[8] Following a meeting of the Defense Committee on November 16, 1942, Churchill set out his thoughts on the conduct of the North African and Italian campaigns, a copy of which was sent to Roosevelt and which stated that British night air attacks "should be brought to bear on Italy whenever the weather is more favorable than for bombing Germany"; that every effort should be made "to make Italy feel the weight of the war"; and that Italian industrial centers should be attacked "in an intense fashion," with every effort made to render them uninhabitable and "to terrorize and paralyse the population."[9]

Gilbert quotes Churchill as saying to Stalin during his 1942 visit to Moscow, with regard to the German civil population, "[W]e looked upon its morale as a military target. We sought no mercy and we would show no mercy."[10] Following a particularly heavy series of raids on the cities of the Ruhr in June 1943, when, according to Gilbert, 15,000 tons of bombs were dropped in seven major attacks, a film was shown during the customary weekend at Chequers, the country house of British Prime Ministers, showing the bombing of German towns from the air. During the course of the film one of Churchill's guests, Richard Casey, is quoted as reporting, "WSC suddenly sat bolt upright and said to me: 'Are we beasts? Are we taking this too far?'"[11] But the air raids went on. Following the terrible air raid on Dresden on February 13, 1945, when, according to Paul Johnson, 135,000 men, women, and children were killed and 4,200 acres of the city completely destroyed,[12] Churchill was sufficiently disturbed to suggest to the Chiefs of Staff Committee "that the moment has come when the question of bombing German cities...should be reviewed."[13] The Air Staff did agree, Gilbert says, that "at this advanced stage of the war" there was no great advantage in bombing "the remaining industrial centres of Germany"[14]; but on the night of April 14, Potsdam, which would hardly qualify as an "industrial center," was bombed. Johnson, in his history, *Modern Times*, calls the destruction of Dresden "the greatest Anglo-American moral disaster of the war." The policy of terror bombing, he goes on to say, "marked a crucial stage in the moral declension of humanity in our times."[15]

As was the case with the air raids on German cities, Churchill had occasional moments of doubt concerning his policy of unlimited, unquestioning support of the Soviet

Union, particularly of how it might affect the future state of
Europe, but in neither case did it have any noticeable
influence on his policies. Churchill was a warrior, he loved
fighting, and for a warrior, the sole objective is to win.
Furthermore, Churchill was a man who lived in the present:
"It is a mistake," he said on February 27, 1945, in a speech
to the House of Commons, "to look too far ahead. Only one
link in the chain of destiny can be handled at one time."[16]
No one can accuse Churchill of "looking too far ahead,"
except, perhaps, when it was too late. In a note to Anthony
Eden, written in 1942 in response to his views on the
postwar organization of the "Four Great Powers," Churchill
added at the end: "It would be a measureless disaster if
Russian barbarism overlaid the cultures and independence
of the ancient states of Europe."[17] In a long message to
Eden written at the time of the San Francisco conference,
there is a foretaste of what was to appear in his famous "Iron
Curtain Speech," given in Fulton, Missouri, on March 5,
1946—"From Stettin in the Baltic to Trieste in the Adriatic,
an iron curtain has descended across the continent of
Europe." In his message to Eden, Churchill set out his fears
for what lay ahead:

> Thus the territories under Russian control would
> include the Baltic provinces, all of Germany to
> the occupational line, all Czechoslovakia, a large
> part of Austria, the whole of Yugoslavia, Hun-
> gary, Roumania, Bulgaria, until Greece in her
> present tottering condition is reached. It would
> include all of the great capitals of Middle Europe

including Berlin, Vienna, Budapest, Belgrade, Bucharest, and Sofia. This constitutes an event in the history of Europe to which there has been no parallel, and which has not been faced by the Allies in their long and hazardous struggle.[18]

The bombing of Dresden did no credit to those responsible for it, but it was no worse than the bombing of Berlin or Hamburg—the number killed was doubtless far less—and while it could have had no effect on the outcome of the war, which by February 1945 was already decided, neither did the air raids on such beautiful old cities as Freiburg or Wurtzburg. Much more disastrous for the future, not only of Europe but of civilization itself, was the policy of unconditional surrender, which made any sort of reasonable peace impossible and required that the war continue to its final, hideous end. The utter failure of Churchill's efforts to secure the independence of Poland made clear that he, as a result of the policy of unconditional surrender and unlimited support of the Soviets was, in effect, a prisoner of Stalin. It was President Roosevelt, of course, who initiated the policy of unconditional surrender; but Churchill, whatever doubts he may have had, accepted it unequivocally. During the Casablanca Conference in January 1943, when this policy was first made public, he informed the War Cabinet in London that it was proposed to include in the statement to be issued at the end of the conference "a declaration of firm intention of the United States and the British Empire to continue the war relentlessly until we have brought about the unconditional surrender of Germany and Japan."[19]

It was, of course, impossible even to negotiate with such a megalomaniac as Hitler, who, it seems clear, was convinced that if the German people were not willing or able to win the war for him, then they deserved to go down in cataclysmic defeat. But there were other possibilities. As has been confirmed in a number of books by responsible and respected historians—the first was Hans Rothfels's *The German Opposition to Hitler* (1948)—there was a responsible, committed opposition to Hitler, which was active before the war started and included men in high places in the army, the Foreign Office, and the Protestant and the Roman Catholic churches, the most visible manifestation of which was the attempt to assassinate Hitler on July 20, 1944. But the policy of unconditional surrender made any encouragement of such efforts impossible. To have negotiated with Hitler was out of the question; but, considering the stakes involved, the millions of lives, the subsequent deportations, the devastation of cities, it is hard to understand why no effort was made to give some encouragement to the high-minded Germans who were willing to, and in thousands of cases did, sacrifice their lives to get rid of Hitler. From Roosevelt one would not have expected much more than such a catchy slogan as "Unconditional Surrender"; as Paul Johnson says of him: "There was an incorrigible element of frivolity in Roosevelt's handling of foreign policy."[20] But of Churchill, with the long tradition of British statesmanship behind him and the example of the appalling results of similar policies following the Great War, one might have expected something better. In retrospect he deplored it all, as in his "Iron Curtain" speech, but by then it was too late.

In *The Secret War Against Hitler*, William Casey, who was head of the O.S.S. office in London, speaks of General Dwight D. Eisenhower's efforts to induce President Roosevelt to redefine unconditional surrender, having reason to believe that the German generals would then be willing to surrender. "Ike would just as soon not have taken the risk of Overlord (the code name for the cross-channel invasion) if other means of winning the war were available."[21] Roosevelt refused, Casey said, and then quotes the President as responding that he was not "willing at this time to say that we do not intend to destroy the German nation."[22] Eisenhower then suggested, Casey says,

> that Allied heads of state announce a "clarified" policy the German generals could accept and that would allow them to quit fighting.... But Hull and FDR turned thumbs down on the idea. Nor did Ike have any more luck with Churchill, although a host of British advisors urged the Prime Minister to press for clarification of unconditional surrender. In a minute dictated on April 19, 1944, Churchill said: "The matter is on the President. He announced it at Casablanca without any consultation. I am not going to address the President on the subject. For good or ill, the Americans took the lead and it is for them to make the first move."[23]

In fairness to Churchill, he probably felt that it would serve no purpose "to address the President on the subject," and that a rebuff would only lessen his already declining influence with him.

"Early in May," Casey goes on to say, "the conspirators inside the Reich came up with a new scheme, a specific military proposal, which Dulles radioed to London. Dulles said: 'The opposition group which includes Beck, Rundstedt and Falkenhausen...were ready to help our armed units get into Germany under the condition that we agreed to allow them to hold the Eastern front.'" Eisenhower, on his part, Casey continues, "was still looking for a way of rephrasing unconditional surrender to make it more palatable to the German generals and their concept of honor and obligation. He even got playwright Bob Sherwood to draft a speech that took another crack at redefining unconditional surrender. Eisenhower planned to deliver it after the landing. Washington, however, remained silent. Finally, Churchill wrote Ike that 'this is a matter that really must be dealt with by governments, and cannot be the subject of friends' talks. I never read anything less suitable for the troops.'"[24] Following the attempt to assassinate Hitler on July 20, 1944, Dulles, so Casey tells us, renewed his efforts to induce those responsible for the conduct of the war to take advantage of the offers of the German generals to end the fighting, but to no avail. "And what came from Washington and London?" Casey quotes Dulles: "The attempt on Hitler's life was dismissed as of no consequence. Churchill suggested that it was merely a case of dog-eat-dog."[25] Casey concludes his revelations of efforts to end the war in 1944 with this somber paragraph:

A little encouragement to those Germans ready to risk their lives to free Germany of Hitler could have brought peace before the Russians had crossed the Vistula and before the Western allies had advanced beyond Normandy. This could have avoided many thousands and perhaps millions of casualties, in gas chambers as well as in battle, and could have saved the freedom of millions of people in Eastern Europe.[26]

Martin Gilbert's book makes it clear that Churchill, old warrior that he was, thoroughly enjoyed the war, at least until its consequences had become evident to him: crossing the Atlantic to confer with Roosevelt, once by battleship and once on the *Queen Mary*, reminders of the days when "Britannia ruled the waves"; the great conferences when decisions were made which decided the destinies of millions to be followed by sumptuous banquets and congratulatory toasts, very satisfying to the ego; the opportunity to employ his great talent for oratory; the reviewing of the troops, taking the salute, and observing the progress of the war from his map room; and perhaps most satisfying of all, the sense of power all this gave him. Gilbert quotes from the notes Churchill had dictated while working on the sixth volume of his war memoirs, when, reflecting on the first meeting of the Yalta Conference with Stalin and Roosevelt, he wrote: "We had the world at our feet. Twenty-five million men marching at our orders by land and sea."[27] So it may have seemed, but as the fate of Poland demonstrated, the independence of which Britain had ostensibly gone to war in the first place to protect, Britain, by the time of the Yalta Conference, had become very much the junior partner in what Churchill liked to refer to as the alliance of "The Three Great Powers," even as Churchill himself had almost no influence on the actual course of events. The policies of unquestioning support of the Soviet Union and unconditional surrender, the first of which Churchill had initiated and the second supported, if reluctantly, had given Stalin a free hand in Eastern Europe, which, the commitments made in the Atlantic Charter notwithstanding, he lost no time taking advantage of.

World War I, it is painful to remember, was concluded with the Peace of Versailles, which did not bring peace but led to what was in reality a continuation of the war it was supposed to end. In contrast, the Congress of Vienna, which followed the Napoleonic wars, resulted in a settlement which lasted for a century without a major European war. France, the defeated, was not subjected to indemnities or territorial annexations, or treated as a moral pariah, as was Germany following World War I. Talleyrand, the French foreign minister, took part in the deliberations leading to the settlement as an equal. The objective at Vienna was to arrive at a peace that would last; Prince Metternich, the Austrian foreign minister, recognized that France, in defeat, was still a major power and a part of Europe.

Following World War II there was not even such a dictated peace as the Treaty of Versailles. The nearest thing we have to a general settlement was represented by the two conferences of Roosevelt, Churchill, and Stalin at Teheran and at Yalta, which did little more, in reality, than divide Europe between the Soviet Union and the Western powers, to the great advantage of the Soviet Union. These two ill-fated conferences have been the subject of acrimonious debate, have fueled political campaigns and accusations of bad faith and broken promises—all of which makes the detailed, objective account in Gilbert's book all the more welcome.

The Teheran Conference opened on the afternoon of November 23, 1943, in the Soviet Embassy in Teheran. The American delegation was housed in a separate building on the grounds of the Soviet Embassy and the British delegation in the British Embassy several miles distant. Roosevelt, as the only head of state, presided. At the first meeting, as Gilbert informs us, Churchill told the group that they represented probably "the greatest concentration of worldly power that had ever been seen in the history of mankind."[28] There were a number of thorny problems and differences among the Allies to be settled: the date of the cross-channel invasion, the Mediterranean strategy, the disposition of Poland and its future frontier with Germany on the west and Russia on the east, and what was to be done with defeated Germany. When the conference ended, a date for the cross-channel invasion had been settled. It was determined that, rather than proceed north from Italy, there should be an invasion of southern France, that the eastern frontier of Poland should be the "Curzon Line" and the western frontier on the Oder, and that Germany should be divided and made incapable of waging war again in the future. Clearly Stalin got everything he wanted.

To fulfill the Soviet demand for a warm-water port, Churchill generously suggested giving Stalin the historic German city of Königsberg. As compensation Poland for its loss of territory to Russia on the east, he proposed giving Poland the rest of East Prussia and the German territory east of the Oder and the western Neisse, which meant that the historic German cities of Danzig, Stettin, and Breslau would be evacuated and turned over to Poland, while Königsberg would go to Russia as its warm-water port. When something was said about the evacuation of the population involved, approximately 8,000,000 people, President Roosevelt, always the humanitarian, inquired if it would be possible to make such transfers on a voluntary basis. Stalin made it clear that the Red Army was already taking care of driving out the population under its control. Churchill had demonstrated the movement of populations with three matches, which Stalin then referred to as "the matter of the three matches,"[29] an easy way to dispose of the lives of 8,000,000 people. As for Poland, Churchill said: "What we wanted was a strong and independent Poland, friendly to Russia."[30]

In connection with all these changes of frontiers and evacuations of populations, it is interesting to recall that while still on board the *Duke of York* on the way back from his first meeting with Roosevelt in 1941, Churchill was informed by Eden that at a conference with Stalin in Moscow the latter insisted, before making any military agreements, that Britain and the United States agree to Stalin's demands concerning the future frontiers of Finland, the Baltic states, and Romania. Churchill replied to

Eden that such demands "were directly contrary to the first, second, and third articles of the Atlantic Charter to which Stalin had subscribed."[31] By the time of the Teheran Conference, obviously, all these solemn assurances had been conveniently forgotten.

When Stalin sensed some hesitation on the part of Churchill concerning the date of the cross-channel invasion, he angrily threatened to withdraw from the war; neither Roosevelt nor Churchill, however, was willing to take a strong stand to support any jointly agreed-to position, whatever it may have been. Certainly they would not speak up for Poland. At the time of the Teheran Conference, with the cross-channel invasion in the future, the Western powers still had much the stronger bargaining position with respect to the Soviet Union; but Roosevelt was too subservient to Stalin to make use of it, and Churchill, having squandered his freedom of action, was powerless except when acting in concert with Roosevelt.

Robert Nisbet is of the opinion that the Cold War began at the Teheran Conference. "It began," he says, "with Stalin's unmistakable and unavoidable perception of a fatal flaw in the U.S.-British alliance, the flaw being chiefly President Roosevelt's ineradicable hatred of all imperialisms and particularly British imperialism. Stalin's perception included also the fact—How could it have not?—that Roosevelt was eager to curry favor with him, Stalin, and wouldn't hesitate to join him faithfully at the conference table at the expense of Churchill and Britain."[32]

When the Yalta Conference began at 5:00 on the afternoon of February 4, 1945, World War II was approaching its end, the Third Reich was in its death throes, and whatever was decided by "The Big Three" really made little practical difference, since the Red Army was in control. It is ironic and says much about the character of each of "The Big Three" that, as Averell Harriman was to recall, "the ailing Roosevelt had decided to travel all the way to the Crimea—4,833 miles by sea from Newport News, to Malta, and then 1,375 by air from Luqa airfield, Malta, to the snowy runway at Saki—because Stalin on the advice of his doctors, refused to leave the Soviet Union."[33] Churchill, at 70, was also not pleased to make the long and arduous journey to Yalta, for, as he had telegraphed to Harry Hopkins, "If we had spent ten years on research we could not have found a worse place in the world."[34] His daughter Sarah, who accompanied Churchill to Yalta, mentions in a letter to her mother that on the way to one of the meetings, while driving across the bleak countryside of the Crimea, her father described it as "the Riviera of Hades." Commenting in his diary on the appearance of "The Big Three" at their first meeting at Yalta, Admiral Cunningham of the British delegation, wrote: "Stalin was good and clear in his points, the PM also very good, but the President does not appear to know what he is talking about and clings to one idea."[35] Insofar as Poland was concerned, all that remained of the original British guarantee of a free and independent Poland was Stalin's assurance, in reply to a question of Roosevelt's as to how soon it would be possible to hold elections, "that he thought it should be possible to hold them within a month unless there was some catastrophe on the front, which he thought was improbable."[36]

As for the future of Germany, Gilbert quotes Churchill as stating: "In principle all three were agreed on the dismemberment of Germany."[37] To this Stalin added that, by the terms of surrender, "they would reserve all their rights over German land, liberties, and even lives."[38] Churchill is then quoted as expressing some concern about the reaction in Great Britain to the evacuation of millions of people from their homeland, but "he himself was not shocked.... [I]f Poland took East Prussia and Silesia as far as the Oder it would mean moving 6,000,000 Germans back to Germany. That might be managed subject to the moral question which he had to settle with his own people." He went on to say that he was "not afraid of the problem of transferring populations so long as it was proportionate to what the Poles could manage and what could be put into Germany."[39] Roosevelt did make some objection to moving the western border of Poland to the western Neisse because of "difficulties involved in large transfers of populations," but apparently this objection did not carry much weight since the border was settled at the western Neisse. The atmosphere of the meeting seems to have been cordial. All those momentous decisions, involving the fate of millions, were followed by a sumptuous dinner and the usual toasts. General Sir Alan Brooke, who attended the conference, remarked in his diary that the standard of the speeches "was remarkably low and mostly consisted of insincere, slimy sort of slush!"[40] Churchill concluded his fantasy to Stalin with a particularly embarrassing oratorical flourish: "I walk through this world with greater courage and hope when I find myself in relation of friendship and intimacy with this great man, whose fame has gone out not only over all Russia but the world."[41]

In reading Gilbert's careful, detailed record of these two lamentable conferences, it is impossible to understand how a man of Churchill's experience and knowledge of history could have accepted, without qualm or protest, the decision to drive millions of people out of their homeland into a country they had never inhabited. "He was not shocked," he said, in view of the fact that such a "disentangling of populations" had been done in connection with the Greeks and Turks after World War I.[42] But Churchill, of all people, should have known that one historic crime does not in any way justify a still greater one. According to official German statistics, the German population of the area east of the Oder-Neisse in the former German Reich was 9,300,000. Of these 1,000,000 did not leave, and 6,943,000 were accounted for in the migration to West Germany and Berlin, leaving 1,257,000 unaccounted for—they may have died in the flight to the west or have been shipped east for forced labor. Whether Roosevelt and Churchill agreed or not to the Russian demands at Teheran and Yalta probably made little practical difference. Stalin knew what he wanted and as a result of the policies of unquestioned support and unconditional surrender was placed in a position to get it. Rather than the "Big Three" making the decisions at Yalta, they were, in reality, made by the "Big One."

At the time of the Teheran conference it would have been possible to have saved Poland and the rest of Eastern Europe from Russian domination, but by the time of the Yalta Conference it was too late. As Churchill was to remark in his *The Second World War*: "I could at this stage only warn and plead." On the other hand, following the Yalta Conference, Churchill reported to the House of Commons in a major speech on February 27, 1945: "Most solemn declarations have been made by Marshal Stalin that the sovereign independence of Poland is maintained." That decision, he went on to say, "is now joined by both Great Britain and the United States."[43] In the same speech, to give further emphasis to the solemnity of the agreements made at Yalta, he added:

> The impression I brought back from the Crimea, and from all my other contacts, is that Marshal Stalin and the Soviet leaders wish to live in honorable friendship and equality with the Western democracies. I feel also that their word is their bond. I know of no government which stands to its obligations even to its own despite, more solidly than the Russian Soviet Government.

It is evident that Churchill had a great facility for self-delusion.

These two old men, both obviously intimidated by "Uncle Joe," as they referred to him, were not prepared, however great our preponderance of military and economic power undoubtedly was, to take a strong position. By agreeing to the expulsion of millions of people from their ancestral homelands and the condemnation of hundreds of thousands to forced labor, Roosevelt and Churchill destroyed whatever claim they may have had to have conducted themselves on a higher moral level than Stalin. In saying this, it is not even implied that Hitler would not have done worse if he had had the power to do so. With the record in Poland and the Holocaust before us, we know what Nazi Germany was capable of, but we like to think of our leaders as operating on a higher moral plane.

As a striking contrast to "The Big Three" of Teheran and Yalta, it is salutary to remember the four men who played a leading part in the restoration of Western Europe— Charles de Gaulle, Konrad Adenauer, Robert Schuman, and Alcide de Gasperi. It was surely no accident that these four men, who, in the face of the animosity and hatred left by the war, were able to conceive of European society in its wholeness, came from Charlemagne's Middle Kingdom— de Gaulle from Lorraine, Adenauer from the Rhineland, Schuman from Alsace, and de Gasperi from the Trentino. During the Yalta Conference, Churchill remarked to Eden, "The only bond of the victors is their common hate,"[44] which was probably also true at Versailles. How fortunate it was, then, that at a critical moment in history there were four men in positions of great moral and political authority who could think and act in terms of peace and reciprocity between nations. In his *Memoirs*, Adenauer describes the dramatic moment on May 11, 1950, when a personal messenger from Robert Schuman, the French Foreign Minister, brought him the proposal to place the entire French and German coal and iron industry under a common higher authority, which, as Adenauer put it, "would create the first firm foundation for the European federation which was indispensable for the preservation of peace."[45]

Martin Gilbert's book is not easy reading; and as an account of human folly on an enormous, unprecedented scale it is, in fact, thoroughly depressing. But it gives every appearance of being an honest account of what happened, of decisions our leaders made, the consequences of which future generations, including our descendants, will have to face. Churchill, who is the subject of these pages, comes out of it a towering public figure—an inspiring wartime leader who never lost his confidence in the darkest hours of the war, a man of enormous vitality and energy, unsparing of himself, but who never lost an opportunity to enjoy what life had to offer, devoted to his family, much beloved by those who worked closely with him, a master of the English language, a great orator. For all that, however, it is difficult to admire a man who, as a wartime leader, could order Italian industrial cities to be bombed in an intensive fashion with every effort made "to terrorize and paralyze the population"; who could recommend that such a city as Königsberg, the city of Immanuel Kant, be handed over to Stalin in order to satisfy the Russian demand for a warm-water port, as though it was his to give; who could acquiesce to the "transfer," as he called it, of millions of people from their homelands; who could agree to the repatriation of thousands of Russian prisoners to what he knew was certain death; who could refer to Joseph Stalin as "that great and good man"; and who could take the position "that we pay no attention to unilateral declarations about Rome being an open city, but continue to bomb remorselessly."[46] He was willing to sacrifice the cultural patrimony of Europe to win a war which could only result in moving the frontier of

Soviet Russia to the middle of Europe.

It was in 1942 that Churchill made his famous statement, "We mean to hold our own. I have not become the King's first minister in order to preside over the liquidation of the British Empire," but that is exactly what he did. And perhaps it was fitting that this descendant of the Duke of Marlborough, the proud offspring of the British Empire at the peak of its power and influence, should have been fated to preside over its liquidation.

IV

Hermann Schnitzler: Remembering a Great Teacher

Max Picard: A Tribute

Richard Strauss: A Classic of Our Time

Richard Strauss   Hermann Schnitzler

Max Picard

10

Hermann Schnitzler:
Remembering a Great Teacher

The man whom I regard as the teacher who had the most lasting and decisive influence on the course of my life was not, officially, a teacher at all but rather a warm friend and a persuasive guide. At the time we met, Hermann Schnitzler, an art historian from Germany, was doing graduate work at Harvard's Fogg Museum on an exchange program, and I was an undergraduate studying mathematics at Massachusetts Institute of Technology. From our first acquaintance, and throughout our long friendship, he was to give depth and direction to my rather haphazard educational efforts.

A Rhinelander, Schnitzler was of medium height and rather well filled out—he liked to eat and enjoyed Mosel wine, which he knew something about. Bespectacled and deliberate in speech, his English having a slight accent, fluent in French and Italian, he was gracious and outgoing. He was born in 1905 in Monschau, a beautiful old town east of the Belgian border, some forty kilometers south of Aachen. It had been founded in the Middle Ages, according to local tradition, by a returning Crusader. Located on a small river which was especially suitable for washing wool, Monschau attracted wool producers. Spinning and weaving were its principal occupations for many years. At one time it produced veils for Turkish women.

Members of his family had lived for generations in Monschau, and Schnitzler's father, like his father before him, was a successful producer of woolen goods. Because there was no local secondary school, Schnitzler had been sent to the gymnasium in Aachen, where he lived with relatives. He was always proud that part of his education had been in the city of Charlemagne, who is revered by the Germans as *Karl der Grosse*. Whenever the shrine of Charlemagne, one of the great relics of the Middle Ages in the cathedral of Aachen, is moved, Schnitzler once told me, as it was during the last war to protect it from air raids, there is a formal inspection to make sure it is still intact. When such a ceremony took place after the last war, Schnitzler, as an expert in such matters, was asked to attend. It was a dreadfully hot and humid day, he said, not a breath of air stirring, and finally, as though Charlemagne himself had had enough, there was a great angry clap of thunder.

Continuing his education, Schnitzler had gone on to study in Berlin, Munich, and, for his doctorate, at the University of Bonn. Earlier, while a student in Berlin in the 1920s, he told me, he received a telegram one day from his father, containing the single word, "*Pleite*," meaning "bankrupt," his father having gone under during the devastating inflation that followed World War I.

To adjust himself to his new situation, Schnitzler, as many Germans have done under such circumstances, not the least of them Goethe, went off to Italy. On the train he got into conversation with a fellow countryman who, as it turned out, was in the travel business. They got on well together and, by the end of the journey, Schnitzler's new friend offered him a job conducting groups of German tourists to Italy. This provided him with the means to continue his studies.

He had hoped to become a concert pianist, but developed problems with his fingers. Although not sufficiently serious to prevent him from becoming an accomplished pianist, this condition made it impossible for him to pursue music as a professional career. He accordingly changed his field of study to the history of art and completed his doctorate at the University of Bonn under the much respected Professor Paul Clemen. Because it was not possible in 1932 to find a suitable job in Germany, he managed to get an invitation for a year or two at the Fogg Museum.

I was twenty-two years old when I first met Hermann Schnitzler. Our backgrounds could hardly have been more different. I had come from the Middle West, growing up in Hinsdale, a prosperous suburb of Chicago with a history, at that time, of less than a century. When I started school, Hinsdale still had many of the characteristics of a prairie village, with two blacksmiths, a harness maker, and a woodworking shop. It was surrounded by woods, open fields, and farms.

The schools were not outstanding but I recall that, in the early grades, the stories we read came largely from Greek and Germanic mythology, which stimulated the interest and imagination of a boy. A teacher, going from school to school on foot, came several times a week to teach us the notes of the scale and the rudiments of music. The high school I attended was rather small and not especially distinguished, but the director of school music was a good musician and teacher and I have him to thank for introducing me to what became an important aspect of my life. There was also an English teacher during my last year who greatly stimulated my interest in literature. Moreover, my father, a successful businessman, self-educated, had read widely as a young man, accumulating an excellent collection of books. Growing up, I went through much of Dickens, Stevenson, and Twain. Later, while in high school, I also read much of Thomas Hardy.

After finishing high school in 1929, I went on to Armour Institute of Technology in Chicago to study engineering. It was, it will be remembered, the age of the engineer. I stayed there for two years, worked hard and did well, standing second in my class, but decided that engineering, and the whole world of technology, was not what I really wanted. An English teacher, the old-fashioned, serious teacher rather characteristic of the American college in those days, had urged me as part of his course to read and to write a paper on *The Education of Henry Adams*. This book made a deep impression, which is still with me. That summer I pressed on to read Adams's *Mont-Saint Michel and Chartres* and the two volumes of his American history.

Another professor, detecting some talent in his field on my part, urged me to transfer to MIT and undertake the serious study of mathematics. This I did, but a year or two convinced me that I did not have the incentive or the talent to become a mathematician. But there were other courses that stirred my interest. Once again I was greatly influenced by an English professor who suggested that I read Goethe's *Wilhelm Meister's Apprenticeship and Travels* in Thomas Carlyle's beautiful translation, my knowledge of German then being inadequate. If I remember correctly, Goethe's advice to a young man was to follow his own inclinations, which at that age was exactly what I wanted to hear.

While attending MIT, I met a German exchange student from Berlin who lived in the same dormitory I did. He was a good pianist, and since I myself played the cello, on Sunday mornings we would often play together. One day he suggested that he bring over a friend whom he thought I would enjoy meeting. That was my introduction to Hermann Schnitzler. He proved to be a born teacher. He quickly took it upon himself to educate the naive, unsophisticated Midwesterner who had fallen into his hands, having sensed, it would seem, some promise in that person that was worth the effort. He soon began a drastic educational program to make up for the deficiencies he observed in my previous training. We went through the Boston museums together, the Fine Arts, the Fogg, the Gardner, examining their treasures and what specifically distinguished them as great art. We also went to recitals and concerts, those of the Boston Symphony, among others.

My extracurricular education was wonderfully enriching, sharing Schnitzler's observations as a well-trained art
historian and his musicianship. He was an accomplished
pianist—I remember the passion with which he played
Schumann's *Carnaval*. He was also at that time going
through a Wagner-Richard Strauss period, which gave me
the opportunity to hear piano arrangements of *Meistersinger*,
Tristan, *Rosenkavalier*, and much more. He also gave me
books to read, among them Thomas Mann's *Tonio Kröger*,
which he insisted I read in German, for me a slow process
at that stage of my development. And we talked. Schnitzler
was a great talker.

Such a stimulating time, coming upon my three years of
hard going in mathematics and all that went with it, years
rewarded with a degree and the realization that I was not
destined to become a mathematician, was an intoxicating
experience. Mindful of Goethe's admonition that a young
man should follow his own inclination, and inspired by my
reading of Henry Adams, I tried to follow, as best I could
in my limited way, in Adams's footsteps, which meant
study at a German university. Schnitzler suggested that I go
to Bonn for a year or two where he had studied, and this is
what I eventually did.

I arrived in Germany in August 1934. I had no idea what
to expect, and was fully prepared to find a country in a state
of turmoil following the Roehm purge, when Hitler had a
number of his close associates murdered for allegedly
conspiring against him. I was relieved to find that all was
outwardly calm and orderly.

Since my friend Schnitzler was then working in Koblenz,

an old city at the confluence of the Mosel and the Rhine which had once been a fortified Roman town, I went directly there. He had suggested that I spend a month or two with him before the start of the university term, which would give me a chance to begin the arduous task of learning German and to see something of the country.

By this time Schnitzler had found a job making an inventory, as it was called, of the artistic monuments in the area around Koblenz. He was living in a large, comfortable Victorian house on a quiet street not far from the Rhine. The house belonged to a lady who took in roomers and he had found a room there also for me.

Schnitzler's assigned task was to catalog any works of artistic or historic importance that he might find in the various villages and towns around Koblenz. For me, fresh from the prairies of the Midwest, it was a rewarding experience to follow along after a trained historian tracking down significant works of art in an area whose history went back to Caesar. It became a stimulating, intensely interesting time for me and an idyllic, if perhaps unrealistic, introduction to Germany. We spent our days measuring churches and taking pictures of sculpture, old houses, castles, and monasteries. The late summer and early autumn were sunny and warm, the countryside lush, the grapes in the vineyards beginning to ripen. To an impressionable young man it all seemed incredibly beautiful and romantic.

Schnitzler, thorough scholar that he was, made a significant discovery at this time. He found a beautiful thirteenth-century figure of Saint Martin, high on the wall of a nineteenth-century church. Through careful research he traced its origin from the great Romanesque cathedral in Mainz. This find subsequently became famous as the *"Bassenheimer Reiter."*

We made innumerable tours of the countryside. I particularly remember a pleasant day exploring the ruins of one of the great medieval castles on the Rhine, Burg Rheinfels, a few kilometers south of Koblenz on the west bank of the river. It had been destroyed, as were many of the castles thereabouts, by the French army in the seventeenth century, but the ruins were of great interest and wonderfully picturesque. In its time it must have been a formidable place, occupying as it did a strategic situation dominating the Rhine Valley.

One summer day Schnitzler suggested that we walk to Bad Ems, several kilometers east of Koblenz on the Lahn. We crossed the Rhine on the old pontoon bridge (since replaced by a great iron structure), went up the route past the fortress of Ehrenbreitstein, enjoying a fine view of the Rhine Valley and of Koblenz, and then followed quiet back roads to Ems. The countryside was well cultivated and orderly, there were fruit trees along the roadside, and the farmers were bringing in their crops, using wagons drawn by horses, oxen, or cows. It all reminded me of the description of a similar countryside in Goethe's *The Sorrows of Young Werther.*

An associate of Schnitzler went with us. He happened to be a member of the Nazi party and a Stormtrooper as well. In fact, he was a mild, scholarly, totally idealistic young man who was later to give up all political activity in disillusionment. But at that time he saw Hitler as the great hope for his country. Schnitzler, on the other hand, took a dim view of Hitler and all his works. They argued about it, but were firm friends and never became angry. On this occasion, at lunch, Schnitzler's associate ordered milk instead of beer. Turning to me in apparent disgust, Schnitzler said, "You can see what these people are doing to this country." Later, as we sat on a grassy hilltop, admiring the landscape stretched out before us, the Stormtrooper turned to me and said, "But if it weren't for Hitler, you wouldn't have been able to come to Germany at all, because we would have been in the midst of a civil war." To which Schnitzler replied, "Yes, of course, because *he* would have started it."

A week or two later, Schnitzler suggested that we make a trip to Trier, some 150 kilometers west of Koblenz on the Mosel. It would be difficult to find a more suitable place for a young man from the Middle West to encounter the depth and variety of European culture. Caesar, we remember, had conquered the country west of the Rhine in 57 B.C. It did not take long for the Romans, great city builders that they were, to recognize the potential of the area of which Trier was to become the center as the site for a city. Whether they appreciated the fine wine that the Mosel hills would produce is not known, but they no doubt had an eye for such possibilities. In any case, the Roman city of Trier, which was given the proud name of *Augusta Treverorum*, was founded in 14 B.C. With its favorable location on the Mosel in a fertile valley where the roads from Paris—one through Rheims, the other through Lyons—converged and offered convenient access to the fortified Roman cities on the Rhine from Cologne to Strasburg, Trier was to grow rapidly.

It was Henry Adams, if I am not mistaken, who expressed the opinion that the age that saw the building of the great cathedrals marked the high point of European civilization. I have been privileged to visit many of the great European cathedrals—Notre Dame, Chartres, and Strasburg in France; Salisbury, Wells, and Canterbury in England; Freiburg, Cologne, Munich, and Ulm in Germany—to mention only a few of the great achievements of the cathedral builders. But of all the cathedrals I have had the opportunity to visit, none made a deeper impact on me than the cathedral at Trier. Every style of church architecture is represented, from Roman, Romanesque, Gothic, to Baroque, all of them combined into a wonderfully coherent structure. Approaching the cathedral from the marketplace, one encounters the west facade, said to be one of the finest examples of eleventh-century architecture. It is 50 meters wide with two square towers surrounding the circular apse in the center. It is a classic example of that early architecture and gives the clear impression that the builders knew where they stood and believed in what they were doing.

After all this inspiring and instructive introduction to the Old World, the time came when it was necessary for me to get down to my work. Schnitzler had recommended the University of Bonn, where Nietzsche had studied, a great university, beautifully situated on the Rhine a few kilometers below Cologne, in the city of Beethoven's birth. By this time I had given up any idea of engineering or mathematics and had decided that economics would be my field.

In October I registered for classes and found a room in a large, airy house in a pleasant section of Bonn, which was then still a quiet university town. My landlady, I soon discovered, was a direct descendant of a prominent, cultivated Bonn family that had befriended Beethoven and had played an important role in his life—a fact of which she was inordinately proud.

During the two years I spent in Germany, I heard all the music I could. The Cologne opera house, built around 1900 in Art Nouveau style, was not beautiful, but performances were of the highest quality. Besides performances of *Figaro*, I heard *Rosenkavalier*, *Magic Flute*, *Don Giovanni*, and *Freischutz*, among others.

In the spring came the Beethoven Festival in Bonn, where one year I heard, besides much Beethoven, Bach's *Art of the Fugue*, played by the organist of the thirteenth-century Church of Saint Thomas in Leipzig. I went to Munich a number of times and particularly remember a performance of Schubert's "Trout Quintet" in the Renaissance court of the Royal Palace, the piano part performed by Elly Ney, and *Don Giovanni* in the eighteenth-century Cuvillies Theater conducted by Richard Strauss.

But the purest music I heard while in Germany was the singing of Gregorian chants by the monks of Maria Laach. I went there a number of times with my friend Schnitzler and later with other friends from the University. It is a beautiful, most impressive place, a twelfth-century Romanesque church on a strangely somber, isolated lake in the Eifel hills west of the Rhine. We would always go at least part of the way on foot, which seemed the appropriate way to approach such a place, and would spend the night at a small hotel near the monastery, coming back for more music the next day. The singing and the liturgy of the Mass in that lovely, austere church were of unforgettable purity and dignity.

I was not the only one to benefit from Schnitzler's tutelage. As a student at the University of Munich and also in Bonn, he had become the leader of a group of students who looked to him for guidance and stimulation. Several remained friends for years afterwards, some of whom I came to know. One of them came from a family of land-owners in Silesia. He invited Schnitzler to spend the Christmas holidays with his family. This was at the time of my first Christmas in Germany, 1934—and Hermann asked if I could be included in the invitation, to which the family kindly agreed. Schnitzler's friend, like him, was a student of the history of art, his particular interest being the German Romantic painters of whom Caspar David Friedrich is probably the best known. He was to become the subject of an attractive book by Schnitzler's friend.

The family included three brothers, including the oldest, the art historian; one was preparing to take over the farm, and the youngest was being trained as a chemist. The father of the family had been a captain in the German army and was killed in World War I. The farm was managed by the mother, whom I came to know as a kind and outgoing lady who presided over her family and managed the farm with complete assurance and competence. She was a remarkable person whom my wife came to know well during the years after the war and admired her as much as I did.

On the trip from Bonn to Silesia we used the opportunity to spend a few days in Dresden, which was still one of the most beautiful cities in Europe. During our stay we visited the art gallery, saw and admired its great treasures, including the Raphael Sistine Madonna and the great collection of Rubens. We were fortunate enough to hear a performance of one of the Strauss operas in the Opera House where most of the great works of Richard Strauss had had their first performances, including *Rosenkavalier*.

We then travelled on to Silesia. We were met at the station by an open carriage drawn by two handsome horses, with a coachman on the box—no self-respecting Silesian landowner at that time, we were told, would have had a car. Not long after we arrived we were taken to the barn to see the stock, among which was an old mule with the letters USA branded on one side—a prisoner of war, apparently, spending his declining years on a Silesian farm. On Christmas Eve the farmhands came in to greet the lady of the house, who had a special word and gift for each. There was much singing and visiting, a Christmas service in the village church, and a goose for Christmas dinner and the traditional carp at New Year's Eve.

It was a great privilege for an American student to be invited to spend the holidays on a Silesian farm, all the more so when one considers that the life and traditions it represented—the well-cultivated and productive farms, the orderly villages and ancient towns—no longer exist, the entire German population of some three million having been driven out at the end of the war under the terms of the Allied agreements.

Aside from such excursions and experiences, studies, of course, commanded most of my attention. While I was registered in the faculty of economics, the first semester was devoted largely to learning German. At that time there were a number of foreign students at Bonn, since the University offered an excellent course in German for them. Attendance brought most of us foreigners together on a regular basis and a number, mostly British and American, formed a little club. We bowled in the relaxed German fashion that seemed to consist largely of drinking beer to congratulate one another for a particularly lucky strike. We made bicycle trips and in the spring several of us took the train to Trier, rented boats, and for several days paddled down the Mosel.

We also studied, of course, several of us managing to earn degrees, and I learned to speak and write quite presentable German. Even as foreign students, we were well aware of the Hitler regime; but it seemed far removed from us, and the University, so far as we could tell, remained intact and largely unaffected—still a center of disinterested scholarship. Although the ugly business of anti-Semitism had started at that time, life on the whole seemed quite normal. The cities were clean and orderly, much more so than those from which we came. We were always courteously treated by professors and fellow students; and most of the people, indeed, nearly all I knew, were either indifferent to National Socialism or strongly opposed to it.

In the summer of 1936 I parted from my friend Schnitzler and the stimulating, privileged existence I had been leading. I came back home to a land of depression and drought, the Middle West looking particularly raw, flat, uninteresting, and the whole country itself seeming terribly dull and matter of fact.

Having made a start with economics, I thought I had better go on with it and in the fall I entered the Graduate School at Harvard. By far the most distinguished man in the Department of Economics at that time was Joseph Schumpeter, who was a product of the Austrian School, from which have come some of the outstanding and farseeing economists of the century, among them Böhm-Bawerk, Menger, Mises, and Hayek.

Schumpeter gave the basic course in economic history in the Graduate School. There were not more than twenty-five students in his lecture course and to be one of them was a great privilege. He was not only a fine scholar but a consummate lecturer. No narrow, academic economist, he was a broadly educated and cultivated man who viewed the world with a certain amused detachment, but saw it whole, and the limited place of economic considerations within it.

He had the quality, which I think is an essential element of the true conservative, of being able to view the present in the long perspective of history, of seeing the present not as the end product or purpose of history, but as a link between the long past and the limitless future. One day in class there was some discussion of the relative productivity and therefore desirability of various economic systems, and whether capitalism is more or less productive than socialism, to which Schumpeter remarked, "It all depends on what you want. If I had a choice, I would take the society that produced the cathedral at Chartres."

After three semesters at Harvard I had completed the course requirements for a Ph.D. and passed the general examination, which entitled me to an M.A. To get my doctorate I would have had to write a thesis; but since I had no intention of going into college teaching, I saw no reason to do it. In any case, I felt that it was about time I got out into the world and did something.

It was a confusing decade in which to start to make one's way, with a world about to destroy itself by total war, and with the difficult decisions and the privations such conflict brings. Events in Germany had in the meanwhile gone from bad to worse and my friend Schnitzler was, I could only hope, somehow surviving. For myself, out of a variety of experiences, I was slowly coming to the idea of becoming a publisher.

In the first letter I received after the war from Schnitzler, which an American soldier had kindly forwarded to me, I learned he had become the director of the Schnüttgen Museum in Cologne, which contained one of the most important collections of medieval art in Europe. During the war he had supervised the transfer of its treasures to a castle, Schloss Alfter, outside the city. After the war, he and his family moved to Alfter as had a number of others, including several prominent artists. Under Schnitzler's guidance, and with the help of others who were attracted to Alfter, it became a lively place, with lectures in the castle, recitals, book reviews, exhibitions, and discussions. The museum was to remain at the castle until a new building had been readied for it, the original museum, a former monastery, having been destroyed by Allied bombing.

In that first letter Schnitzler strongly urged me to read a book written in German by Max Picard, a Swiss author, with the title *Hitler in Our Selves*. This book, he said, would help to explain the catastrophe that had overtaken European civilization. I immediately wrote to the Swiss publisher, Eugen Rentsch in Zurich, asking for an option on the American publication rights and a reading copy. I read the book at once and made up my mind that it would be on our first publication list.

Picard, who was a wise man, felt that the German catastrophe should be taken as a warning of what could happen to any modern society. He described the various features of modern life that were manifestations of its sickness, among them its discontinuity and fragmentation, its emptiness, destructiveness, materialism, and its lack of faith in a higher order. Modern man, he said, regards the environment not as the circumstance in which we live out our lives, but as enemy territory to be conquered and occupied; language, not as a gift of God to discover and to communicate truth, but as a means of propaganda to influence other people.

Having determined to go into publishing and to have the Picard book among my first efforts, I decided to go to Europe early in 1949, armed with letters of introduction and hopeful of meeting Picard and his publisher, among others. After a pleasant meeting with Dr. Rentsch and his wife, who was as much a part of the publishing firm as he, I took the train to Tessin, the Italian-speaking part of Switzerland where Picard had made his home since the early 1920s.

It was a wonderful visit and was to be the beginning of a long and friendly relationship. Max Picard was a wise man, with a deeply felt faith, who not only understood and appreciated as few others do, the great works of the past, but most acutely the problems of the modern world. I am proud to say that his *Hitler in Our Selves* was among the first books that I published, for all the difficulties it involved, and that it was my friend Schnitzler who was responsible for calling my attention to his work.

Looking back over the many years that have passed, I have tried to recall those times when, as a young man from the Middle West, seeking an education, I had the good fortune to encounter an older European, already advanced in learning, who was kind enough to share his Old World culture with me. This involved not only his taste and talent in art and music, but also a profound appreciation of the intellectual facets of life.

This friendship, which began in America, was to be further enriched, as I have recounted here, by time spent together in Germany. Despite the darkness that descended on Europe, despite the ravages of war and their aftermath, the culture and character that my friend Hermann Schnitzler represented not only survived but also were preserved, mostly through efforts of men like himself. He was a great friend and a great teacher who helped me to appreciate what the human spirit is capable of achieving as well as to give direction and purpose to my life. To have had such a friend was a great privilege, for which I have every reason to be grateful.

11

Max Picard:
A Tribute

The *Time* magazine issue of February 4, 1952, under the heading "Religion," concluded its review of Max Picard's *The Flight from God* with the following:

> Is there any hope for the man of the *Flight?* Picard has no answer, except his own faith. Concluding, he tries to express for his century what Francis Thompson said for the 19th, George Herbert and John Donne for the 17th, and the Psalmist centuries before.
>
> Writes Max Picard: 'Whithersoever they may flee, there is God.... Ever more desperately they flee, but God is already in every place, waiting for them to come.'

The name Max Picard was first mentioned to me by a German friend in the first letter I received from him after the war. After describing the suffering, the destruction, the hopelessness and then the anguish of knowing that if his own country won the war it would be a catastrophe for humanity, he went on to say, "To understand what has happened, and why, you must read a book called *Hitler in Our Selves* by Max Picard."

I did read it and it was because of this book that I became a publisher. I remember very clearly making the decision to accept the contract for American rights that the original Swiss publisher, Dr. Eugen Rentsch, offered me. Up to that time, I had published a series of pamphlets and had brought out American editions of two books by the prominent English publisher Victor Golancz, which I had published in offset editions because I thought they had something to say which at that time very much needed to be said and which no other American publisher would even look at.

I had published those books and the pamphlets as a part-time activity. If I undertook to publish such a book as *Hitler in Our Selves*, which had to be translated from the German original, it would have to be done professionally. I realized at the time that to accept the offer of American rights I would have to become a full-time publisher. For my decision to become a publisher, therefore, I have an additional reason to be grateful to Max Picard.

A final compensation for having become his American publisher was the privilege of coming to know Dr. Picard. The human, friendly letters I received from him were an experience in themselves and gave me some idea of what to expect when I met him, but only a little. In the fall of 1949 I met his publisher in Zurich and then went down to Caslano, where Picard lived in the Italian-speaking canton of Tessin, in southern Switzerland. I remember exactly how he looked when I arrived that first time at the tiny station in Caslano. He was standing somewhat apart from the small group waiting for the train, a friendly but rather distant smile on his face, his blue eyes bright and penetrating.

When I first saw him I began to understand something he had written to me, that with him there was no becoming. "As I am," he said, "I always was," and so he looked. He was rather short, solidly built, with a fringe of white hair around an otherwise bald head, intensely blue eyes, a broad, ruddy, expressive face with strongly marked features. His movements were short and deliberate, and his voice rather high pitched; he had a warm sense of humor and told amusing stories very well, but there always seemed a distant look of sadness in his eyes. He was most cordial and friendly, but also reserved.

We talked as we walked to his house; there was no need of small talk to establish a relationship. I felt that I had always known him, and on future visits it seemed there had been no break, that we simply took up where we had left off, without interruption. While on this first visit I was to be with him hardly more than twenty-four hours. When I look back, it seems to have been much longer, so vivid was the experience and so much, in retrospect, having seemed to take place.

We strolled along the shores of Lake Lugano; we sat, saying nothing, looking out over the water and into the mountains from a favorite spot of his. Later, we talked, had a wonderful roast duck for dinner, and walked to Ponte Tresa on the Italian frontier to buy cheese and tomatoes. We drank wine, I met his very engaging son, who, after our delightful evening, insisted that we finish it off with a special kind of local schnapps, which, he assured me, "the Romans had drunk when they were here."

With Picard, and this was to me one of the most revealing aspects of the experience of being with him, everything was in its place, everything belonged together—he was a whole man. Here was a man with the vision of a prophet of the Old Testament, who understood, as few others, the sickness of the modern world, who wrote books the world will long remember. Yet here was the same man, selecting tomatoes in a tiny Italian store, haggling with the market woman to their mutual pleasure, and eating roast duck and drinking wine. I understood what he was talking about in that beautiful passage in one of his books when he describes Goethe at the Battle of Valmy. "In Goethe's time bread and wine had their place; life and cannons and war had another, separated from each other and yet connected to each other. Today there is nothing beyond the totality of war: bread and wine appear the extraneous remnants of a bygone world."

Max Picard came from a Jewish family which had lived in Switzerland for generations, but he himself was born in 1888 in Baden, at the southern end of the Black Forest. He studied medicine in Heidelberg and practiced for a time in Munich—very successfully, it seems—but gave up medicine, because its orientation, he felt, had become too mechanical, too positivistic, Darwinistic. He moved to Tessin in the early 1920s for the sake of his wife's health, stayed on after her early death, and spent the rest of his life there. He was eventually converted to Catholicism, but he was more than either Christian or Jew: he was both and above all, a complete person. He was a wise man who had a deeply felt faith, and who understood and appreciated, as do few others, the great works of the past.

In a letter to André Gide, written in 1921, Rilke called Picard "the most unpretentious, purest man I know." He was not a systematic philosopher, but a critical thinker, specifically, a critic of modern civilization and all that goes with it. His most profound and prophetic book, perhaps, is *The Flight from God*, first published in 1934, and in our translation in 1951. Wyndham Lewis once said something to the effect that when Shakespeare wrote *King Lear* he must have been in a kind of trance. In another place he remarks that he found it difficult not to believe that the creative artist is in possession of an experience the equal, at least, to that of the mystic. Picard's description of modern civilization as a gigantic flight from God can only have been the result of such an experience. It is, as one critic described it, a prophetic vision.

His book on silence is equally remarkable; for Picard, silence is not merely the absence of sound, it has a positive, creative quality, it is the counter-pole of language. Without silence, language becomes nothing more than idle chatter. For Picard, language also has a sacred character: "When language is destroyed, man loses his relationship with the

Original Word from which his own words and their measure are derived."

Picard felt strongly that one of the things lacking in modern life is the true encounter—people see and talk to each other but do not really encounter one another; the one gives nothing of himself to the other. To have met Max Picard was an encounter, and to meet him in his works can be just as much so. He gave generously of himself; his heart is in his work. If his reader meets him only part way, he will take something away with him that will make him a more complete and better person.

At the time of another visit to Dr. Picard, some seven years after the first, I was struck by how unchanged he was, and how unchangeable. Again the overpowering impression was his wholeness, the feeling he gave that he belonged. By then he lived in a different house, a half mile or so from the lake, just below the Convent of the Sisters of Neggio, with whom, of course, he was on the best of terms. He told me wonderful stories on those first two visits, of peasants and wine growers of Swiss factory owners, gentle stories the Mother Superior of the Convent had told him; stories of an elemental kind of humor and directness about them, full of understanding, and told with great energy and skill. Fully to understand Max Picard as a writer, I think, one should have heard him tell his stories.

A characteristic story was the one about the man he had ordered to hang himself in his (Picard's) own living room. He was working in his study one day, he told me (this was when he was living in a house directly on the Lake of Lugano) when he heard the sound of people talking excit-

edly in his living room. Thinking they were uninvited
visitors, and being busy, he at first paid no attention. When
the voices became too loud, he stopped his work and went
to see what was going on. He found two men, both dripping
wet, and a woman, all very excited. One of the men and the
woman were almost hysterical. After some difficulty, he
discovered that the more excited of the two men and the
woman were a married couple who had been walking along
the lake, quarreling about a divorce. The man wanted to
marry another woman but his wife refused to give him his
freedom. The man had threatened to drown himself unless
his wife agreed to divorce him; and finally, in desperation,
he really did throw himself into the lake, only to be pulled
out by the second man, who happened to be at hand.

All had come into the house of Dr. Picard, which stood
nearby. Upon hearing all this, Dr. Picard turned to the
estranged husband and, in his strong, rather high-pitched,
commanding voice, told him, "Go ahead, drown yourself,
you have my permission." Somewhat taken aback by this,
the man did nothing, whereupon Dr. Picard said, "Then
hang yourself from the lighting fixture; it will be strong
enough, and I will get a rope. No one has ever hanged
himself in my living room; it would be a new experience for
me, and since I am a physician by profession, an interesting
one." At this, the man's wife became furious, and flew at
Picard in defense of her husband. When peace was restored,
the man and wife went off happily together.

At the conclusion of the story, Dr. Picard remarked,
"You see, morality, right or wrong, means nothing to
modern man—he can only understand a concrete situation.

If I had talked to them, as a priest would have, of the obligations and duties of marriage, they would have been bored, and would have had no idea of what I was talking about. They could only understand the concrete situation of being drowned in the lake or hanged from my lighting fixture, and that is why I said what I did. I understand they are still living more or less happily together."

Dr. Picard's style of writing is as elemental as his stories. There is no development, no carefully worked out exposition, only the presentation of certain basic ideas and conceptions, which he offers to the reader in every possible way, and from every possible aspect. His approach is that of a poet. Needless to say, it is not a style which is easily translated into such a matter-of-fact language as modern English, nor is it a style the American reader finds easy to read and understand. Not surprisingly, then, none of the four books we published in translation were great popular successes. Several of them were, however, well and intelligently reviewed.

The academic philosophers were somewhat puzzled by his style, by his "formlessness," by his lack of system; and, of course, they found him difficult to categorize, but they were aware that here was a man of profound insight. Professor M.H. Hartshorne, for example, in his review of *The Flight from God* in the *Philosophical Review* concluded, "While this is not a book that would be of technical interest to philosophers, it is one that commends itself to all who take thought about the ultimate hollowness of our anxious self-confidence." F.A. Harkins in his review of *The World of Silence*—in the Jesuit weekly *America*—speaks of the exasperation with which metaphysicians will read Picard, of the absence of a tightly woven system of abstract statements. He then ended his review with this beautiful tribute to the author; "To this same world of silence, wondrously recreated in these pages by a poet's art, Max Picard invites his reader, here to be refreshed and healed, here to be given back power to taste the true savor of existence."

12

Richard Strauss:
A Classic of Our Time

When Richard Strauss appeared in London in 1947 at a special concert arranged in his honor by Sir Thomas Beecham, many people found it difficult to believe that the composer of *Salomé* and *Rosenkavalier* was still alive. In the grim world of 1947, when most of the great opera houses of Europe were bombed-out shells, when that jewel of the old Europe, Dresden, where many of the Strauss operas had had their first performances, was a wasteland of rubble and under Soviet Russian occupation, Richard Strauss must have appeared to be a revenant from a long-since vanished past.

Ludwig II of Bavaria, whom the world considered mad, but whose first act as king was to send his chancellor to find Richard Wagner and bring him to Munich, was in the first year of his reign when Richard Strauss was born in his capital on the Ysar in 1864. In the Royal Opera of Munich, a few months later, *Tristan* had its first performance. Franz Strauss, the father of Richard, played the first horn. Although a confirmed anti-Wagnerian, the elder Strauss on another occasion won the master's praise for the artistry of his playing.

The life of Richard Strauss, from his birth in the placid Munich of Ludwig II to his death in 1949 in a shattered, divided Europe spanned a period of violent change. He came at the end, and may well represent the last gift to the world of a great musical tradition. In contrast to most of the great composers, Richard Strauss enjoyed not only a long life, but a life, one can believe, that came about as close to complete success and fulfillment as is permitted to man, flawed and imperfect creature that he is.

His father came from a family which for generations had occupied the office of tower warden in a small town in northern Bavaria. One of the responsibilities of the tower warden was to play the horn for festive occasions. As a young man, Franz Strauss came to Munich and made himself the leading horn player of his time. Besides occupying the chair of first horn in the Munich opera, he was also professor in the conservatory. In the words of his son, "He was a so-called character. He would have considered it dishonorable to revise a musical judgment he had once considered correct.... His musical faith embraced the trinity of Mozart (above all), Haydn, Beethoven. To these were added Schubert, as a composer of lieder, Weber, and, at a distance, Mendelssohn and Spohr."

Richard Strauss's mother came from the Pschorr family, who were well-to-do and respected Munich brewers. His musical education began with piano lessons at the age of four, followed by instruction in violin, theory, and composition, all from friends or colleagues of his father. There were family gatherings on Sunday afternoons in the garden of an uncle, where music, played by friends and members of the family, was the central attraction. His first compositions were performed at such affairs by an amateur orchestra, the *"Wilde Gung,'"* which was conducted by his father and in which he himself played violin.

Franz Strauss was a demanding father and saw to it that his son was given an exacting and thorough musical education. He had, his son said, an infallible sense of time as well as a violent temper, so that to make music with him, as Strauss put it, could be a "somewhat unpredictable pleasure, but I learned how music should be played from the innumerable times I had to accompany him in the beautiful Mozart horn concertos and the Beethoven horn sonatas."

As a reward for his graduation from the classical Gymnasium, where he did well, his father took him to Bayreuth. The following winter, with proper introductions, he sent him to Vienna, where he played the piano for a public performance of his violin concerto, and received the only favorable comment from the redoubtable critic Eduard Hanslick he was ever to have.

The next year his father let him go to Berlin where, among others, he met Hans von Bülow—the great conductor of the day—who before their meeting had arranged to have his orchestra play Strauss's serenade for winds, and on the occasion of their meeting, asked him to compose a suite for winds. This was completed the following summer, and in the winter of 1884, when Strauss was eighteen, Bülow had his orchestra play the piece at a public performance in Munich with Strauss as conductor, his formal debut. A conservatory would have had nothing to offer Strauss; instead, he spent two years at the University of Munich, where he studied philosophy and the history of art. He was now ready to begin his musical career.

In 1885, Bülow arranged for Strauss to come as his assistant to Meiningen, a small principality, which had one of the best orchestras and theaters in Germany, and where Bülow was musical director. Strauss has written an amusing account of his debut with the Meiningen orchestra, first as a soloist in the Mozart C-minor piano concerto and then conducting his own F-minor symphony:

> Although I had practised faithfully all summer, I was by no means a fully trained pianist, and was terribly nervous about playing the piece under Bülow's direction. After the first movement had gone reasonably well, the very generous maestro encouraged me with the words, 'If you weren't something better, you could become a pianist.' While I didn't feel that the compliment was entirely deserved, it raised my self-confidence sufficiently so that I was able to throw myself into the last movements with more freedom.

Among those in the audience that day was no less a figure than Johannes Brahms. Strauss, of course, was most anx-

ious to have Brahms's opinion of his symphony. He reported their conversation as follows: "In his laconic way, he
said only, 'Quite nice,' but then added an encouraging piece
of advice, 'Young man, study the Schubert dances and try
your hand in the invention of eight-bar melodies.' I am
grateful," Strauss added, "chiefly to Johannes Brahms, that
since then I have never been ashamed to use a popular
melody (as little as they are regarded by the school-wisdom
of contemporary criticism, they come to one rarely, and
then only at a fortunate moment)."

Strauss spent only one winter an Meiningen, but the
opportunity to work under such a man as Bülow, with an
excellent orchestra and before a discerning audience, gave
him superb training and invaluable experience. Meiningen
was followed by engagements first in Munich as third
conductor of the opera, then in Weimar for four years as
second conductor. He then returned to Munich, where he
was given the title *königlicher Kapellmeister* (royal conductor) of the opera. It was in Weimar, after long and careful
preparation, that he conducted *Tristan* for the first time—
"the most beautiful experience of my life," he wrote to
Cosima Wagner. It was also in Weimar that his first opera,
Guntram, had its premiere, and in Weimar where he
conducted the first performance of Humperdinck's *Hansel
and Gretel*, which the composer, then entirely unknown,
had sent to Strauss. Through Strauss's efforts, the opera
became successful and Humperdinck famous almost over-
night.

Strauss's first compositions, not surprisingly, were in the
traditional forms: besides a gavotte, a "*Festmarch*," and early

symphony, the violin concerto already mentioned, there was a horn concerto, a quartet, a cello sonata, etc. The winter in Meiningen was followed by a trip to Italy, which led to his first serious attempt to strike out on his own, to develop his own manner of musical expression—the four movement, impressionistic *Aus Italien*. It is not often played, overshadowed as it is by his later works, but it has many beautiful passages, and is the work of a young musician who knew where he was going. *Guntram*, his first opera, was given a friendly reception in Weimar, but in Munich was a dismal failure. The Munich tenor, after the first performance, declared he would sing it again only if guaranteed a higher pension, and the orchestra threatened to strike.

Strauss's first tone poem, *Macbeth*, was another of the compositions of this period. In a letter to Bülow, explaining the poetic relationship of the work, he wrote: "If one wished to create a work of art that is coherent in tone and structure, and if it is to have such an effect on the listener, then what the composer wishes to say must have taken form in his mind. This is only possible in consequence of the inspiration of a poetical idea, whether this accompanies the work as program or not." In its first form, *Macbeth* was not satisfactory to Strauss, especially in its instrumentation; and following suggestions from Bülow, he completely revised it. It was then performed in Berlin, under Bülow's direction, with great success—Bülow wrote to a friend that it sounded "overpowering," and was enough to make him into an optimist.

Macbeth was soon followed by *Don Juan*, which is the

first work of Strauss to become part of the regular symphonic repertoire. After the first rehearsal for the first performance, which took place in Weimar in November, 1889, Strauss wrote to his father: "I am happy to see that I have again made progress in instrumentation; everything sounded fine, and comes out superbly, even if it is horribly difficult. I felt sorry for the poor horn and trumpet players. They blew themselves blue, it is so difficult—it is fortunate that the piece is so short.... The sound was wonderful, of enormous intensity and voluptuousness; the thing is going to make a great impression here. The oboe passage in G-major with the basses divided into four parts are especially beautiful; the divided violas and cellos, all with mutes, the horns also all muted, had a perfectly magical sound...." (Strauss, it should be remembered, was then twenty-five.) Within a year *Don Juan* was followed by another tone poem, *Death and Transfiguration*.

In 1898 Strauss became First Conductor of the Royal Opera in Berlin. During the first ten years of his association with the Berlin Opera, he appeared as conductor 700 times, and directed 69 different works, the first, characteristically, being *Tristan*, which was followed, in less than two weeks, by *Carmen*, *Hansel and Gretel*, *The Merry Wives of Windsor*, *La Muette de Portici*, and *Fidelio*. He was now at the height of his immense vitality and creative powers—three further tone poems, *Till Eulenspiegel*, *Also Sprach Zarathustra*, and *Don Quixote*, were behind him, as well as a number of songs and smaller works. A second opera, *Feuersnot*, was in preparation, and he soon completed another tone poem, the immense *Heldenleben*, which was first performed in

1899. Romain Rolland heard it soon after in Cologne, and was overwhelmed. Years later he wrote: "...it was clear to me that the mediocrity of his melodic sense scarcely exceeded that of a Mendelssohn, but the harmonic-rhythmic invention, the brilliance of the instrumentation, the dramatic intelligence, the will, were gigantic. I think still today that the vital arrow of Strauss has never risen higher than it did then."

Besides his heavy schedule as conductor of the Berlin Opera, his creative work, and his appearances as a guest conductor in cities from London to Moscow, Strauss found time to found his own orchestra for the performance of works by contemporary composers. In 1904 he made an American tour, which became a great triumph. It included twenty-one concerts in four weeks with twenty different orchestras, recitals of his own songs with his wife Pauline as soloist, and the world premiere of a new work, the *Sinfonia Domestica* on March 21, 1904, in New York's Carnegie Hall. Strauss was now the acknowledged great figure of contemporary music; the successor, one might say, of Wagner and Brahms.

The two tone poems written during the first years of Strauss's engagement as conductor in Berlin, *Heldenleben* and the *Sinfonia Domestica*, are his last works in this form. One has the impression that he had carried "program music" to the extreme limits of its possibilities. *Heldenleben* is written for a very large orchestra, which Strauss uses with the complete mastery now at his command. It opens with the presentation of the hero in a wonderfully clear, strong theme played by the horns and strings in E-flat, the key of

Beethoven's *Eroica*; but in spite of many beautiful passages, the work, to my mind, lacks coherence—perhaps Strauss tried to do too much.

Strauss has been accused of glorifying himself in *Heldenleben*. But while the hero's "help-mate" is clearly a picture of Strauss's own wife Pauline—as he told Romain Rolland—and the depiction of the hero's enemies a portrayal of his own critics, it is hardly plausible that Strauss thought of himself as a hero, or intended the piece as a representation of himself in a heroic cast. In the opinion of the excellent English musician and critic Norman Del Mar, "Strauss had too much of a sense of humor pompously to proclaim himself a hero to all the world."

In the *Sinfonia Domestica*, Strauss, as he said, undertook "to give a musical picture of married life. I know that some people believe the work to be a humorous representation of domestic happiness...but it is my intention that the work be taken seriously." Romain Rolland, with whom Strauss maintained a friendly and doubtless mutually stimulating relationship for many years, objected to the "programmatic division" of the *Domestic Symphony*. In his letter of reply, Strauss undertook to explain his reasons for using a program. "You may be right," he wrote to Rolland, "in what you say about the program of the *Domestica*, and in this you agree with Gustav Mahler, who completely damns the whole business of a program.... For me, the poetical program is nothing more than the means by which the expression and purely musical development of my feelings are given form; it is not, as you believe, merely a musical description of certain events of life. That would be utterly contrary to the spirit of music. But for music not to lose itself in complete arbitrariness, to dissolve in emptiness, it needs the limits of form, and such a boundary is formed by a program." Many years later, Strauss remarked that he had "no particular liking" for *Heldenleben*, but he chose to conduct the *Domestic Symphony*, particularly lovingly, we are told, for the celebration of his eightieth birthday in 1944 in Vienna.

Strauss himself must have thought that he had gone as far as he could with program music. His second opera, *Feuersnot*, although given its first performance in Dresden, and soon after in Frankfurt, Vienna, Berlin and Bremen, was not successful—at least partly, it seems, because of the inadequacy of the story. Oscar Wilde's *Salomé*, which had been translated into German and very successfully presented in his Berlin theater by Max Reinhardt, appeared to offer Strauss exactly the dramatic material he was looking for. After setting the opening lines, "*Wie schon ist die Prinzessin heute Nacht!*," Strauss wrote to a friend: "The piece cried out for music."

It was first performed on December 9, 1905, in Dresden, and caused a great sensation. Some were horrified, especially by the idea of basing an opera on this gruesome story of degeneracy, but Gustav Mahler welcomed it as "a work of genius...one of the great masterpieces of our time." When, two years later, it was performed in New York at the Metropolitan, the house was sold out at double prices and extra policemen had to be called to handle the crowds. Whatever Mahler may have thought, the New York critics were utterly appalled, and after one performance it was withdrawn. It was an enormous success, however, in Europe, and with the proceeds—Strauss knew the value of his work—the composer built his country house in Garmisch, which became his home for the rest of his life, and where he died.

In the meantime, Strauss had met the Austrian poet and playwright Hugo von Hofmannsthal, who became his close friend and collaborator, and remained so until Hofmannsthal's death in 1929. The first result of this meeting was *Electra*, which Strauss finished in Garmisch on September 22, 1908, and which was first performed under Ernst von Schuch in Dresden on January 25, 1909.

Ernst Krause, in his book on Strauss, sums it all up as follows: "In *Electra* Strauss plunged into the abyss on the dark side of existence with all the vehemence of his vital musical nature, although he later asserted that he had approached the subject 'very coolly and at a distance.' Disease here is not restricted to Klytemnestra's liver; everything in this snake pit is rotten, putrid, decaying, while the music, in its unprecedented demands on the orchestra, a truly gigantic apparatus even larger than that of *Salomé*, glitters, shines, seduces, underlines every word and gesture."

Strauss himself wrote that *Salomé* and *Electra* "stand alone among all my works; in them I went to the extreme limits of harmony, psychical polyphony...and the receptive ability of modern ears." I particularly remember a performance of *Electra* many years ago in Cologne, the dramatic effect of which was heightened, if possible, by the Electra collapsing at the climax of her great, incredibly demanding aria at the beginning of the opera.

After *Electra* Strauss remarked, "Now I want to write a Mozart opera." Hofmannsthal made several suggestions, none of which seemed too satisfactory until—after a meeting and a long, fruitful conversation in Weimar with his friend Count Harry Kessler—Hofmannsthal brought Strauss the bare outline of what was to become *Rosenkavalier.* Strauss was delighted, and urged his friend to go home at once and set to work. After receiving the first pages, Strauss wrote to Hofmannsthal: "The scene is charming, and will compose itself like oil and butter, I am already hatching it out."

The correspondence that followed between poet and musician, both intent on producing a work of art and each submerging his personality in the task at hand, is of the greatest interest. One can almost see the finished opera taking form in their exchange of letters: "For the end of the third act, the concluding duet of Sophie and Octavian, I have a very pretty melody. Would it be possible for you to give me 12 to 16 verses in the following rhythm...." From this beginning we have that beautiful, magical duet, *"Ist ein Traum, kann nich wirklich sein..."* that ends the opera, but nowhere, it seems to me, does Strauss's sense of the relationship between music and text show itself more clearly than in the setting of the Marschallin's words, *"Jedes Ding hat seine Zeit,"* which marks the transition in the first act from the amorous exchange between Octavian and the Marschallin, with which the opera opens, to the development. These few bars have the unmistakable touch of genius.

Rosenkavalier was an immediate success, and is still one of the most popular operas, not only in Germany and Austria, but wherever opera is given. The first performance in Dresden on January 26, 1911, was a great international event. Reinhardt had come down from Berlin, at Strauss's suggestion, to supervise the staging, and as before, Ernst von Schuch, whom Strauss greatly respected, was the conductor. Every principal paper in Europe and the United States sent correspondents. In a letter to his friend Ottonie Degenfeld (dated 5 AM, January 27, 1911), Hofmannsthal left an impression of that memorable evening:

> I can only write very hurriedly, so many people everywhere, in the hotel, on the stairs, constantly knocking at the door, incredibly exciting, and very nice. It was a wonderful evening, how happy I would have been if you had been there. Everything so festive, especially so in this small city; the hundreds of vehicles, the crowds of curious people in the streets, then the beginning of the tension, then, after the second act, the sense of success. I went to the loge of Frau Strauss to offer my congratulations. At that moment, the people saw me from below; the whole main floor turned around and began to applaud, people called out from all the boxes, it was a very pleasant moment, and more gratifying than the stupid, conventional appearance on the stage.... Afterward there was a dinner, for, I think, four hundred. I saw it all as through a mist....

Before going on to another opera—while waiting for Hofmannsthal to get a libretto ready for him, he said—Strauss began his last great orchestral work, the *Alpensymphonie*, but did not finish it until the winter of 1914-15. It is written for a huge orchestra, and in its variety of color and atmosphere demonstrates again Strauss as the complete master of instrumentation. For all its complexity, however, and the variety and number of instruments, which include a wind and thunder machine, glockenspiel, etc., it is a work of great majesty and classic dignity.

Rosenkavalier, perhaps, marked the high point of Strauss's collaboration with Hofmannsthal and of his own creative achievement, but much of great substance was to follow. There was the one-act ballet, *Josephslegende*, which was first performed in Paris in 1914 by the Diaghileff company, then the three-act opera *Frau Ohne Schatten*, which had its first performance in Vienna in 1919. There were several smaller works, including *Intermezzo*, which was based on a rather ridiculous incident from his own life. Frau Strauss, while her husband was on a concert tour, opened a note addressed to him which was signed "Your ever loving Mitzi." She suspected the worst and, by the time Strauss returned, had consulted a lawyer about a divorce, etc. When the smoke had finally cleared, it turned out that Mitzi had confused Strauss with another musician, and was only trying to get two free tickets for the opera.

The last collaboration with Hofmannsthal was *Arabella*, which is a return to the spirit of *Rosenkavalier*, although the setting is the Vienna of the 1860s rather than that of Maria Theresa. One misses the exuberance and melodic drive of its predecessor, but it is a work of great charm and, obviously, of a master.

There were several other collaborators after Hofmannsthal's sudden death in 1929. The first was Stefan Zweig, whose literary gifts Strauss greatly admired. In his memoirs (published in Stockholm in 1944) Zweig has the following to say about Strauss:

> I was well aware of the honor of such an offer.... I knew of no creative musician of our time I would have been more willing to serve than Richard Strauss, the last of the great race of full-blooded German musicians, which extends from Handel and Bach through Beethoven and Brahms into our own day. I declared myself ready, and at the first meeting proposed the theme of *The Silent Woman* of Ben Jonson as a motive for an opera, and was pleasantly surprised at how quickly and clearly Strauss accepted all my suggestions. I had not expected...such astonishing dramatic understanding. While one was explaining the material to him he would be putting it into a dramatic form, and, what was even more astonishing, adjusting it to the limits of his own capacity, which he grasped with unbelievable clarity. I have met many great artists in my life, but never one who knew how to maintain such abstract and unerring objectivity toward himself. At our very first meeting Strauss let me know quite frankly that a composer of seventy no

longer possessed the original power of musical inspiration. Such symphonic works as *Till Eulenspiegel* and *Death and Transfiguration* would no longer be possible for him, since pure music required the highest degree of creative spirit, but the word still inspired him. He could take something that was formed and ready and illustrate it dramatically, because musical themes developed spontaneously from situations and words, which is why, in his later years, he had turned exclusively to opera. He was well aware that as a form of art opera was through. Wagner was such an enormous summit that no one can go beyond him. 'But,' he added with a broad Bavarian laugh, 'I helped myself by making a detour.' He gave me complete freedom.... He would be grateful, however, if I could construct a few complicated forms which would give him the possibility of particularly colorful development. 'I don't invent long melodies like Mozart. Mine are always short themes. But what I know how to do is to turn such a theme around, paraphrase it, get everything out of it that is in it, and in this no one can come close to me any more.'

Die Schweigsame Frau had its first performance in Dresden in 1935 under Karl Boehm. Zweig was Jewish, and when Strauss discovered that Zweig's name was not to appear on the program, he let it be known that in this case he would not come to the first performance. Zweig's name did finally appear and Strauss attended the performance, but Hitler stayed away. Although Strauss urged Zweig to continue to work for him, Zweig felt it would be better if he did not; he eventually left Austria, and, finally, a homeless and tragic figure, took his own life in Brazil.

There were other operas. The last, *Capriccio*, for which Clemens Krauss wrote the text, was completed during the war, in 1941, when Strauss was seventy-seven, and first performed in Munich in 1942, not long before the stately old Munich opera house was destroyed. The subtitle of the work is *A Conversation Piece for Music*, which is exactly what it is. It takes place in a country house outside Paris, about 1775, when, in Strauss's description, "Gluck was beginning his work on the reform of the opera." The two central figures are the countess, an enlightened French lady of twenty-seven and an admirer of Gluck, and her brother, who is a serious patron of the theater. Besides these two there are the poet and the musician, both devoted friends, each demonstrating the superiority of his art over the other, and each trying to win the favor of the countess. Her dilemma is increased when the composer sets the sonnet of the poet to music, thus, in accordance with the theories of Gluck, bringing both to a higher level of expression. There is also the theater director, representing Italian opera, whom Strauss uses as the means to express his own ideas.

In *Capriccio* it is not the composer's intention to over-whelm us, as it was, perhaps, in *Heldenleben*, not to plumb the depths of human emotion and desire, as in *Salomé*, but to express his love for the opera and his conception of the true purpose of art; in spite of having been written during

World War II, it is a work that radiates the serenity of a great artist nearing the close of a full and creative life.

Although Strauss, particularly as a younger man, was regarded as a revolutionary and a destructive influence, there can be no doubt that Stefan Zweig was right when he said that with Strauss the great tradition that goes back to Handel and Bach was continued into our own day. He was also very much a man of his time: in such music as *Heldenleben* and *Zarathustra* he doubtless expressed the spirit and inadequacies of his time, but because he never cut himself off from a great tradition, he was also able to rise above his time, which is one reason that his music is not merely a period piece, but has something to say to us still and can raise our eyes to a higher view of life, which is the purpose of true art.

Heldenleben, as its critics say, may reflect the bombast of its age, which was not, by the way, confined to William II—but in its lovely violin passages which describe the hero's "helpmate" and in the "Works of Peace" it does much more: it expresses another aspect of heroism. "Modern!" Strauss once said, "What does it mean to be modern? The word should be emphasized differently. Have inspiration like Beethoven, write counterpoint like Bach, be able to orchestrate like Mozart, and be genuine and true children of your own time; then you will be modern."

Not long before his death, in a conversation with a friend in Zurich, Strauss is reported to have said that his affirmation of faith included "the Mozart melody as the purest expression of the human soul, and the Wagner opera, in which he saw the peak of cultural development of the

West." As for his own work, he said, "I know well that my symphonic work cannot approach the immense genius of Beethoven, and I am equally well aware of the distance of my operas (in the magnitude of conception, primary melodic invention, cultural wisdom) from the eternal works of Richard Wagner, but the facts of the development of the art of the theater justify me in the modest but beautiful feeling that my operas, in the many-sidedness of their dramatic material and in the forms of their treatment, will take an honorable place at the end of the rainbow in their relationship to all earlier works of the theater—leaving the works of Richard Wagner out of account."

Two fairly recent, widely heralded books, I should perhaps mention, take a rather different view of Richard Strauss and his achievement than is indicated in the foregoing. In his book *Richard Strauss*, George R. Marek speaks highly, and with understanding, of some of the music of Strauss, especially of his earlier period, but as the subtitle of his book indicates, *The Life of a Non-Hero*, deprecates him as a man. The book contains all the conventional, stupid generalizations about pre-World War I Germany—Munich a city of beer and sausages, Berlin of bombast and militarism, the universal subservience to petty officials and the military, the music "foursquare and heavy as the German furniture," the school system "grey and intolerant" where the usual teacher "was a dreary official whose small salary was compensated for by his own sense of importance," the family dominated by a tyrannical father, etc. One wonders how such a society was able to function at all, let alone produce such music as that of Wagner,

Brahms, and Richard Strauss.

Marek makes much of Frau Strauss's habit of insisting that guests wipe their shoes before coming into her house, and resents the fact that during both World Wars Strauss continued to compose music, and, under Hitler, instead of emigrating or getting himself thrown into a concentration camp, went right on composing music. Marek unhesitatingly informs us that because Strauss did not indulge in extra-marital affairs and was happily married, "He was not highly sexed," and that Strauss himself was the subject of his tone poem *Heldenleben.* "Without Strauss," asks Mr. Marek, "who can this hero be?" But one may equally ask, Why Strauss? Why, because Marek needed to make the point to justify the theme of his book, Strauss as a "non-hero."

Strauss did indeed continue to write music during the two world wars, as Beethoven did during the Napoleonic wars. Was Mozart a hero, did Beethoven rush off to enlist to fight against the Hitler of his time? Shocking as it may sound, for Strauss to have stayed in Germany during the Hitler period may well have been the more honorable and courageous course than to emigrate. Had Strauss left Germany after the difficulties he experienced in connection with the fact that his librettist, Stefan Zweig, was Jewish, and then presented himself in New York as a victim of Nazi persecution, he would have been received with open arms. There would have been special performances of his music, especially of *Heldenleben,* editorials in the *New York Times* and the *Saturday Review,* invitations and honorary degrees from Harvard and Yale, etc.

His first loyalty was to music; if he made compromises to the powers of the world, he remained true to his art. Do we criticize Shostakovich because he stayed in Russia, Solzhenitsyn because he would not leave until he was forced to? If Strauss had emigrated, it is doubtful that we would have *Capriccio*, the beautiful orchestral piece *Metamorphosen*, or the haunting, almost mystical last songs, composed a few months before his death. "Decay, mental and moral, attacked him," Mr. Marek tells us, "as it attacked his people. Strauss's mind was not strong enough to wing above the times." I must say that I fail to see much winging above the times by Mr. Marek's mind, with his clichés, his assumption, appropriate to the age of Camelot and *Playboy*, that if a man is loyal to his wife it can only be because he is not "highly sexed." Before leaving Mr. Marek, it is rather revealing that his own photograph on the jacket of the book is larger than that of Richard Strauss.

In Barbara Tuchman's *The Proud Tower*, Strauss is presented as the embodiment of all that was wrong, in Mrs. Tuchman's opinion, with the Germany of William II. The portrait of himself in *Heldenleben*—and she takes it for granted that it is a portrait of himself—was a reflection of the "national mood." He was unable to keep his "technical facilities and command over ideas in bounds"; and if, she said, German home life is as Strauss pictured it in the *Sinfonia Domestica*, "German history becomes understandable." Strauss's wife, Pauline, who was a fine singer—the best interpreter of his songs, he said—becomes at the hands of Barbara Tuchman a teutonic fury: she "practiced housewifery," we are told, "with ruthless fanaticism," shrieked at the maids if the linen closets were not arranged in "mathematically perfect rows," and treated visitors with "arrangements which exhibited a talent for organization...not inferior to that of the late Field Marshall von Moltke."

As for Strauss's music, *Electra* is "two hours of demonic intensity," *Rosenkavalier* "a silver rose, beautiful, glittering and tarnished," the violin solo in *Heldenleben* "alternately seductive and shrewish," and in the work as a whole there is "evidence of a deep-seated flaw in the composer." Mrs. Tuchman's omniscience and readiness to sit in judgment on nations, composers, composers' wives, music, or whatever it may be, are truly staggering. One has the impression that she learned how to write history from *Time* magazine.

Whatever flaws there may be in the music of Richard Strauss or were in him as a person—and who among us is without flaws?—he continued a great tradition into our own time and left us works which will remain a part of our cultural heritage. As a conductor he brought new life to the great masterworks of the past, and as a composer gave new color and powers of expression to the orchestra. In his tone poems, his songs, and in such operas as *Salomé*, *Rosenkavalier*, and *Capriccio*, he enriched our lives. Finally, for all the horrors our century has been guilty of, it is worthwhile to remind ourselves that he was also a man of our time.

V

Eliot, Pound, and Lewis: A Creative Friendship

George F. Kennan: A Gift to America

Alexander Solzhenitsyn: The Man and the Problem

Ezra Pound

T. S. Eliot

Wyndham Lewis

George F. Kennan

Alexander Solzhenitsyn

13

T.S. Eliot, Ezra Pound, and Wyndham Lewis:
A Creative Friendship

It may be a source of some pride to those of us fated to live out our lives as Americans that the three men who probably had the greatest influence on English literature in our century were all born on this side of the Atlantic. One of them, Wyndham Lewis, to be sure, was born on a yacht anchored in a harbor in Nova Scotia; his father, however, was an American, served as an officer in the Union Army in the Civil War, and came from a family that had been established here for many generations. The other two were as American in background and education as it is possible to be.

Our pride at having produced men of such high achievement, however, must be considered against the fact that all three spent their creative lives in Europe. For Wyndham

Lewis the decision was made for him by his mother, who hustled him off to Europe at the age of ten, but it was he who chose to remain in Europe, and to study in Paris rather than accept the invitation of his father to go to Cornell, and except for an enforced stay in Canada during World War II, he spent his entire life in Europe. The other two, Ezra Pound and T.S. Eliot, went to Europe as young men out of college, and it was as part of European, not American, cultural life that they made their contribution to literature. Lewis was a European in training, attitude, and point of view, but Pound and Eliot were Americans, and Pound, particularly, remained aggressively American; whether he was living in London or Italy his interest in American affairs never waned.

The lives and achievements of these three men were closely connected. They met as young men, each was influenced and helped by the other two, and they remained friends, in spite of occasional differences, for the rest of their lives. When Lewis, who had gone blind, was unable to read the proofs of his last book, it was his old friend T.S. Eliot who did it for him. And when Pound was confined in Saint Elizabeths in Washington, Eliot and Lewis always kept in close touch with him, and it was at least partly through Eliot's influence that he was finally released. Many may remember the picture in *Time* of Pound as a very old man attending the memorial service for Eliot in Westminster Abbey in 1965. The lives and association of these three men, whose careers started almost at the same time shortly before World War I, are an integral part of the literary and cultural history of this century.

The careers of all three may be said, in a certain way, to have been launched by the publication of Lewis' magazine *Blast*. Both Lewis and Pound had been published before and had made something of a name for themselves in artistic and literary circles in London, but it was the publication in June, 1914, of the first issue of *Blast* that put them, so to speak, in the center of the stage. The first *Blast* contained 160 pages of text, was well printed on heavy paper, its format large, typography extravagant, its cover purple. It contained illustrations, many by Lewis, stories by Rebecca West and Ford Maddox Ford, poetry by Pound and others, but it is chiefly remembered for its "Blasts" and "Blesses" and its manifestoes.

It was in this first issue of *Blast* that "vorticism," the new art form, was announced, the name having been invented by Pound. Vorticism was supposed to express the idea that art should represent the present, at rest, and at the greatest concentration of energy, between past and future. "There is no present—there is Past and Future, and there is Art," was a vorticist slogan. English humor and its "first cousin and accomplice, sport" were blasted, as were "sentimental hygienics," Victorian liberalism, the Royal Academy, the Britannic aesthete. Blesses were reserved for the seafarer, the great ports, for Shakespeare "for his bitter Northern Rhetoric of humor" and Swift "for his solemn, bleak wisdom of laughter." A special bless, as if in anticipation of our hairy age, was granted the hairdresser. Its purpose, Lewis wrote many years later, was to exalt "formality and order, at the expense of the disorderly and the unkempt. It is merely a humorous way," he went on to say, "of staging the classic standpoint as against the romantic."

The second, and last, issue of *Blast* appeared in July 1915, by which time Lewis was serving in the British army. This issue again contained essays, notes, and editorial comments by Lewis and poetry by Pound, but displayed little of the youthful exuberance of the first—the editors and contributors were too much aware of the suicidal bloodletting taking place in the trenches of Flanders and France for that. The second issue, for example, contained, as did the first, a contribution by the gifted young sculptor Gaudier-Brzeska, together with the announcement that he had been killed while serving in the French army.

Between the two issues of *Blast*, Eliot had arrived in London via Marburg and Oxford, where he had been studying for a degree in philosophy. He met Pound soon after his arrival, and through Pound, Wyndham Lewis. Eliot's meeting of Pound, who promptly took him under his wing, had two immediate consequences—the publication in Chicago of *Prufrock* in Harriet Monroe's *Poetry* magazine, and the appearance of two other poems a month or two later in *Blast*. The two issues of *Blast* established Lewis as a major figure—as a brilliant polemicist and a critic of the basic assumptions and intellectual position of his time, two roles he was never to surrender. Pound had played an important part in *Blast*, but Lewis was the moving force. Eliot's role as a contributor of two poems to the second issue was relatively minor; still, the enterprise brought them together, and established an association and identified them with a position in the intellectual life of their time which was undoubtedly an important factor in the development and achievement of all three.

Lewis was born in 1882 on a yacht off the coast of Nova Scotia, as mentioned earlier. Pound was born in 1885 in Hailey, Idaho, and Eliot in 1888 in St. Louis. Lewis was brought up in England by his mother, who had separated from his father. He was sent to various schools, the last one Rugby, from which he was dropped, spent several years at an art school in London, the Slade, and then went to the continent, spending most of the time in Paris, where he studied art, philosophy under Bergson and others, talked, painted, and wrote. He returned to England to stay in 1909. It was in the following year that he first met Ezra Pound, in the Vienna Café in London. Pound, he wrote many years later, did not greatly appeal to him at first—he seemed overly sure of himself and not a little presumptuous. His first impression, he said, was of "a bombastic galleon, palpably bound to, or from, the Spanish Main," but, he discovered, "beneath its skull and cross-bones, intertwined with *fleurs de lis* and spattered with star-spangled oddities, a heart of gold." As Lewis became better acquainted with Pound he found, as he wrote many years later, that "this theatrical fellow was one of the best." And he went on to say, "I still regard him as one of the best, even one of the best poets."

By the time of this meeting, Lewis was making a name for himself, both as a writer and an artist. He had exhibited in London with some success; and shortly before his meeting with Pound, Ford Maddox Ford had accepted a group of stories for publication in the *English Review*, stories he had written while still in France and in which appeared some of the ideas he was to develop in the more than forty books that were to follow.

But how did Ezra Pound, this young American poet who was born in Hailey, Idaho, and looked, according to Lewis, like an "acclimatized Buffalo Bill," happen to be in the Vienna Café in London in 1910, and what was he doing there? The influence of Idaho, it must be said at once, was slight, since Pound's family had taken him at an early age to Philadelphia, where his father was employed as an assayer in the U.S. Mint. The family lived first in west Philadelphia, then in Jenkintown, and when Ezra was about six bought a comfortable house in Wyncote, where he grew up. He received good training in private schools and developed a considerable proficiency in Latin, which enabled him to enter the University of Pennsylvania shortly before reaching the age of sixteen.

It was at this time, he was to write some twenty years later, that he made up his mind to become a poet. He decided at that early age that by the time he was thirty he would know more about poetry than any man living. The poetic "impulse," he said, came from the gods, but technique was man's responsibility, and he was determined to master it. After two years at Pennsylvania he transferred to Hamilton, from which he graduated with a Ph.B. two years later. His college years, in spite of his assertions to the contrary, must have been stimulating and developing—he received excellent training in languages, read widely and well, made some friends, including William Carlos Williams, and wrote poetry. After Hamilton he went back to Pennsylvania to do graduate work; there he studied Spanish literature, Old French, Provençal, and Italian. He was granted an M.A. by Pennsylvania in 1906 and a Fellowship in Romantics, which gave him enough money for a summer in Europe, part of which he spent studying in the British Museum and part in Spain. The Prado made an especially strong impression on him—thirty years later he could still describe the pictures in the main gallery and recall the exact order in which they were hung. He left the University of Pennsylvania in 1907, gave up the idea of a doctorate, and after one semester teaching at Wabash College in Crawfordsville, Indiana, went to Europe, to return to his native land only for longer or shorter visits, except for the thirteen years he was confined in Saint Elizabeths in Washington.

Pound's short stay at Wabash College was something of a disaster—he found Crawfordsville, Indiana, confining and dull, and Crawfordsville, in 1907, found it difficult to adjust itself to a Professor of Romance Languages who wore a black velvet jacket, a soft-collared shirt, flowing bow tie, patent leather pumps, carried a malacca cane, and drank rum in his tea. The crisis came when he allowed a stranded chorus girl he had found in a snow storm to sleep in his room. It was all quite innocent, he insisted, but Wabash did not care for his "bohemian ways," as the president put it, and was glad for the excuse to be rid of him. He wrote some good poetry while at Wabash and made some friends, but was not sorry to leave, and was soon on his way to Europe, arriving in Venice, which he had visited before, with just $80.

While in Venice he arranged to have a group of his poems printed under the title *A Lume Spento*. This was in preparation for his assault on London, since he believed, quite correctly, that a poet would make more of an impression with a printed book of his poetry under his arm than some pages of unpublished manuscript. He stayed long enough in Venice to recover from the disaster of Wabash and to gather strength and inspiration for the next step, London, where he arrived with nothing more than his confidence in himself, three pounds, and the copies of his books of poems.

He soon arranged to give a series of lectures at the Polytechnic on the Literature of Southern Europe, which gave him a little money, and to have the *Evening Standard* review his book of poetry. The review ended with the sentence, "The unseizable magic of poetry is in this queer paper volume, and words are no good in describing it." He managed to induce Elkin Mathews to publish another small collection, the first printing of which was 100 copies and soon sold out; then came a larger collection, *Personae*. The Polytechnic engaged him for a more ambitious series of lectures, and he began to meet people in literary circles, including T.E. Hulme, William Butler Yeats, and Ford Maddox Ford, who published his "Ballad of the Goodley Fere" in the *English Review*. His book on medieval Latin poetry, *The Spirit of Romance*, which is still in print, was published by Dent in 1910. The introduction to this book contains the characteristic line, "The history of an art is the history of masterworks, not of failures or of mediocrity." By the time the first meeting with Wyndham Lewis took place in the Vienna Café, then, which was only some two years after Pound's rather inauspicious arrival in London, he was, at the age of twenty-six, known as a poet and had become a man of some standing in literary circles.

It was Pound, the discoverer of talent, the literary impresario, as I have said, who brought Eliot and Lewis together. Eliot's path to London was as circuitous as Pound's, but, as one might expect, less dramatic. Instead of Crawfordsville, Indiana, Eliot had spent a year at the Sorbonne after a year of graduate work at Harvard, and was studying philosophy at the University of Marburg with the intention of obtaining a Harvard Ph.D. and becoming a professor, as one of his teachers at Harvard, Josiah Royce, had encouraged him to do, but the war intervened and he went to Oxford. Conrad Aiken, one of his closest friends at Harvard, had earlier tried, without success, to place several of Eliot's poems with an English publisher, had met Pound, and had given Eliot a letter of introduction to him.

The results of that first meeting with Pound are well known—Pound wrote instantly to Harriet Monroe in Chicago, for whose new magazine, *Poetry*, he had more or less made himself European editor, as follows: "An American called Eliot called this P.M. I think he has some sense tho' he has not yet sent me any verse." A few weeks later Eliot, while still at Oxford, sent him the manuscript of *The Love Song of J. Alfred Prufrock*. Pound was ecstatic, and immediately transmitted his enthusiasm to Miss Monroe. It was, he said, "the best poem I have yet had or seen from an American. *Pray God it be not a single and unique success.*" Eliot, Pound went on to say, was "the only

American I know who has made what I call an adequate preparation for writing. He has actually trained himself *and* modernized himself *on his own.*"

Pound sent *Prufrock* to Miss Monroe in October, 1914, with the words, "The most interesting contribution I've had from an American. P.S. Hope you'll get it *in* soon." Miss Monroe had her own ideas—*Prufrock* was not the sort of poetry she thought young Americans should be writing; she much preferred Vachel Lindsay, whose *The Firemen's Ball* she had published in the June issue. Pound, however, was not to be put off; letter followed importuning letter, until she finally surrendered and in the June 1915 issue of *Poetry,* now a collector's item of considerable value, the poem appeared which begins

> *Let us go then, you and I,*
> *When the evening is spread out against the sky*
> *Like a patient etherized upon a table....*

It was not, needless to say, to be a "single and unique success," as Pound had feared, but the beginning of one of the great literary careers of this century. The following month two poems appeared in *Blast.* Eliot had written little or nothing for almost three years. The warm approval and stimulation of Pound plus, no doubt, the prospect of publication, encouraged him to go on. In October *Poetry* published three more new poems. Later in the year Pound arranged to have Elkin Mathews, who had published his own two books of poetry, bring out a collection which he edited and called *The Catholic Anthology,* and in which he included the poems that had appeared in *Poetry* and one of the two from *Blast*. The principal reason for the anthology, Pound remarked, "was to get sixteen pages of Eliot printed in England."

If all had gone according to plan and his family's wishes, Eliot would have returned to Harvard, obtained his Ph.D., and become a professor. He did finish his thesis—"to please his parents," according to his second wife, Valerie Eliot—but dreaded the prospect of a return to Harvard. It did not require much encouragement from Pound, therefore, to induce him to stay in England—it was Pound, according to his biographer Noel Stock, "who saved Eliot for poetry." Eliot left Oxford at the end of the term in June 1915, having in the meantime married Vivienne Haigh Wood. That fall he took a job as a teacher in a boys' school at a salary of 140 pounds a year, with dinner. He supplemented his salary by book reviewing and occasional lectures; but it was an unproductive, difficult period for him, his financial problems increased by the illness of his wife.

After two years of teaching, he took a position in a branch of Lloyds Bank in London, hoping that this would give him sufficient income to live on, some leisure for poetry, and a pension for his wife if she should outlive him. Pound at this period fared better than Eliot—he wrote music criticism for a magazine, had some income from other writing and editorial projects, which was supplemented by the small income of his wife, Dorothy Shakespear, and occasional checks from his father. He also enjoyed a more robust constitution than Eliot, who eventually broke down under the strain and was forced, in 1921, to take a rest cure in Switzerland. It was during this three-month stay in

Switzerland that he finished the first draft of *The Waste Land*, which he immediately brought to Pound.

Two years before, Pound had taken Eliot on a walking tour in France to restore his health, and besides getting Eliot published, he was trying to raise a fund to give him a regular source of income, a project he called "Bel Esprit." In a letter to John Quinn, the New York lawyer who used his money, perceptive critical judgment and influence to help writers and artists, Pound, referring to Eliot, wrote, "It is a crime against literature to let him waste eight hours vitality per diem in that bank." Quinn agreed to subscribe to the fund, but it became a source of embarrassment to Eliot who put a stop to it.

The Waste Land marked the high point of Eliot's literary collaboration with Pound. By the time Eliot brought him the first draft of the poem, Pound was living in Paris, having left London, he said, because "the decay of the British Empire was too depressing a spectacle to witness at close range." Pound made numerous suggestions for changes, consisting largely of cuts and rearrangements. In a letter to Eliot explaining one deletion he wrote, "That is nineteen pages, and let us say the longest poem in the English langwidge. Don't try to bust all records by prolonging it three pages further."

A recent critic described the process as one of pulling "a masterpiece out of a grab bag of brilliant material"; Pound himself described his participation as a "Caesarian operation." However described, Eliot was profoundly grateful, and made no secret of Pound's help. In his characteristically generous way, Eliot gave the original manuscript to Quinn, both as a token for the encouragement Quinn had given to him, and for the further reason, as he put it in a letter to Quinn, "that this manuscript is worth preserving in its present form solely for the reason that it is the only evidence of the difference which [Pound's] criticism has made to the poem." For years the manuscript was thought to have been lost, but it was recently found among Quinn's papers which the New York Public Library acquired some years after his death, and is now available in a facsimile edition.

The first publication of *The Waste Land* was in the first issue of Eliot's magazine *Criterion*, October 1922. The following month it appeared in New York in *The Dial.* Quinn arranged for its publication in book form by Boni and Liveright, who brought it out in November. The first printing of 1,000 was soon sold out, and Eliot was given the Dial award of $2,000. Many were puzzled by *The Waste Land*; one reviewer even thought that Mr. Eliot might be putting over a hoax, but Pound was not alone in recognizing that in his ability to capture the essence of the human condition in the circumstances of the time. Eliot had shown himself, in *The Waste Land*, to be a poet.

To say that the poem is merely a reflection of Eliot's unhappy first marriage, his financial worries and nervous breakdown, is far too superficial. The poem is a reflection, not of Eliot, but of the aimlessness, disjointedness, sordidness of contemporary life. In itself, it is in no way sick or decadent; it is a wonderfully evocative picture of the situation of man in the world as it is. Another poet, Kathleen Raine, writing many years after the first publication of *The Waste Land* on the meaning of Eliot's early poetry to her generation, said it "enabled us to know our generation imaginatively. All those who have lived in the Waste Land of London can, I suppose, remember the particular occasions on which, reading T.S. Eliot's poems for the first time, an experience of the contemporary world that had been nameless and formless received its apotheosis."

Eliot sent one of the first copies he received of the Boni and Liveright edition to Ezra Pound with the inscription "for E.P. miglior fabbro from T.S.E. Jan. 1923." His first volume of collected poetry was dedicated to Pound with the same inscription, which comes from Dante and means "the better craftsman." Explaining this dedication Eliot wrote in 1938, "I wished at that moment to honour the technical mastery and critical ability manifest in [Pound's]...work, which had also done so much to turn *The Waste Land* from a jumble of good and bad passages into a poem."

Pound and Eliot remained in touch with each other—Pound contributed to the *Criterion*, and Eliot, through his position at Faber and Faber, saw many of Pound's books through publication and himself selected and edited a collection of Pound's poetry, but there was never again the close collaboration which had characterized their association from their first meeting in London in 1914 to the publication of *The Waste Land* in the form given it by Pound in 1922.

As has already been mentioned, Pound left London in 1920 to go to Paris, where he stayed only until about 1924—long enough for him to meet many people and for the force of his personality to make itself felt. He and his wife were frequent visitors to the famous bookshop, Shakespeare and

Company, run by the young American Sylvia Beach, where Pound, among other things, made shelves, mended chairs, etc. He also was active in gathering subscriptions for James Joyce's *Ulysses* when Miss Beach took over its publication.

The following description by Wyndham Lewis of an encounter with Pound during the latter's Paris days is worth repeating. Getting no answer after ringing the bell at Pound's flat, Lewis walked in and discovered the following scene:

> A splendidly built young man, stript to the waist, and with a torso of dazzling white, was standing not far from me. He was tall, handsome and serene, and was repelling with his boxing gloves— I thought without undue exertion—a hectic assault of Ezra's. After a final swing at the dazzling solar plexus (parried effortlessly by the trousered statue) Pound fell back upon the settee. The young man was Hemingway.

Pound, as is well known, took Hemingway in hand, went over his manuscripts, cut out superfluous words as was his custom, and helped him to find a publisher, a service he had performed while still in London for another young American, Robert Frost. In a letter to Pound, written in 1933, Hemingway acknowledged the help Pound had given him by saying that he had learned more about "how to write and how not to write" from him "than from any man alive, and had always said so."

When we last saw Lewis, except for his brief encounter with Pound and Hemingway wearing boxing gloves, he had just brought out the second issue of *Blast* and gone off to the war to end all war. He served for a time at the front in an artillery unit, and was then transferred to a group of artists who were supposed to devote their time to painting and drawing "the scene of war," as Lewis put it—a scheme devised by Lord Beaverbrook, through whose intervention Lewis received the assignment. He hurriedly finished a novel, *Tarr,* which was published during the war, largely as a result of Pound's intervention, in Harriet Shaw Weaver's magazine, *The Egoist,* and in book form after the war had ended. It attracted wide attention; Rebecca West, for example, called it "a beautiful and serious work of art that reminds one of Dostoievsky." By the early twenties, Lewis, as the editor of *Blast,* the author of *Tarr,* and a recognized artist, was an established personality; but he was not then, and never became, a part of the literary and artistic establishment, nor did he wish to be.

For the first four years following his return from the war, and his recovery from a serious illness that followed it, little was heard from Lewis. He did bring out two issues of a new magazine, *The Tyro,* which contained contributions from T.S. Eliot, Herbert Read, and himself, and contributed occasionally to the *Criterion,* but it was a period, for him, of semi-retirement from the scene of battle, which he devoted to perfecting his style as a painter and to study.

It was followed by a torrent of creative activity—two important books on politics, *The Art of Being Ruled* (1926) and *The Lion and the Fox* (1927), a major philosophical work, *Time and Western Man* (1927), followed by a collection of stories, *The Wild Body* (1927) and the first part of a long novel, *Childermass* (1928). In 1928 he brought out a completely revised edition of his wartime novel *Tarr*, and if all this were not enough, he continued his contributions to the *Criterion*, engaged in numerous controversies, painted and drew. In 1927 he founded another magazine, *The Enemy*, of which only three issues appeared, the last in 1929. Lewis, of course, was "the Enemy." "The names we remember in European literature," he wrote in the first issue, "are those of men who satirized and attacked, rather than petted and fawned upon, their contemporaries. Only *this* time exacts an uncritical hypnotic sleep of all within it."

One of Lewis's best and most characteristic books is *Time and Western Man*; it is in this book that he declared war, so to speak, on what he considered to be the dominant intellectual position of the twentieth century—the philosophy of time, the school of philosophy, as he described it, for which "time and change are the ultimate values." It is the position which regards everything as relative, all reality as a function of time. "The Darwinian theory and all the background of nineteenth century thought was already behind it," Lewis wrote, and further "scientific" confirmation was provided by Einstein's theory of relativity. It is a position, in Lewis's opinion, which is essentially romantic, "with all that that word conveys in its most florid, unreal, inflated, self-deceiving connotation."

The ultimate consequence of the time philosophy, Lewis argued, is the degradation of man. With its emphasis on change, man—the man of the present, living man—ends up, for the philosophy of time, as little more than a minute link in the endless process of progressive evolution—his value lies not in what he *is*, but in what he as a species, not an individual, may *become*. As Lewis put it, "You, in imagination, are already cancelled by those who will perfect you in the mechanical time-scale that stretches out, always ascending, before us. What you do and how you live has no worth in itself. You are an *inferior*, fatally, to all the future."

Against this rather depressing point of view, which deprives man of all individual worth, Lewis offers the sense of personality, "the most vivid and fundamental sense we possess," as he describes it. It is this sense that makes man unique; it alone makes creative achievement possible. But the sense of personality, Lewis points out, is essentially one of separation, and to maintain such separation from others requires, he believes, a personal God. As he expressed it, "In our approaches to God, in consequence, we do not need to 'magnify' a human body, but only to intensify that consciousness of a separated and transcendent life. So God becomes the supreme symbol of our separation and our limited transcendence.... It is, then, because the sense of personality is posited as our greatest 'real,' that we require a 'God,' a something that is nothing but a *person*, secure in its absolute egoism, to be the rationale of this sense."

It is exactly "our separation and our limited transcendence" that the time philosophy denies us; its God is not, in Lewis's words, "a perfection already existing, eternally there, of which we are humble shadows," but a constantly emerging God, the perfection toward which man is thought to be constantly striving. Appealing as such a conception may on its surface appear to be, this God we supposedly attain by our strenuous efforts toward perfection turns out to be a mocking God. "Brought out into the daylight," Lewis said, "it would no longer be anything more than a somewhat less idiotic you."

In *Time and Western Man* Lewis publicly disassociated himself from Pound, Lewis having gained the erroneous impression, apparently, that Pound had become involved in a literary project of some kind with Gertrude Stein, whom Lewis hated with all the considerable passion of which he was capable. To Lewis, Gertrude Stein, with her "stuttering style" as he called it, was the epitome of the "time philosophy" in action. The following is quoted by Lewis in another of his books, *The Diabolical Principle*, and comes from a magazine published in Paris in 1925 by the group around Gertrude Stein; it is quoted here to give the reader some idea of the reasons for Lewis's strong feelings on the subject of Miss Stein: "If we have a warm feeling for both [the Superrealists] and the Communists, it is because the movements which they represent are aimed at the destruction of a thoroughly rotten structure....We are entertained intellectually, if not physically, with the idea of [the] destruction [of contemporary society]. But...our interests are confined to literature and life.... *It is our purpose purely and simply to amuse ourselves.*"

The thought that Pound would have associated himself with a group expounding ideas on this level of irresponsibility would be enough to cause Lewis to write him off forever, but it was not true; Pound had met Gertrude Stein once or twice during his stay in Paris, but did not get on with her, which is not at all surprising. Pound did not particularly like Paris, and in 1924 moved to Rapallo, a small town on the Mediterranean a few miles south of Genoa, where he lived until his arrest by the American authorities at the end of World War II.

In an essay written for Eliot's sixtieth birthday, Lewis had the following to say about the relationship between Pound and Eliot: "It is no secret that Ezra Pound exercised a very powerful influence on Mr. Eliot. I do not have to define the nature of this influence, of course. Mr. Eliot was lifted out of his lunar alley-ways and *fin de siècle* nocturnes, into a massive region of verbal creation in contact with that astonishing didactic intelligence, that is all." Lewis's own relationship with Pound was of quite a different sort, but during the period from about 1910 to 1920, when Pound left London, it was close, friendly, and doubtless stimulating to both. During Lewis's service in the army, Pound looked after Lewis's interests, arranged for the publication of his articles, and tried to sell his drawings. They even collaborated in a series of essays, written in the form of letters, but Lewis, who in any case was inordinately suspicious, was quick to resent Pound's propensity to literary management.

After Pound settled in Rapallo they corresponded only occasionally, but in 1938, when Pound was in London, Lewis made a fine portrait of him, which hangs in the Tate Gallery. In spite of their occasional differences and the rather sharp attack on Pound in *Time and Western Man*, they remained friends; and Lewis's essay for Eliot's sixtieth birthday, which was written while Pound was still confined in Saint Elizabeths, is devoted largely to Pound, to whom Lewis pays the following tribute: "So, for all his queerness at times—ham publicity of self, misreading of the part of the poet in society—in spite of anything that may be said Ezra is not only *himself* a great poet, but has been of the most amazing use to other people. Let it not be forgotten for instance that it was he who was responsible for the all-important contact for James Joyce—namely Miss Weaver. It was *his* critical understanding, *his* generosity, involved in the detection and appreciation of the literary genius of James Joyce. It was through him that a very considerable sum of money was put at Joyce's disposal at the critical moment." Lewis concludes his comments on Pound with the following, "He was a man of letters, in the marrow of his bones and down to the red-rooted follicles of his hair. He breathed Letters, ate Letters, dreamt Letters. A very rare kind of man."

Two other encounters during his London period had a lasting influence on Pound's thought and career—the Oriental scholar Ernest Fenollosa and Major Douglas, the founder of Social Credit. Pound met Douglas in 1916 in the office of the *New Age*, a magazine edited by Alfred R. Orage, and became an almost instant convert. From that point on usury became an obsession with him, and the word "usurocracy," which he used to denote a social system based on money and credit, an indispensable part of his vocabulary. Social Credit was doubtless not the panacea Pound considered it to be, but that Major Douglas was entirely a fool seems doubtful too, if the following quotation from him is indicative of the quality of his thought; "I would... make the suggestion...that the first requisite of a satisfactory government system is that it shall divest itself of the idea that it has a mission to improve the morale or direct the philosophy of any of its constituent citizens."

Ernest Fenollosa was a distinguished Oriental scholar of American origin who had spent many years in Japan, studying both Japanese and Chinese literature, and had died in 1908. Pound met his widow in London in 1913, with the result that she entrusted her husband's papers to him, with her authorization to edit and publish them as he thought best. Pound threw himself into the study of the Fenollosa material with his usual energy, becoming, as a result, an authority on the Japanese Noh drama and a lifelong student of Chinese. He came to feel that the Chinese ideogram, because it was never entirely removed from its origin in the concrete, had certain advantages over the Western alphabet. Two years after receiving the Fenollosa manuscripts, Pound published a translation of Chinese poetry under the title *Cathay*. The *Times Literary Supplement* spoke of the language of Pound's translation as "simple, sharp, precise." Ford Madox Ford, in a moment of enthusiasm, called *Cathay* "the most beautiful book in the language."

Pound made other translations, from Provençal, Italian, Greek, and besides the book of Chinese poetry, translated Confucius, from which the following is a striking example, and represents a conception of the relationship between the individual and society to which Pound attached great importance, and frequently referred to in his other writing:

> The men of old wanting to clarify and diffuse
> throughout the empire that light which comes
> from looking straight into the heart and then

acting, first set up good government in their own states; wanting good government in their states, they first established order in their own families; wanting order in the home, they first disciplined themselves; desiring self-discipline, they rectified their own hearts; and wanting to rectify their hearts, they sought precise verbal definitions of their inarticulate thoughts; wishing to attain precise verbal definitions, they sought to extend their knowledge to the utmost. This completion of knowledge is rooted in sorting things into organic categories.

When things had been classified in organic categories, knowledge moved toward fulfillment; given the extreme knowable points, the inarticulate thoughts were defined with precision. Having attained this precise verbal precision, they then stabilized their hearts, they disciplined themselves; having attained self-discipline, they set their own houses in order; having order in their own homes, they brought good government to their own states; and when their states were well governed, the empire was brought into equilibrium.

Pound's major poetic work is, of course, *The Cantos*, which he worked on over a period of more than thirty years. One section, *The Pisan Cantos*, comprising 120 pages and eleven cantos, was written while Pound was confined in a U.S. Army detention camp near Pisa, for part of the time in a cage. Pound's biographer, Noel Stock, himself a poet and a competent critic, speaks of the *Pisan Cantos* as follows: "They are confused and often fragmentary; and they bear no relation structurally to the seventy earlier cantos; but shot through by a rare sad light they tell of things gone which somehow seem to live on, and are probably his best poetry. In those few desperate months he was forced to return to that point within himself where the human person meets the outside world of real things, and to speak of what he found there. If at times the verse is silly, it is because in himself Pound was often silly; if at times it is firm, dignified and intelligent, it is because in himself Pound was often firm, dignified and intelligent; if it is fragmentary and confused, it is because Pound was never able to think out his position and did not know how the matters with which he dealt were related; and if often lines and passages have a beauty seldom equalled in the poetry of the twentieth century it is because Pound had a true lyric gift."

As for the *Cantos* as a whole, I am not competent to make even a comment, much less to pass judgment. Instead I will quote the distinguished English critic Sir Herbert Read on the subject: "I am not going to deny that for the most part the Cantos present insuperable difficulties for the impatient reader but, as Pound says somewhere, 'You can't get through hell in a hurry.' They are of varying length, but they already amount to more than five hundred pages of verse and constitute the longest, and without hesitation I would say the greatest, poetic achievement of our time."

When *The Waste Land* was published in 1922 Eliot was still working as a clerk in a London bank and had just launched his magazine, the *Criterion*. He left the bank in 1925 to join the newly organized publishing firm of Faber and Gwyer, later to become Faber and Faber, which gave him the income he needed, leisure for his literary pursuits and work that was congenial and appropriate. One of his tasks at Faber, it used to be said, was writing jacket blurbs. His patience and helpfulness to young authors was well known—from personal experience I can bear witness to his kindness to inexperienced publishers; his friends, in fact, thought that the time he devoted to young authors he felt had promise might have been better spent on his own work.

In spite of the demands on his time and energy, he continued to edit the *Criterion*, the publication of which was eventually taken over by Faber. He attached the greatest importance to the magazine, as is evidenced by the following from a letter to Lewis dated January 31, 1925, which is devoted entirely to the *Criterion*, and his wish for Lewis to continue to write regularly for it: "Furthermore I am not an individual but an instrument, and anything I do is in the interest of art and literature and civilization, and is not a matter for personal compensation." As it worked out, Lewis wrote only occasionally for the *Criterion*, not at all for every issue as Eliot had proposed in the letter referred to above.

The closeness of their association, however, in spite of occasional differences, may be judged not only from Eliot's wish to have something from Lewis in every issue, but from the following from a letter to Eliot from Lewis; "As I understand with your paper that you are almost in the position I was in with *Tyro* and *Blast* I will give you anything I have for nothing, as you did me, and am anxious to be of use to you: for I know that every failure of an exceptional attempt like yours with the *Criterion* means that the chance of establishing some sort of critical standard here is diminished."

Pound also contributed frequently to the *Criterion*, but at least pretended not to think much of it. "...a magnificent piece of editing, i.e. for the purpose of getting into the Athenaeum Club, and becoming permanent," he remarked on one occasion. He, by the way, accepted some of the blame for what he considered Eliot's unduly cautious approach to criticism. In a letter to the Secretary of the Guggenheim Foundation, written in 1925, to urge them to extend financial assistance to Eliot and Lewis, he made the following comment:

> I may in some measure be to blame for the extreme caution of his [Eliot's] criticism. I pointed out to him in the beginning that there was no use the two of us butting a stone wall; that he'd never be as hefty a battering ram as I was, nor as explosive as Lewis, and that he'd better try a more oceanic and fluid method of sapping the foundations. He is now respected by the *Times Lit. Sup.* But his criticism no longer rouses my interest.

What Pound, of course, wished to "sap" was not the "foundations" of an orderly society, but of established stupidity and mediocrity. The primary aim of all three, Pound, Eliot, and Lewis, each in his own way, was to defend civilized values. For Eliot, the means to restore the health of Western civilization was Christianity. In his book *The Idea of a Christian Society* he pointed out the dangers of the dominant liberalism of the time, which he thought "must either proceed into a gradual decline of which we can see no end, or reform itself into a positive shape which is likely to be effectively secular." To attain, or recover, the Christian society which he thought was the only alternative to a purely secular society, he recommended, among other things, a Christian education.

The purpose of such an education would not be merely to make people into pious Christians, but primarily, as he put it, "to train people to be able to think in Christian categories." The great mass of any population, Eliot thought, necessarily occupied in the everyday cares and demands of life, could not be expected to devote much time or effort to "thinking about the objects of faith"; their Christianity must be almost wholly realized in behavior. For Christian values, and the faith which supports them to survive there must be, he thought, a "Community of Christians," of people who would lead a "Christian life on its highest social level."

Eliot thought of "the Community of Christians" not as "an organization, but a body of indefinite outline, composed of both clergy and laity, of the more conscious, more spiritually and intellectually developed of both." It will be their "identity of belief and aspiration, their background of a common culture, which will enable them to influence and be influenced by each other, and collectively to form the conscious mind and conscience of the nation." Like William Penn, Eliot did not think that the actual *form* of government was as important as the moral level of the people, "for it is the general ethos of the people they have to govern, not their own piety, that determines the behaviour of politicians." For this reason, he thought, "A nation's system of education is much more important than its system of government."

When we consider the very different personalities of these three men, all enormously gifted, but quite different in their individual characteristics—Pound, flamboyant, extravagant; Eliot, restrained, cautious; Lewis, suspicious, belligerent—we can not help but wonder how it was possible for three such men to remain close friends from the time they met as young men until the ends of their lives. Their common American background no doubt played some part in bringing Pound and Eliot together, and they both shared certain characteristics we like to think of as American: generosity, openness to others, a fresher, more unencumbered attitude toward the past than is usual for a European, who, as Goethe remarked, carries the burden of the quarrels of a long history.

But their close association, mutual respect, and friendship were based on more than their common origin on this side of the Atlantic. In their basic attitude toward the spirit of their time, all three were outsiders; it was a time dominated by a facile, shallow liberalism, which, as Eliot once remarked, had "replaced belief in Divine Grace" with "the myth of human goodness." Above all they were serious men, far more interested in finding and expressing the truth than in success as the world understands it. The English critic E.W.F. Tomlin remarked that a characteristic of these three "was that they had mastered their subjects, and were aware of what lay beyond them. The reading that went into *Time and Western Man* alone exceeded the life-time capacity of many so-called 'scholars.'" The royalties Lewis earned from this book, one of the most important of our time, which represented an immense amount of work and thought of the highest order, did not amount to a pittance; but Lewis's concern, as he put it toward the end of his life, was for "the threat of extinction to the cultural tradition of the West." It was this mutual concern, on a very high level, and an utterly serious attitude toward creative work that brought them and held them together.

Why did Pound and Eliot stay in Europe, and what might have happened to them if they had come back to this country, as both were many times urged to do, or to Lewis if he had gone to Cornell and stayed over here? In Pound's case, the answer is rather simple, and was given in essence by his experience in Crawfordsville, Indiana, as a young man, and the treatment he received following the war. There is no doubt that in making broadcasts on the Italian radio during wartime he was technically guilty of treason; against this, it seems to me, must be weighed the effect of the broadcasts, which was zero, and his achievement as a poet and a critic, which is immense. One can not expect magnanimity from any government, and especially not in the intoxication of victory in a great war and overwhelming world power, but one might have expected the academic and literary community to have protested the brutal treat-ment meted out to Pound. It did not, nor was there any protest of his long confinement in a mental institution except on the part of a few individuals; his release was brought about largely as a result of protests from Europe, in which Eliot played a substantial part. When, however, during his confinement in Saint Elizabeths, the Bollingen prize for poetry was given him for *The Pisan Cantos*, the liberal establishment reacted with the sort of roar one might have expected had the Nobel Prize been awarded to Adolf Hitler.

Lewis spent some five years in Toronto during World War II, which, incidentally, provided him with the background for one of his greatest novels, *Self-Condemned*. He was desperately hard up, and tried to get lecture engagements from a number of universities, including the University of Chicago. A small Canadian Catholic college was the only representative of the academic institutions of North America to offer this really great, creative intelligence something more substantial than an occasional lecture. Since his death, Cornell and the University of Buffalo have spent large sums accumulating Lewis material—manuscripts, letters, first editions, drawings, etc. When they could have done something for Lewis himself, to their own glory and profit, they ignored him. The American intellectual establishment, on the other hand, did not ignore the Communist apologist Harold Laski, who was offered all the honors and respect at its command, the Harold Laski who, in 1954, at the height of Stalinism—mass arrests, millions in slave labor camps and all the rest—had lectured at the Soviet Institute of Law.

The following taken from letters from Ezra Pound, the first written in 1926 to Harriet Monroe, and the second in

1934 to his old professor at the University of Pennsylvania, Felix Schelling, puts the problem of the poet in America as he saw it very graphically:

> Poetry here is decent and honourable. In America it lays one open to continuous insult on all sides.... Re your question is it any better abroad for authors: England gives small pensions; France provides jobs...Italy is full of ancient libraries; the jobs are quite comfortable, not very highly paid, but are respectable, and can't interfere with the librarians' time.
>
> As for 'expatriated'? You know damn well the country won't feed me. The simple economic fact that if I had returned to America I shd. have starved, and that to maintain anything like the standard of living, or indeed to live, *in* America from 1916 onwards I shd. have had to quadruple my earnings, i.e. it wd. have been impossible for me to devote *any* time to my REAL work.

Eliot, of course, fared much better than Pound at the hands of the academy. As early as 1932 he was invited to give the Charles Eliot Norton lectures at Harvard; many universities honored themselves by awarding him honorary degrees; he was given the Nobel Prize, etc. One cannot help but wonder, however, if his achievement would have been possible if he had completed his Ph.D. and become a Harvard professor. He wrote some of his greatest poetry and founded the *Criterion* while still a bank clerk in London. One can say with considerable justification that as a clerk in Lloyds Bank in London Eliot had more opportunity for creative work and got more done than would have been possible had he been a Harvard professor. It was done, of course, at the cost of intensely hard work—in a letter to Quinn in the early twenties he remarks that he was working such long hours that he did not have time either for the barber or the dentist, but he had something to show for it.

It is impossible, of course, to sum up the achievement of these three men. They were very much a part of the time in which they lived, however much they rejected its basic assumptions and point of view. Both Lewis and Eliot described themselves as classicists, among other reasons, no doubt, because of the importance they attached to order; Lewis at one time called Pound a "revolutionary simpleton," which in certain ways was probably justified, but in his emphasis on "precise verbal definitions," on the proper use of language, Pound was a classicist too.

All three, each in his own way, were concerned with the health of society. Eliot founded the *Criterion* to restore values; in such books as *Time and Western Man*, *Paleface*, *The Art of Being Ruled*, Lewis was fighting for an intelligent understanding of the nature of our civilization and of the forces he thought were undermining it. The political books Lewis wrote in the thirties, for which he was violently and unfairly condemned, were written not to promote fascism, as some simple-minded critics have contended, but to point out that a repetition of World War I would be even more catastrophic for civilization than the first.

In many of his political judgments Pound was undoubtedly completely mistaken and irresponsible; but he would

deserve an honored place in literature if only for his unerring critical judgment, for his ability to discern quality, and
for his encouragement at a critical point in the career of each
of such men as Joyce, Hemingway, Eliot, Frost; and then
there are his letters—letters of encouragement and criticism to aspiring poets, to students, letters opening doors or
asking for help for a promising writer, the dozens of letters
to Harriet Monroe. "Keep on remindin' 'em that we ain't
bolcheviks, but only the terrifyin' voice of civilization,
kultchuh, refinement, aesthetic perception," he wrote in
one to Miss Monroe, and when she wanted to retire, he
wrote to her, "The intelligence of the nation [is] more
important than the comfort of any one individual or the
bodily life of a whole generation."

In a letter to H.L. Mencken thanking him for a copy of
the latter's *In Defense of Women*, Pound remarked, almost
as an afterthought, "What is wrong with it, and with your
work in general is that you have drifted into writing for your
inferiors." Could anyone have put it more precisely? Who-
ever wants to know what went on in the period from about
1910 to 1940, whatever he may think of his politics or
economics, or even his poetry, will have to consult the
letters of Ezra Pound—the proper function of the artist in
society, he thought, was to be "not only its intelligence, but
its 'nostrils and antennae.'" And this, as his letters clearly
show, Pound made a strenuous and, more often than not,
successful effort to be.

How much of Lewis's qualities were a result of his
American heritage it would be hard to say, but there can be
no doubt that much in both Pound and Eliot came from

their American background. We may not have been able to give them what they needed to realize their talents and special qualities, they may even have been more resented than appreciated by many Americans, but that they did have qualities and characteristics which were distinctly American cannot be doubted. To this extent, at least, we can consider them an American gift to the Old World. In one of Eliot's most beautiful works, *The Rock*, a "Pageant Play written on behalf of the forty-five churches' Fund of the Diocese of London," as it says on the title page, there are the lines, "I have said, take no thought of the harvest, but only of perfect sowing." In taking upon themselves the difficult, thankless task of being the "terrifying voices of civilization," Eliot and his two friends, I am sure, did not give much thought of the possible consequences to themselves, of what there "might be in it for them," but what better can one say of anyone's life than "He sowed better than he reaped"?

14

George F. Kennan:
A Gift to America

In his latest book, *Around the Cragged Hill*, George F. Kennan, statesman, scholar, and author, offers a summing up described in the subtitle as "a personal and political philosophy." This is a departure from earlier books which were based on his years in the foreign service, first as a specialist on the Soviet Union and as U.S. Ambassador, then as head of the State Department's first policy planning staff, and finally as historian at the Institute for Advanced Studies in Princeton. His previous works on diplomatic history and his memoirs won, among other honors, two Pulitzer Prizes and a National Book Award. His own distinguished public service has been recognized by a Presidential Medal of Freedom. These achievements lead us to expect much from his new book and in this we are not disappointed—it is wonderfully thought-out and skillfully written, a gift of Kennan's accumulated wisdom for the consideration of his fellow countrymen.

The title is taken from several lines of John Donne's verse describing truth as attainable only through a long and arduous climb up a steep hill, an appropriate metaphor for Kennan's struggle to draw conclusions from his life experience, disdaining as he does idle abstractions and having witnessed firsthand the awful forces that have made this century, the most destructive in history. The first part of his book contains "reflections and reactions that might have relevance to situations of mankind everywhere," that is, to universal rather than to national realities. The second part is more contemporary, treating the present conditions of American society.

The opening chapter is entitled, "Man, the Cracked Vessel." Having served several years in Moscow during the regime of Stalin and as head of the American mission to Berlin during the opening days of World War II when Adolf Hitler appeared to have Europe at his feet, Kennan has observed man at his very worst, and, not surprisingly, sees our species as seriously flawed. He asserts that man's

> nature is the scene of a never-ending and never quite resolvable conflict between two very profound impulses. One of these built into him from birth and not a matter of his own choice is something he shares with the animals: namely, the imperative impulse to preserve and proliferate his own kind, with all the powerful compulsions that engenders. The other is the need—a

need underlying the entire historical development of civilization—to redeem human life, at
least partially of its essentially animalistic origins
by lending to it such attributes as order, dignity,
beauty, and charity—this last meaning the love
of or at least the respect for one's fellow man and
a capacity for compassion.

So rending is this conflict, he goes on to say, so irreconcil-
able are "the two within a single frame," that the individual
has to seek outside help, which could come only through
faith to make it endurable.

Following this rather stark statement of the human
condition, Kennan presents a thoughtful, clearly written,
and deeply felt chapter on faith. Faith, he contends, is the
only answer to the dilemma of man and that never-ending
conflict between the contradictions that "destroy the unity
and integrity of his undertakings, confuse his efforts, place
limits on his possibilities for achievement, and often cause
one part of his personality to be the enemy of the other."

Kennan then offers his own personal creed: "I regard
myself, if anyone wants to know, as a Christian, although
there are certainly others who would question my right to
that status." For his belief in Jesus, he says, he needs no
"historical evidence or explication, faith suffices." There are
those, he admits, who would deny him the right to claim to
be a Christian insofar as he finds "great difficulty in
reconciling the figure of the Almighty God, the presumed
Creator of our universe, with that of the supposedly loving
and benevolent God to whom we are taught to pray." This

Creator he designates as the "Primary Cause," and he goes on to point out how implausible is

> the suggestion that this Primary Cause, having created such an order and laid down the laws of its development should in response to the prayers of creatures such as ourselves interfere on a day-to-day basis and in the greatest detail, in the working of those laws, thus vitiating the very concept that lay behind them.

To make the map of his "cosmology," as he describes it, more human, Kennan introduces what he calls a "Merciful Deity":

> Simultaneously with the emergence of the soul there seems to me to have become evident the existence of the involvement with human life of a Deity of another sort—not the Primary Cause this time, but something quite different: a Deity filled with understanding and compassion for the agonies inflicted on man by the conflict between his two natures unable, to be sure, to spare him the realities of his animalistic one, but ready to help him, capable of helping him, to come to terms with it. The Deity could do this only by becoming part of man's consciousness, by giving him an awareness of the divine presence and by rendering him capable of the act of faith.

He further explains this concept as follows:

For the spirit is not, as I sense it and conceive it, some distant and all-powerful authority, standing wholly outside our predicament and disposing autocratically over all the factors affecting our lives. It is rather a participant in our struggle—a spirit infused with understanding and sympathy for our situation, involved as we are in the conflict between our physical and spiritual natures, and prepared to give us such assistance as we deserve and can accept.

Kennan concludes this account of his own faith with this thought: "Nevertheless, all of that being said, the problem of religious faith has remained, for me, essentially an individual one: the effort of a single man to establish his relationships to forces beyond reach of his own rational perception—forces upon interaction with which he knew the ultimate value of his own life to depend."

Now, whether or not one accepts George Kennan's cosmology, one must certainly admire his conviction, the manner in which he has tried to fathom the unfathomable, and the fine language in which it is expressed. Having unburdened himself on the subject of faith, which I am sure was not easy for a man of New England and Protestant background, Kennan takes up the problem of power in chapters on government, on nationalism, and on ideology. As a responsible member of the diplomatic service for nearly three decades, he had worked closely with heads of state in positions of great power, though he himself did not experience such power. Having witnessed the consequences of power on those who aspire to it or wield it, Kennan is in a unique position to judge its consequences. There is, of course, as he says, no alternative to government, which by its very nature always involves power: "No government *can* be without it. It is government's most effectual attribute. It lies in the very definition of government and represents the greatest center of power in any national community." Government, he makes clear, whether we like it or not, however large or small the community, whether free or oppressive, is essential to civilized life. But necessary as it is, it must always be suspect. In this connection, Kennan quotes Henry Adams, who, he says, best describes such distortions:

> The effects of power and publicity on all men is the aggravation of self, a sort of tumor that ends in killing the victim's sympathies; a diseased appetite like a passion for drink or perverted tastes; one can scarcely use expressions too strong to describe the violence of egotism it stimulates.

For Kennan, then, the exercise of power by government must be regarded with considerable reservations:

> Its doings are something that should be viewed by an outsider only with a sigh for its unquestioned necessity and by the participant only with a prayer for forgiveness for the many moral ambiguities it requires him to accept and for the distortions of personality it afflicts upon him.

He finishes his discussion of the influence of governmental

power on those who wield it with the following wise admonition:

> ...it must be recognized as one of the uniformities embracing all government, democratic and otherwise, that they attract to themselves, and function within, an atmosphere of inflamed ambitions, rivalries, sensitivities, anxieties, suspicions, embarrassments, and resentments, which, to put it mildly, seldom, if ever, bring out the best in the personalities involved, and sometimes provoke the worst. Government, in short, is, for unavoidable, compelling reasons, an unpleasant business. It cannot be otherwise. And we find in this fact another reason why, whatever else one may think of government, it should not be idealized.

He also has some wise things to say on the subject of "Human Rights," as enumerated in the Universal Declaration of Human Rights, approved by the General Assembly of the United Nations on December 10, 1948, and passed without a dissenting vote. What does it mean, he asks "that everyone has the right to a standard of living adequate for the health and well-being of himself and his family, including food, clothing, housing and medical care, and necessary social services..."? To whom does one apply to obtain such rights? In the incessant demands for the recognition of such rights, as our leaders are in the habit of making, Kennan detects an aura of sanctimoniousness. He confesses, "I still find myself wishing that we could be more discriminating in our choice of official language, and a bit more demanding of ourselves in bringing gesture into some sort of visible relationship with reality."

Kennan is equally forthright in assessing nationalism. He brings to us again the benefit of his own great experience in international affairs when he asserts that "In the course of two centuries that have passed since its emergence, nationalism had developed into the greatest emotional-political force of the age." It was one of the fundamental causes of the First World War and also became the source of the two great totalitarian movements ultimately leading to the catastrophe of World War II. His thoughts on nationalism confirm, if any confirmation is needed, that Kennan is a realist who sees things as they are.

Kennan concluded the first part of his book with a chapter on ideology, his conception of which is somewhat bland and benign. He defines ideology "as a system of secular thought about contemporary politics and social change on a level higher than just the national one, and capable of serving as a guide for public policy." He chooses to believe that one of the aims of ideology "in a healthy and well-balanced society" is that of finding "useful and, if possible, creative work for every mature human being." Kennan even quotes the definition of ideology from the *Encyclopedia Britannica* as a "comprehensive theory of human nature and requiring a protracted social struggle to enact."

For a tougher and sharper critique of ideology, however, the reader will do well to turn to another great American man of letters, Russell Kirk, who views ideology as "the politics of passionate unreason" and as an "inverted religion, denying the Christian doctrine of salvation through grace in death, and substituting collective salvation here on earth through violent revolution." One can, of course, agree with Kennan that a major goal of human reason should be that of creating a vigorous, rational society which undertakes, among other things, to provide a decent and balanced life for its citizens.

But for the ideologue, as Kirk reminds us, and as history itself forcefully confirms, the objective is ultimately the totalitarian state, which claims jurisdiction over all life, public and private, and absolute submission to its demands. Here we need only recall the "social struggle" which the two most notorious ideologues of the twentieth century, Lenin and Hitler, managed to impose upon their people and which led, inevitably and cataclysmically, to the Gulag Archipelago and to the Holocaust. Like that other great phenomenon of the century, nuclear fission, ideology, we must admit, is not harmless.

When, in the second and longer part of his book, Kennan addressed directly the realities of present-day America, his thoughts are more sharply focussed and convey convictions of great relevance and importance. In his chapter, "Dimensions," we encounter the following sentence: "If I were asked by a foreigner what strikes me most about my own people, two points, I think, would come most readily to mind: first, that we are a nation of bad social habits and, second, that there are too many of us." He goes on to cite some of the bad social habits he has in mind, a catalog of our woes: "The list would include such things as environmental deterioration; crime; drug abuse; in general, the dreadful conditions in the urban ghettos; the national budget deficit; the continued inability of our government to meet its financial obligations without massive borrowing at the expense of future generations; the decline of personal savings; and, in general, the excessive dependence on credit to sustain both governmental and personal activity."

He goes on to enumerate other "troublesome social conditions: attitudes of hopelessness, skepticism, cynicism, and bewilderment, particularly among the youth— that have led many observers to characterize this society (and, I think, not unjustly) as a 'sick one.'" In the following chapter, "Addictions," he specifies what he judges to be the greatest contemporary hazards to the well-being of American society: the automobile, advertising, and television. He insists, in particular that the automobile has virtually destroyed public transportation and ruined as well "the densely populated urban centers of the nineteenth century, with all the glories of economic and cultural life that had flowed from their very unity and compactness" and left us instead with what has come to be known as "urban sprawl."

Kennan not only deplores the constant din of advertising, the clutter of junk mail, and the blatant urging to spend more, buy more, but also questions the underlying drive for greater and greater economic growth:

> I react skeptically...to the ideal of economic growth that preoccupies so intensely almost all thought on economic problems in the United States.... Why growth? The assumption that without constant growth a national economy

could not be what it was supposed to be—would not, that is, serve the purpose of a society that it was meant to serve—seems to me without substantiation.

And he asks, "If a given economy adequately serves, at a given time, the needs of the population, provides food and housing and consumer goods in adequate quantities to assure a healthy and comfortable life for all concerned, why should it constantly have to be growing?"

Television, as we all know, has had its most invidious and destructive influence on the young. It is, Kennan declares, like the automobile, essentially antisocial. He specifically condemns the time spent watching television:

How much of this precious time, then, can the child afford to waste on a form of diversion that is passive, physically enervating and contributes nothing to the growth of the mind or body or emotional capacity, if only for the simple reason that it exercises none of these faculties?

In the failure of television to challenge the viewer's faculties, he discerns a deeper threat and offers a warning that Americans would do well to heed:

The public of a great country that lets a large portion of its leisure time be wasted by a steady exposure to media that provided none of this challenge is depriving itself in the most serious way of something that will be vitally needed if it is to retain its competitive importance in the

world. There are other parts of the world where
want, poverty, or the cruelty of social pressure is
producing a more serious and relentless discipline of both mind and body; and this difference,
if not corrected, must someday make itself felt in
the 'dust and heat' of international life.

Returning to his earlier observation, that "there are too
many of us," Kennan makes two telling points: first, that
immigration should be restricted, although, after making a
convincing case for this step, he admits, "Unfortunately it
appears, as things stand today, to lie beyond the vigor and
capacity for firm decision of the American political establishment to draw any rational limits to further immigration." That being the case, and considering the fact that the
country has simply become too populous and diverse to be
governed without excessive bureaucracy and remoteness
from the true needs of the people, Kennan makes a second
and even more startling suggestion: that if the country has
grown too large, beyond the capacity of the government to
administer it properly, then divide it up into something like
a dozen constituent republics, absorbing not only the
powers of the existing states, but a considerable part of
those powers of the federal establishment. Each of the
dozen or so regional units, he suggests, should be distinguished by cultural and social qualities that would set it off
from the others. "Ease, flexibility, intimacy of government,
not a quest for racial or ethnic uniformity," he asserts,
"could be the purpose of such a reform."

Turning to foreign policy, Kennan is predictably direct and down-to-earth in his observations. First, he rejects the preoccupation with nuclear weapons that had haunted the world for nearly half a century: "The nuclear weapon was, in fact, from the start an essentially useless weapon, useless at least for any rational purpose...." With 15,000 nuclear warheads in world arsenals, "[o]bviously it would never have been possible to use more than a very small fraction of these weapons in combat without creating, in addition to millions of directly caused casualties, a worldwide environmental catastrophe." Second, in looking to the future, he believes that "the sort of war we *do not* have to plan for...is a great war among the great powers. Experience of this past century has made that plain, in the light of modern military technology, no all-out war among the great industrial powers...can now be other than suicidal. If wars of this sort cannot be ruled out, civilization will be." Finally, in following this line of reasoning, Kennan urges the withdrawal of American forces from Europe, and he hopes "that in the search for a new European security structure designed to meet the changed situation, prevailing in the light of the Soviet breakdown, the accent would be put on a European organization of which the United States was not a member."

In dealing with the U.S. State Department and the Foreign Service, Kennan continues to be provocative, describing them as "in a dreadful state; vastly over staffed, poorly organized internally, so over elaborate and cumbersome" that they are "practically useless." He sees some fourteen billion dollars leaving our Treasury each year to end up in one way or another in the hands of foreign regimes. "One shudders to think," he says, "of the number and complexity of the various written agreements these programs must have involved." Of the military assistance, Kennan asserts, half went to African nations and, as he observes, "They are not greatly involved in international conflicts. It is hard to imagine against whom they would use these weapons and the training we are supposedly giving them if not against their neighbors or, in civil conflicts, against themselves. Is it our business to prepare them for that?"

Kennan makes it clear that he is "wholly and emphatically rejecting any and all messianic concepts of America's role in the world: rejecting, that is, the image of ourselves as teachers and redeemers of the rest of humanity, rejecting the illusion of unique and superior virtues on our part...the prattle about Manifest Destiny or the 'American Century....'" Instead, he urges "a very modest and restricted foreign policy directed to the curtailment of external undertaking and involvement wherever this is in any way possible." His long experience in these matters and his record of clear thinking lend weight to Kennan's judgments. Consider, as an example, his stand on the issue of unconditional surrender:

> By and large, it must be said, there are many drawbacks to unconditional surrender as a way to end a war. In excluding the regime of the defeated country from any significant participation in the drawing up of the post-hostilities regime, it also absolves them of all responsibility, while

saddling the victors with total responsibility, for what is to come. But it also assumes that it is both desirable and possible to exclude an entire population from participating in the designing of its own future. While this can perhaps be done for a short time, it cannot be done for very long. The results of...two great wars, ostensibly ended by unconditional surrender, afford a startling demonstration of its reality. In less than two decades after the end of World War One, Germany, nominally the defeated power, was again the greatest military power in Europe. Within two or three decades after the ending of the Second World War, Germany and Japan, the two defeated powers, were the most prosperous and economically powerful countries in their respective regions. All of these reflections stand as a warning against moving into future wars without taking into account the experience of the two great European wars of this century and of their consequences.

The concluding chapter, entitled "What is to be Done?" makes it clear that our country faces serious problems, problems which our present political system seems unable to confront with any degree of seriousness, particularly because they are all long-term problems which we try to confront with short-term solutions. The members of our political establishment are all indebted, he contends, to the constituencies that have elected them; by necessity, their first concern is the next election. The Founding Fathers attempted a partial solution to this problem by prescribing that members of the Senate should serve for six years and be elected by the state legislators; but in the enthusiasm for popular voting, the seventeenth amendment ordained the popular election of senators, with results as might have been expected. In discussing these matters, Kennan makes this devastating statement, which is unfortunately only too true:

> The principle by which our government appears to have been guided for many years and decades in the past is that among the qualifications for public office, experience counts for precisely nothing—that for the great majority of executive positions anyone whose qualifications meet the political requirements of the moment will obviously be preferable to anyone else who may have had rich experience in the respective field but whose political qualifications fail the test.

In contrast to those often chosen for public office, this country has a great wealth of citizens who have made contributions to our national life in their capacities as business leaders, scholars, academic administrators, scientists, publicists, as well as ex-presidents, ex-cabinet members, ex-governors, former distinguished legislators or jurists, and many others whose rich experience is simply allowed to rot away, unused. Kennan proposes to make use of such experience by setting up what he calls a Council of State, a non-political advisory body, "one that permits the tapping of the greatest source of wisdom and experience that the private citizenry of the country can provide." He envisages a body of perhaps nine members who would be chosen by the President from a carefully selected panel of some 100 members of quality and distinction. "One might hope that selection to this panel would come to be considered the highest form of distinction that could be conferred on any ordinary citizen not serving in elected or other governmental office."

This Council of State would be purely advisory, would have no legislative or judicial authority, and in no way would infringe or interfere with the ordinary operations of government. "The Council's task," he goes on to say, "would be confined to telling the country, including the politicians, what ought to be done in the long-term interest of American society." Kennan concludes his discussion of the Council of State with the following observation:

> There are, as has been seen, a number of serious national problems the solution of which has been shown to be beyond the capacity of our governmental establishment as it now stands. The result has been, as I see it, something close to a major crisis in the life of the nation. In the question as to whether this deficiency can be corrected, it is nothing less than the adequacy of our form of government to meet the unprecedented challenges of the modern age that is at stake.

What is ultimately to be drawn from his writings, Kennan hopes, are "some rather basic *preferences*—a preference for the small over the great, for the qualitative over the quantitative, for the personal over the impersonal, for the discriminate over the indiscriminate, and for the varied over the uniform "in most major aspects of social life." He acknowledges his aversion to the American tradition of handling social and political problems according to all-inclusive, programmatic categories; instead he longs for intelligent discrimination in the treatment of both persons and situations, with an emphasis on the importance of means over ends. Finally, he believes "that if we are to have hope of emerging successfully from the great social bewilderment of this age, weight must be laid predominantly upon the spiritual, moral and intellectual shaping of the individual."

Quoting J.R.R. Tolkien—"despair is only for those who see the end beyond all doubt"—he concludes on a confident note: "The hour may be late, but there is still nothing that says it is too late....The challenge is to see what could be done, and then to have the heart and the resolution to attempt it." In his examination of the troubles of modern times, George Frost Kennan, elder statesman and sage, invariably reflects not only his many years of experience but also his courage of judgment. This most thoughtful and compelling book is truly a gift to America.

15

Alexander Solzhenitsyn:
The Man and the Problem

Those great personalities who appear among us from time to time with the compulsion to tell us the truth about ourselves are rarely given a warm welcome, and least of all by those who regard themselves as the custodians of society. Solzhenitsyn is a problem because he is just such a personality. The Russian authorities found him to be a most uncomfortable man to have around, and unable to think of anything better to do with him, sent him into exile.

His book, *The Oak and the Calf,* makes clear how repugnant he must have been to them; while an unwilling guest in our country, still driven by the compulsion to tell the truth as he sees it, he made himself almost as repugnant to those who consider themselves the intellectual leaders of our society—the liberal left. Consideration of the problem of Solzhenitsyn, therefore, involves not only Communist Russia, but our own country as well.

The Oak and the Calf begins in 1962 with the publication of *One Day in the Life of Ivan Denisovich* and ends with Solzhenitsyn's expulsion from Russia in 1974. The calf, of course, is Solzhenitsyn and the oak the Soviet state, but toward the end of the book the author remarks that he used the metaphor only for the sake of the Russian proverb from which it comes and not because the Soviet state deserves to be compared to an oak tree—an "oversized oaken cudgel," he says, would have been more appropriate. The publication of *Ivan Denisovich* in the literary magazine *Novy Mir* during the brief "thaw" that followed Khrushchev's denunciation of Stalin may well stand out in the future as the turning point in the history of our time: the appearance of that book established once and for all the realities of the slave labor system as an undeniable feature of the Soviet State, and it vaulted Solzhenitsyn from the obscurity of a mathematics teacher in a provincial school to one of the towering and most important men of our time.

The Oak and the Calf was clearly not written for reasons of self- justification, but so that the world might know, and particularly so that future generations of Russians might know, what it was like to be a writer under a Communist regime, when manuscripts that might be considered subversive by the authorities had to be carefully hidden, and when, as a result of the rigid control of publishing, the secret, or *samizdat* method of publication developed and became, in spite of the great risks involved, remarkably effective. This is both a wonderfully revealing and a wonderfully inspiring book: it lets us see, vividly and uncompromisingly, one aspect of the modern world at its worst, the suppression of all values in the interest of an ideology. It also lets us see, in its striving for fulfillment on the highest level, the human spirit at its best and noblest.

Novy Mir and its editor, Alexander Tvardovsky, occupy a central position in Solzhenitsyn's literary career and, as well, in his account of it. That such a book as *Ivan Denisovich* could have been published at all was nothing short of miraculous. Solzhenitsyn's life had been spared as an artillery officer at the front, from eight years in the death camps of the Soviet Union, and then from what he had been told was a fatal cancer, and, he felt very deeply, for a purpose. "I must write simply to ensure that it was not all forgotten, that posterity might someday come to know of it. Publication in my own lifetime, I must shut out of my mind, out of my dreams." The works he composed in the camps, when it was impossible to write, he memorized; when he was later in a position to write it down, the manuscripts had to be carefully hidden. Discovery of such manuscripts as his, and as an ex-prisoner he was always subject to suspicion and search, could lead to instant execution. The apparently more relaxed atmosphere following the XXII Congress, and especially a remark by Tvardovsky in a speech he had given at the Congress—that *Novy Mir* "might publish bolder and more polemical things, if only it had them"—convinced Solzhenitsyn that the time had come to abandon the caution he had acquired as a *zek*, a political prisoner, and offer a "lightened" version of *Ivan Denisovich* to *Novy Mir*. It was brought to the magazine by a friend, another ex-prisoner, and somehow attracted the attention of a woman on the editorial staff, Anna Samoilevna, who was determined that it be published. She had it copied, knowing that no editor would read it in the form it had come in, and by skillful maneuvering managed to circumvent the four sub-editors who, she was quite sure, would not approve of it, and to get it into the hands of Tvardovsky himself, with the words, "a prison camp as seen through the eyes of a peasant, a work in which you could hear the voice of the Russian people." This aroused the interest of Tvardovsky, who was of peasant background; he read it and was overwhelmed by the conviction that he had made a great discovery. The next hurdle was Khrushchev himself, who also, as it happened, was of peasant background:

> I cannot say that I precisely planned it, but I did accurately foresee that the muzhik Ivan Denisovich was bound to arouse the sympathy of the superior muzhik Tvardovsky and of the supreme muzhik Nikita Khrushchev. And that was just what happened: it was not poetry nor politics that decided the fate of my story, but that unchanging peasant nature, so much ridiculed, trampled underfoot and vilified in our country since the Great Break, and indeed earlier.

Solzhenitsyn's attitude toward Tvardovsky is ambivalent and not always consistent: he had great respect for him as an editor, was grateful to him for what he had done for him as a writer and for Russian literature through his magazine, and he liked and enjoyed him as a person, but as a former *zek* and knowing the realities of life in Soviet Russia as he did, he found it impossible to forgive Tvardovsky for the compromises which were an inevitable part of his position as editor of the leading literary magazine. When, however, Tvardovsky once spoke of resigning, Solzhenitsyn, in trying to dissuade him, says that he told him "*Novy Mir* was preserving our cultural tradition; *Novy Mir* was the only honest witness to the times we lived in; there were two or three good articles in every issue, and even one would be enough to redeem the rest...."

Tvardovsky's own father, on the other hand, had been arrested and sent off somewhere to die in misery only because he was a *kulak*, a more prosperous than ordinary peasant. The son managed to excuse or even forget that as one of the necessary steps toward the society of the future; and at the time of the occupation of Czechoslovakia, when Solzhenitsyn was trying to induce prominent writers to sign a letter of protest, Tvardovsky refused. When, finally, it had become apparent that Tvardovsky would be forced to resign, Solzhenitsyn thought that he should go down fighting. He speaks of the humiliations Tvardovsky had endured through the years for the sake of the magazine; why, then, when the final blow came, he asked, did the magazine have "to go down on its knees?" But in spite of his criticisms and disagreements, Solzhenitsyn could send a most generous and affectionate telegram to Tvardovsky on the occasion of his sixtieth birthday: "I wish you spacious days, precious discoveries, a happy creative life in your ripe years! Through all our constant quarrels and disagreements

I remain immutably your deeply affectionate and grateful Solzhenitsyn," and after Tvardovsky's death from cancer only six months following his dismissal from *Novy Mir* Solzhenitsyn issued the following public statement (he, of course, was still in Russia):

> There are many ways of killing a poet. The method chosen for Tvardovsky was to take away his beloved child—his passion—his journal. They were not satisfied with sixteen years of insults, meekly endured by this hero so long as his journal survived, so long as literature went on without interruptions, so long as people could be printed in it, so long as people could go on reading it. They were not satisfied! So they lit fires around him: scattered his forces, destroyed his journal, dealt with him unjustly. And within six months those fires had consumed him. Within six months he was mortally sick; and only his characteristic fortitude sustained him till now, conscious to the last. Suffering to the last.

However many insults and humiliations Tvardovsky was made to suffer, and however many compromises he made to keep his position and to maintain his journal, it all culminated in the publication of the book which established Solzhenitsyn and which may well finally prove to be a fatal blow to the Soviet system. Who then can say that all this did not have a higher purpose?

With the worldwide attention showered on him following the success of his first book, Solzhenitsyn had gained a vantage point from which to continue his assault on the system of which the Gulag was an integral part. Much of the present book is an account of this fight, of attacks and strategic retreats, all carefully planned and as carefully executed, always with the knowledge that overstepping the limits of his precarious position could lead to disaster. He issued public statements, gave interviews to the foreign press, sent letters of protest to prominent officials—one to Comrade Suslov, for example, Secretary of the Central Committee of the Communist Party of the Soviet Union; another to the Minister of State Security, this one objecting to the tapping of his telephone and the search of his house by agents of the secret police. Following his dismissal from the Writer's Union he sent a letter to the Secretariat of the Union which concludes:

> It is high time to remember that we belong first and foremost to humanity, and that man has separated himself from the animal world by thought and by speech. These, naturally, should be free. If they are put in chains, we shall return to the state of animals.
>
> Openness, honest and complete openness— that is the first condition of health in all societies, including our own. And he who does not want this openness for our country cares nothing for his fatherland and thinks only of his own interest. He who does not want this openness for his fatherland does not want to purify it of its own diseases, but only to drive them inward, there to fester.

The granting of the Nobel Prize for literature to Solzhenitsyn in 1971 provided a new opportunity for attack and gave him a stronger position from which to launch it. It was made clear to him that an exit permit would readily be granted so that he could go to Stockholm to receive the prize, but it was made equally clear that in this event he would not be allowed to return. He had no desire to leave his native land, however attractive the many offers of asylum may have appeared: he was a Russian writer, Russian was his language, and it was to his own people that he wished to speak; to leave voluntarily would be, he thought, an act of cowardice, and would weaken his position. The Swedish ambassador refused to permit the investiture to take place in the Swedish embassy for fear of annoying the Russian government; it was finally to be held in a private apartment with a small group of writers and friends in attendance, but this had to be cancelled because the secretary of the Nobel Committee—for whom, by the way, Solzhenitsyn had the highest respect—was unable to attend. In spite of such difficulties Solzhenitsyn found ways to use the prestige of the Nobel Prize and his acceptance lecture to continue his battle against the masters of the Gulag. All this is fascinating to read, and in spite of Solzhenitsyn's obvious regret that it took him away from writing, which he felt was his mission in life, one cannot help but feel, old fighter that he is, that he enjoyed the battle.

In reading all this the question comes constantly to mind, How was it possible? How, for nearly eight years, was this former prisoner able to defy the most powerful and ruthless government on the face of the earth? Solzhenitsyn himself seems to feel that the authorities hesitated to arrest or kill him, a fate they had meted out to millions, because of the effect that this may have had on public opinion abroad, but the fear of such opinion certainly did not prevent the masters of the Kremlin from putting down revolts in Poland, East Germany, and Hungary ruthlessly and with the shooting, execution, and arrest of thousands, women and children alike, nor did it prevent the occupation of Prague following the "Czech spring" which was also followed by the usual arrests, imprisonments, and executions. Solzhenitsyn did, of course, occupy a unique position, but he was also, old *zek* that he was, a wily and skillful fighter. He had arranged, for example, to send copies of his manuscripts abroad, and he had given careful instructions concerning how and in what order they were to be published in case of his arrest or disappearance. The secret police had located and seized a collection of his manuscripts, which included large parts of *The Gulag Archipelago* and *The Oak and the Calf,* so that the authorities knew the explosive nature of what he had written; they were also, of course, aware that his arrest would only add to its effectiveness if and when it was published.

The decision, finally, to arrest him and send him out of the country (he wasn't even told where he would be going when he was put on the plane) must have been made only after the most careful deliberation: it was in the power of the authorities to imprison or execute him, but because his manuscripts were already abroad, it was not in their power to silence him. They had tried various means to discredit him, by spreading rumors that he had been a German prisoner, even a German agent, that he was a Jew. They had even arranged for the publication of a slanderous book by his former wife. None of all this seems to have had much effect: the credibility of the Soviet authorities is nowhere very high (except among liberals), and least of all in Russia.

The final decision to exile Solzhenitsyn may well have been motivated by the conviction that once abroad, those old, reliable defenders of the Soviet Union, the intellectuals of the liberal left, could be relied upon to do everything in their power to do what the bosses in the Kremlin, armed as they were with thousands of tanks, guns, atomic weapons of every variety, the most ruthless police force, and the most effective propaganda apparatus in the world, had been unable to do, discredit the testimony of Alexander Solzhenitsyn.

One would like to think that the sheer magnitude of Solzhenitsyn as a person, his uncompromising integrity, his conviction that he was called upon to speak for the millions who had suffered and died in the camps, and the great artistry with which his message is expressed, might have had some effect on the men of the Kremlin, and perhaps it did. Still, if they based their decision to send him into exile on the supposition that the liberal intellectuals of the West would do everything in their power to discredit him and to lessen the authority of his message, they calculated correctly. It must be said also that they had sound basis for such a supposition: the desire of the liberal intellectuals to see Communist Russia as the hope of mankind had been unshaken by such events as the murder of millions of peasants during the period of forced collectivization (they were *kulaks*), the purge trials of the thirties, the Hitler-Stalin pact, which triggered World War II, the ruthless occupation and Stalinization of Poland, Roumania, Hungary, East Germany, Czechoslovakia, and the Baltic countries, and much else besides.

For the rulers of Russia, Solzhenitsyn is a danger because he speaks the truth, and does it with enormous authority and conviction; what he says, all of them, I am sure, if pressed would admit: they are well aware of what they are doing now and of what was done in the past to gain and maintain power. For the liberals, however, Solzhenitsyn presents quite a different problem: he has destroyed their illusions, the basis of their faith, and in particular the illusion that Russian Communism, as a form of socialism, is the wave of the future and the hope of mankind. In a different way, it is just as difficult for the liberals to confront Solzhenitsyn as it is for the Communists.

A thorough study of the response of American liberals to Solzhenitsyn would be most revealing, not only of the intellectual disarray of contemporary liberalism, but of the moral and spiritual crisis of our time. In the present article there is room only for a few examples, the first from reviews of Solzhenitsyn's books. This seems justified by the fact that book reviewing is largely the domain of the liberal left, and because most reviews say more about the reviewer than about the book supposedly under consideration. The reviewer for the *Library Journal*, to give a rather conspicuous example, described the Harvard speech as "less than inspiring...the bitter invective of an aging, frustrated, vain man." *Letter to the Soviet Leaders,* the same publication decided, "...falls far short of the achievement of his creative works...some of his arguments are cogent, and dramatically offered, but they betray naivete and his own confusion on theology." Robert Conquest, who is one of the great authorities on the Soviet Union and no liberal, in his review in the *New Republic* of *Lenin in Zurich* pronounced the book "a work of art which conveys...some of the reality of Lenin and the great vortex centered on him." On the other hand, the *Library Journal* was of the opinion that in this book the author had "trapped himself" because he was "unable to explore the enigma of Lenin's power." The reviewer of *Cancer Ward* in the *New York Times* spoke of the author's "lack of measure and sometimes of control over the material and a penchant for simplistic moralizing," and the review of *Warning to the West* in *Harper's* magazine of Solzhenitsyn's "intellectual vulgarities" and "comical simplifications of systematic philosophy." Such words as "simplistic," "naive," "moralistic" appear frequently in the reviews of Solzhenitsyn's books, but it remained for the *New Yorker* to compare him to the Ayatollah—both, the *New Yorker* informs us, are religious fanatics, anti-modern, and anti-West. It is easy, of course, to dispose of Solzhenitsyn's message as "simplistic"—one can say the same thing of the Sermon on the Mount—or by asserting that he is a religious fanatic; but it is something else again to confront and come to terms with the reality of what he has to say about the crisis of our time, of which Communist Russia is only a part.

One of the most unscrupulous attacks on Solzhenitsyn appeared in the May 1980 issue of *Harper's*—"The Dark

Side of Solzhenitsyn," by George Feifer. It is one of those "yes...but" affairs: to demonstrate his objectivity Mr. Feifer begins by acknowledging Solzhenitsyn's "courage, toughness, and resourcefulness" (he could hardly do otherwise), and, as well, his achievement as a writer—"*The First Circle* and *Cancer Ward* are among the most powerful novels published anywhere"—and then proceeds to denigrate him with all the nasty tricks journalists have developed to use against people who are bigger than they are—misrepresentation, innuendo, blowing isolated incidents and remarks out of all proportion to their circumstances, quoting unknown "authorities," appearing to have knowledge they could not possibly possess. Solzhenitsyn, according to Mr. Feifer, is disloyal to his friends, a "mystical authoritarian," a purveyor of "moralistic, painfully simplistic solutions to social problems," a man guilty, while in the death camps (how could he possibly know?) of "compromises and tactical hesitations," who assumes a "posture of moral superiority," and "has taken on...many of the characteristics of the tyranny he opposes." "For all his detestation of Lenin," Feifer informs us, "Solzhenitsyn is closer to him on the most fundamental social and political questions than to prerevolutionary Russian, let alone Western, democrats. Wags touched something deep," Feifer goes on to say, "when they called *Lenin in Zurich* 'Solzhenitsyn in Zurich.'" What wags, besides Mr. Feifer? To attempt to put A in a bad light by saying that he is closer to C than B is meaningless unless B, C, and the basis of comparison are clearly defined; that Feifer does nothing of the sort is another example of his journalistic sleight of hand. Finally, to attempt to compare a man of the profound religious conviction and selflessness of Solzhenitsyn to the utterly ruthless Lenin, driven as he was by an insatiable thirst for power, is not only dishonest, it is contemptible.

Mr. Feifer makes much of Solzhenitsyn's alleged un-kindness and lack of gratitude toward Tvardovsky, whom according to Feifer, he "flays," in *The Oak and the Calf,* "with almost as much derision and contempt as *The Gulag Archipelago* flung at the Soviet rulers." This is not true, as a careful reading of the book will make clear. In connection with all this it should be remembered that Tvardovsky occupied a high position in the Soviet hierarchy and in consequence enjoyed many favors—a chauffeur-driven car, a pleasant dacha in the country, trips abroad, etc.—while Solzhenitsyn had been sentenced, by the same society that had showered favors on Tvardovsky, to eight years in the death camps and three years as an exile in a remote part of the country, all for having made critical remarks about the "leader" in a private letter, written from the front. In a normal society their relations would doubtless have been open and cordial, Tvardovsky an able, discerning editor and gifted poet, and Solzhenitsyn a strong willed writer of genius, but the circumstances of their lives in the poisoned society of Soviet Russia made such a relationship impos-sible, as Solzhenitsyn makes perfectly clear. Following a visit to Tvardovsky during his last illness, Solzhenitsyn says of him, in *The Oak and the Calf:*

Alas, Aleksandr Trifonijchi! Do you remember our discussion of "Matryona's Home"? ...How you dreaded to think what would have become of you if the October Revolution had never taken place?

I will tell you what you would have become: the poet of the people, greater than Kolzov or Nikitin. You would have written as freely as a man breathes, you would not have needed to seek relief in vodka, you would not have contracted cancer as a result of injustice and persecution.

These are hardly the words of a man "flaying" another.

There is, doubtless, a "dark side" to Solzhenitsyn, as, I am sure, he would be the first to admit: he is a man, and man is a flawed creature. But rather than dwell on his dark side, and exaggerate and misrepresent it, let us be grateful for his creative achievement, which derives from his conviction that his life has a purpose larger than himself.

In the first part of *Witness*, which is called "Letter to My Children," Whittaker Chambers undertakes to explain to us the attraction Communism held for his generation. This derived, he said, from the conviction that "it was necessary to change the world." It was the commitment of Communists to this conviction, and their willingness to live or die for it, "to bear witness," as Chambers says, in a world which had lost the power to hold convictions and to die for them, that was the source of their power and influence. And what was the faith that lay at the root of this conviction? It was not a new faith, Chambers tells us:

It is, in fact, man's second oldest faith. Its promise was whispered in the first days of Creation under the Tree of the Knowledge of Good and Evil: "Ye shall be as gods." It is the great alternative faith of mankind. Like all great faiths, its force derives from a simple vision. Other ages have had great visions. They have always been different versions of the same vision: the vision of God and of man's relationship to God. The Communist vision is of the vision of Man without God.

It is the vision of man's mind displacing God as the creative intelligence of the world. It is the vision of man's liberated mind, by the sole force of its rational intelligence, redirecting man's destiny and reorganizing man's life in the world. It is the vision of man, once more the central figure of Creation, not because God made him in His image, but because man's mind made him the most intelligent of the animals.

Solzhenitsyn has shown, once and for all, and for all the world to see, the consequences of the Communist vision of man without God, and in so doing, has shattered the whole basis of Communism. Soviet Russia, as the center of the world Communist movement, had the physical power to do enormous harm; but it is doubtful that it would be possible to find a really convinced Communist anywhere in Russia, and certainly not in the Kremlin. *The Oak and the Calf,* probably unintentionally, clearly demonstrates that by their insecurity in dealing with Solzhenitsyn the Soviet authorities, who had it within their power to crush him at will, were well aware that he was their better.

The movement created by the Russian dissidents, in which Solzhenitsyn, of course, played a central part, is not counterrevolutionary in the usual sense, nor political, but moral. This is doubtless the source of its strength and the reason that the Soviet authorities, with all their ruthlessness, found it impossible to combat. On one of the first pages of *The Oak and the Calf* (page 10, to be exact) Solzhenitsyn remarks that the Soviet regime "could certainly have been breached only by literature. The regime has been reinforced with concrete to such an extent that neither a military coup nor a political organization nor a picket line of strikers can knock it over or run it through. Only the solitary writer would be able to do this. And the Russian younger generation would move on into the breach."

The Oak and the Calf, as the account of one "solitary writer's" successful attempt to undermine a government whose power is felt throughout the world, must be counted one of the most important books of our time. Let us hope that "the younger generation" will have the wit and the strength to move into the breach he had made for them—and for us.

Notes

Notes

I. This Liberal Age: *A Critical Appraisal*

1. John Dos Passos, *Occasions and Protests* (Chicago, 1964), p. 175.
2. Ronald Berman, *America in the Sixties* (New York, 1968), p. 20.
3. For a detailed discussion of this phenomenon, with many examples, see Paul Hollander, "The Ideological Pilgrim," *Encounter*, November 1973.
4. Eliseo Vivas, *Two Roads to Ignorance* (unpublished manuscript), Chapter VII, p. 25.
5. Quoted in Berman, p. 176.
6. George F. Kennan, *Memoirs, 1925-1950* (Boston, 1967), p. 82.
7. Joseph E. Davies, *Mission to Moscow* (New York, 1942), p. 44.
8. *Ibid.*
9. Kennan, p. 83.
10. Davies, p. 67.
11. *Ibid.*
12. *Foreign Affairs*, April 1942.
13. *Pacific Affairs*, March 1942.
14. *The Saturday Review of Literature*, January 10, 1942.
15. *The New Republic*, January 12, 1942.
16. "These territorial changes seemed to me to be doubly pernicious, and the casual American acquiescence in them all the less forgivable, because of the fact that they served, like other territorial concessions to the Russians, simply to extract great productive areas from the economy of Europe and to permit the Russians, for reasons of their own military and political convenience, to deny these areas and their resources to the general purposes of European reconstruction.... The disaster that befell this area [East Prussia] with the entry of Soviet forces has no parallel in modern European

experience. There were considerable sections of it where, to judge by all existing evidence, scarcely a man, woman, or child of the indigenous population was left alive after the initial passage of Soviet forces." Kennan, pp. 264-265.

17. Dos Passos, p. 175.

18. From a letter to W.T. Couch from William Miller, quoted in "The Sainted Book Burners," *The Freeman*, April 1955, p. 423.

19. *The New Republic*, January 1, 1945.

20. *The Library Journal*, September 15, 1944.

21. *Kirkus Book Review Service*, September 1945.

22. *New York Times*, December 9, 1945.

23. Richard M. Weaver, *Ideas Have Consequences* (Chicago, 1948), p. 2.

24. *New York Times*, February 22, 1948.

25. *Ibid.*, March 22, 1948.

26. *The Nation*, May 29, 1948.

27. *Annals of the American Academy*, July 1948.

28. Weaver, p. 172.

29. F.A. Hayek, "The Intellectuals and Socialism," *The University of Chicago Law Review*, Spring 1949, reprinted in *Studies in Philosophy, Politics and Economics* (Chicago, 1967), p. 178.

30. Joseph Schumpeter, *Capitalism, Socialism, and Democracy* (New York, 1942), p. 147.

31. *Ibid.*, p. 151.

32. *Ibid.*, p. 161.

33. Hayek, p. 184.

34. *Ibid.*, p. 185.

35. *Ibid.*, p. 189.

36. Vivas, Chapter IV, p. 7.

37. *Ibid.*, p. 26.

38. *Ibid.*, p. 30.

39. *Ibid.*, pp. 30-31.

40. Eric Voegelin, "On Classical Studies," *Modern Age*, Winter 1973.

II. Albert J. Nock: *An Appreciation*

Books consulted for this article, and from which the quotations have been taken:

Crunden, Robert M., *The Mind and Art of Albert J. Nock,* (Henry Regnery Co., Chicago, 1964).

Francis Rabelais (with C.R. Wilson), (Harper & Bros., New York, 1929).

"Isaiah's Job," reissued in *American Conservative Thought in the Twentieth Century,* edited by William F. Buckley, Jr., (Bobbs-Merrill Company, Indianapolis, 1970).

Memoirs of a Superfluous Man, (Harper & Bros., New York, 1943; Henry Regnery Co., Chicago, 1964).

On Doing the Right Thing, (Harper & Bros., New York, 1928).

Our Enemy, the State, (Caxton Printers, Caldwell, Idaho, 1946).

The Book of Journeyman, (Books for Libraries Press, Freeport, N.Y., 1967).

The Theory of Education in the United States, (Harcourt, Brace, New York, 1932; Henry Regnery Co., Chicago, 1949).

IV. Russell Kirk: *Making of the Conservative Mind*

1. Russell Kirk, *The Conservative Mind* (Chicago, 1953), p. 3.
2. *Ibid.,* p. 7.
3. *Ibid.,* pp. 7-8.
4. *Ibid.,* p. 24.
5. *Ibid.,* p. 32.
6. *Ibid.,* p. 26.
7. *Ibid.,* p. 295.
8. *Ibid.,* p. 296.
9. *Ibid.,* p. 297.
10. *Ibid.,* p. 311.
11. *Ibid.,* p. 313.
12. *Ibid.,* pp. 315-316.
13. *Ibid.,* p. 325.

14. *Ibid.*, p. 364.

15. *Ibid.*, p. 316.

16. *Ibid.*, p. 372.

17. *Ibid.*, p. 372.

18. *Ibid.*, p. 377.

19. *Ibid.*, p. 385.

20. *Ibid.*, p. 386.

21. *Ibid.*, p. 400.

22. F.A. Hayek, "Why I Am Not a Conservative," reprinted as a postscript in *The Constitution of Liberty* (Chicago, 1972), p. 398.

23. *Ibid.*, p. 401.

24. *Ibid.*, pp. 401–402.

25. *Ibid.*, p. 402.

26. *Ibid.*, p. 400.

27. Willmoore Kendall, *The Conservative Affirmation* (Chicago, 1963), p.xi.

28. Russell Kirk, *John Randolph of Roanoke, A Study in American Politics* (Chicago, 1964), p. 1.

29. William F. Buckley, Jr., *God and Man at Yale* (Chicago, 1951), p. 190.

30. Russell Kirk, *Academic Freedom, An Essay in Definition* (Chicago, 1955).

31. *Ibid.*, p. 4.

32. George A. Nash, *The Conservative Intellectual Movement in America, Since 1945* (New York, 1976), p.145.

VII. Historical Revisionism and World War II: *Part I*

*Robert E. Sherwood, one of President Roosevelt's speechwriters, was later to remark on the subject of this speech: "I burn inwardly whenever I think of those words 'again-and-again-and-again' ...unfortunately for my own conscience, I happened at the time to be one of those who urged him to go to the limit on this, feeling as I did then that any risk of future embarrassment was negligible as compared with the risk of losing the election."

Roosevelt and Hopkins: An Intimate History (New York, 1948), p. 874.

1. Charles A. Beard, *President Roosevelt and the Coming of the War*, 1941 (New Haven, Conn., 1948), p. 3.
2. *Ibid.*, pp.15-16.
3. *Ibid.*, p. 19.
4. *Ibid.*, p. 22.
5. *Ibid.*, p. 595.
6. Howard K. Beale, "The Professional Historians," *Pacific Historical Review* (August 1953), p. 249.
7. Charles A. Beard, "Written History as an Act of Faith," *American Historical Review*, 1934, pp. 219-231.
8. Beale, p. 250.
9. William Henry Chamberlin, *America's Second Crusade* (Chicago, 1950), p. 22.
10. *Ibid.*, p. 353.
11. Charles C. Tansill, *Back Door to War* (Chicago, 1952), p. 3.
12. *Ibid.*, p. 9.
13. *Ibid.*, p. 625.

VIII. Historical Revisionism and World War II: *Part II*

14. *New York Times*, January 25, 1942, as quoted by Beard, p. 221.
15. Beard, p. 309.
16. Sherwood, p. 674.
17. Elliott Roosevelt, *As He Saw It* (New York, 1946), p. 68.
18. *The Conferences at Cairo and Teheran, 1943*, Department of State Publication 7187 (Washington, 1961), p. 554.
19. George N. Crocker, *Roosevelt's Road to Russia* (Chicago, 1959), pp. 222-223.
20. *The Conferences at Cairo and Teheran*, p. 487.
21. Crocker, p. 315.
22. *Ibid.*, p. 226.

23. Henry L. Stimson and McGeorge Bundy, *On Active Service in War and Peace* (New York, 1947), p. 574.

24. Crocker, p. 280.

25. *Ibid.*, p. 21.

26. *Ibid.*, p. 29.

27. *The Conferences at Cairo and Teheran*, p. 486. In Sherwood's account, it is worth noting, the phrase "somewhat along the Soviet line" is omitted.

28. Crocker, p. 18.

29. *Ibid.*, p. 48.

30. *Franklin D. Roosevelt, His Personal Letters*, edited by Elliott Roosevelt (New York, 1947-50), Vol. 2, 1204-1205.

31. *The Holy See and the World War*, 1941-1942, 202-210.

32. Crocker, p. 20.

33. *Perpetual War for Perpetual Peace*, edited by Harry Elmer Barnes (Caldwell, Idaho, 1953), p. 10.

34. *Wisconsin Magazine of History*, Summer 1973.

35. Quoted by Marguerite J. Fisher in "Harry Elmer Barnes: An Overall Preview," *Harry Elmer Barnes, Learned Crusader* (Colorado Springs, 1968), p. 25.

IX. Winston Churchill: *A Question of Leadership*

1. Martin Gilbert, *Winston Churchill: Road to Victory 1941-1945*, 7 vols. (Boston, 1986).

2. *Ibid.*, 7:2.

3. *Ibid.*, pp. 9-10.

4. *Ibid.*, p. 94.

5. *Ibid.*, p. 185.

6. Quoted from a letter to Lord Beaverbrook, Minister for Aircraft Production, in Paul Johnson, *Modern Times* (New York, 1983), p. 370.

7. Gilbert, p. 295.

8. *Ibid.*, p. 391.

9. *Ibid.*, p. 259.

10. *Ibid.*, p. 179.
11. *Ibid.*, p. 437.
12. Johnson, p. 404.
13. Gilbert, p. 1257.
14. *Ibid.*, p. 1258.
15. Johnson, p. 404.
16. Gilbert, p. 1234.
17. *Ibid.*, p. 239.
18. *Ibid.*, pp. 1329-1330.
19. *Ibid.*, p. 300.
20. Johnson, p. 344.
21. William Casey, *The Secret War Against Hitler* (Washington, D.C., 1988), p. 66.
22. *Ibid.*
23. *Ibid.*
24. *Ibid.*, p. 67.
25. *Ibid.*, p. 120.
26. *Ibid.*
27. Gilbert, pp. 1173-1174.
28. *Ibid.*, p. 570.
29. *Ibid.*, p. 588.
30. *Ibid.*, p. 589.
31. *Ibid.*, p. 15.
32. Robert Nisbet, *Roosevelt and Stalin: The Failed Courtship* (Washington, D.C., 1988), p. 102.
33. Gilbert, p. 1158.
34. *Ibid.*
35. *Ibid.*, p. 1175.
36. *Ibid.*, p. 1193.
37. *Ibid.*, p. 1178.
38. *Ibid.*, p. 1179.
39. *Ibid.*, p. 1189.
40. *Ibid.*, p. 1194.
41. *Ibid.*
42. *Ibid.*, p. 1189.
43. *Ibid.*, p. 1234.

44. *Ibid.*, p. 1196.
45. Konrad Adenauer, *Memoirs: 1945-53* (Chicago, 1966), p. 257.
46. Gilbert, p. 474.

XIV. George F. Kennan: *A Gift to America*

George F. Kennan, *Around the Cragged Hill,* (New York: Norton, 1993).

XV. Alexander Solzhenitsyn: *The Man and the Problem*

The Oak and the Calf, translated from the Russian by Harry Willetts (New York: Harper & Row, 1980).